THE NATAL PAPERS
OF 'JOHN ROSS'

Killie Campbell Africana Library Publications

View of the anchorage at Port Natal.

Maclean's chart

CHARLES RAWDEN MACLEAN

THE NATAL PAPERS
OF 'JOHN ROSS'

Loss of the Brig *Mary* at Natal
with Early Recollections of that Settlement

and

Among the Caffres

Edited by
STEPHEN GRAY

Killie Campbell Africana Library
Durban
University of Natal Press
Pietermaritzburg
1992

© University of Natal 1992
Box 375, Pietermaritzburg, 3200 South Africa

ISBN 0 86980 851 6
ISBN 0 86980 529 0 (Set)

Typeset in the University of Natal Press
Pietermaritzburg
Printed by Kohler Carton and Print (Natal.)

Contents

Illustrations

Acknowledgements

The editor wishes to express his gratitude to the following individuals and institutions for assistance given during the preparation of this work:

Ms Gillian Berning, Director of the Local History Museum, Durban; Ms J.F. Duggan, Director of the Killie Campbell Africana Library, University of Natal, Durban; Mr Michael Green, University of Natal, Durban; Mrs Thompson and her colleagues, Aberdeen Family History Shop, Aberdeen and North-East Scotland Family History Society, Aberdeen; Mrs L. Noble and Mr George Dey, Fraserburgh Public Library, Fraserburgh, Aberdeenshire; Mr Robert Devaux and his staff, Saint Lucia National Trust, Castries; Mr R.R. Aspinall and his staff, Library and Archive of the Museum of London in Docklands Project; Dr Robert Green, Registrar's Office, University of Southampton; Mr David Dixie and his staff, Hydrographic Office, Taunton; Ms Tamara Semevsky; Mr Mark Hunt, Audio-Visual Unit, University of Natal; and Dr C. Engelbrecht, National Museum, Bloemfontein.

The financial assistance of the Institute for Research Development of the Human Sciences Research Council, Pretoria, towards this research is also acknowledged. Opinions expressed by the editor in this publication are those of the editor and are not necessarily to be attributed to the Institute for Research Development or the Human Sciences Research Council.

Illustrations and charts

The publishers acknowledge the courtesy of the following in making illustrative material available and granting permission for its use:

Mr George Dey of Fraserburgh: pictures of Fraserburgh.

Hydrographic Office, Taunton: Maclean's Chart of Port Natal and the accompanying drawings, View of the anchorage *and* First interview with the natives. Reproduced from an Admiralty Survey with the permission of the Controller of Her Majesty's Stationery Office.

Local History Museum, Durban: King's Chart of Port Natal; photo of Francis Farewell; King's sketch of Shaka from Isaacs' *Travels*.

National Museum, Bloemfontein: Hoffman's drawing of Farewell's camp.

PLA Collection, Museum in Docklands Project, London: pictures of West India Docks.

Public Record Office, Kew: Hawes' Chart of Port Natal (CO 700 Natal 3) *and* Haddon's Chart of Port Natal (CO 700 Natal 1). Crown copyright; reproduced with the permission of the Controller of Her Majesty's Stationery Office.

Ms Tamara Semevsky: photograph of the editor and the 'John Ross' memorial.

Cover
Mr Mark Hunt: cover artwork based on Maclean's original.

Introduction

To introduce the Natal Papers of C.R. Maclean is no easy task. Who was he, and how is he related to 'John Ross'? Why has his work never appeared in book form before, and how come is it of such importance to the very basics of history in Natal? All these questions will be answered in the course of what follows.

The body of this book consists of Maclean's own work under the heading *The Natal Papers*. The bulk of this is his *Loss of the Brig 'Mary' at Natal, with Early Recollections of that Settlement*, which was frequently referred to much more simply as his *Recollections of Natal*, his *Memoirs of Natal* or just as his *Zulu Narrative*. The work was serialised in the eleven instalments as they appear here. The twelfth item included here, the only other piece he wrote to do with Natal, is a letter written to *The Times*, which serves to round off and conclude the serial. All this material appeared in print during his lifetime, but has never been collected in book form before.

The editor's supportive material to the main texts is divided as follows. The Introduction contains all the biographical evidence available to establish who 'John Ross' was and how he relates to the author, Charles Rawden Maclean, together with what has been made of them by South African and other writers before this material became generally available. Following Maclean's own texts a Commentary is included; this deals with the background to Maclean's own writing and many matters arising, instalment by instalment, from his version of Natal history and his involvement with it. The Bibliography following this lists all Maclean's extant work and other works frequently referred to in what follows.

Life

The adventurous young pioneer hero of Natal − known in the settler legends of South Africa as 'John Ross' − was in real life called Charles Rawden Maclean. Because much mystery attaches to his name, it is as well to give a bald account of the facts of his biography here. As will be shown in the second half of this introduction, the 'John Ross' story has been peculiarly subject to speculation on the part of writers and historians since as early as Nathaniel Isaacs' account of

1

him in 1836. Such speculation may now cease in the light of the following factual profile.

According to the Parish Records of Fraserburgh in Scotland of 1817,[1] Charles Rawden Maclean was born there on 17 August 1815. His father was Lieutenant Francis Maclean, RN, whose first child, Charlotte, had been born in 1804 and christened in Romney, Kent. The second, Rebekah, was born in 1806 and baptised at another port, Orford in Suffolk. The next daughter, Isabella (b. 1809) was the first to be christened in Fraserburgh, suggesting that after an unsettled naval life the Maclean family moved there at that time. Francis and Alexander Maclean followed, and then Charles Rawden. The occasion of the entry in the register is the birth and baptism of Henry (b. 1817).

At least we know from this entry that Charles Rawden was the sixth child out of seven, and the third son. By 1817 the family had been in Fraserburgh for eight years, so had settled there. The name of Francis Maclean's wife is not recorded, nor can we tell if there were further siblings and if the family remained there.

The family surname on the entry is spelled Mclean, but in the early nineteenth century such variant spellings, depending on the scribe rather than the subject, were common: Maclane and Maclaine are also found. Charles Rawden himself, according to his signature, considered himself Maclean.[2]

The records of the parish were kept by the Church of Scotland, but that was not necessarily the church to which the Macleans belonged. The Episcopalians and Presbyterians were also strong in the north-east of Scotland, as were some dozen others. Later Maclean would be a member of a 'Presbyterian Committee', but that body sat merely to serve the interests of non-Catholics. All that is certain is that, unlike some children of Fraserburgh, he belonged to a family of church members who believed in having their particulars recorded.

The detail that Maclean's father described himself as a lieutenant of the Royal Navy is important. Lieutenant Francis Farewell, RN, and Mr J.S. King, the would-be RN lieutenant – the pioneers of Natal – who were both to play influential roles in Charles Maclean's young life, were of his father's generation and had both been half-pensioned out of the navy thanks to cutbacks in the officer class after the defeat of Napoleon at sea.[3] As there was no Royal Navy base at Fraserburgh, Maclean senior must likewise have been retrenched and decided to 'retire' there. He kept his title, however. Exactly two months after the Battle of Waterloo, which finally put paid to the threat of Napoleon on land, Maclean's son Charles was born.

According to many available sources on the Clan Maclean, no further information on either the father or the son is recorded.[4] The Maclean clan originated on the Isle of Mull in the Western Hebrides, where a Maclean Clan

Line still runs between the islands. But in Scotland Macleans are commonly thought of as Highlanders; in Fraserburgh Charles Maclean's father would have been considered an outsider, the name never having been common in Aberdeenshire. The Maclean clan is closely related to another Highland family, the great clan Ross – so it is more than fortuitous that Charles should have been renamed after them.

At the time of his birth Macleans and Rosses were considerably dispersed overseas, particularly as the first settlers of Nova Scotia (Captain King's birthplace) – in Toronto there is a popular magazine called *Maclean's* – and even in the port of Wilmington, NC, which they founded. Another Maclean, Colonel John, became Lieutenant-Governor of Natal (1864–7). As the current head of one branch of the Clan Maclean, Lorne Maclaine of Lochbuie, lives today in Westville, Natal, so we may see in what a wide diaspora the clans became scattered. The Macleans include one of the world's most famous spies. The name is used by toothpaste manufacturers and movie stars as well, and really is as common as Smith or Jones among the Sassenachs.

The first name Charles narrows the field only somewhat, for among patriotic Scotsmen the name of the Bonnie Prince was liberally bestowed. Charlotte, the family's first-born, had presumably been expected to be the boy that would carry Scotland's favourite Christian name. But we need not conclude that the family felt itself to be fiercely Scottish; the other children's names indicate they were British royalist. In all his voluminous writings Charles Maclean was to mention Scotland only once in passing, so it held no particular patriotic call for him.

According to John R. Ross, by 1810 one Charles Maclean, recently emigrated from Scotland, was a major landholder on the eastern seaboard of Canada. Another Charles Maclean, as recently as 1978, published a book called *The Wolf Children*, recounting sightings of children kidnapped by and brought up as wild animals. We may understand why our Charles Maclean insisted on using his middle name, Rawden, on every document he signed.

Had he really been named 'John Ross', there was an equally bewildering list of characters with whom he could be muddled. 'Ross' is the name of one of the noblemen who sides with Macduff in Shakespeare's *Macbeth*, after all. In Maclean's own lifetime there was, for example, Captain Sir John Ross, rear-admiral, who over 1828–30 attempted to voyage to the North Pole via the North-West Passage. In 1836 the Principal Chief of the Cherokees led a delegation of his people to the Senate of the United States to plead for their ancestral land-rights; the name the whites had given him was 'John Ross'.[5] To add to our difficulties, in 1824 another John Ross, an agent of the Glasgow Missionary Society, was the co-founder of Lovedale Mission Station, near Fort

Hare in the Ciskei; he brought the first press from Scotland to the Eastern Frontier and was the first to print Xhosa.[6] Possibly details from his biography have contributed to our 'John Ross' legend that he was born in Glasgow, but in this case not as a noble ecclesiastic, but as a Clydeside skellum. The name was as common – and as extraordinary – as Charles Maclean.

Fraserburgh (pron. Fraserbro' or just the Broch) has an interesting history, and in 1815 was very different from what it is today. An hour's bus-ride north of the flourishing oil-rich Aberdeen, the desolate modern town stands on the shoulder of Scotland, known by the locals as World's End. Developed by the Fraser clan around a castle on the head, in the sixteenth century it boasted one of the few universities of Europe, rivalling Aberdeen's. The harbour faces the Moray Firth and the chill North Sea, and is the entire focus of the community's main activity, fishing. In competition with the Dutch herring fleets, Fraserburgh by the birth of Charles Maclean had become of some importance. By 1818 the second part of the harbour, capable of holding up to a thousand drifters, had been completed. It is hard not to conclude that Francis Maclean was drawn there, at the very time of its improvements, to serve in some capacity as a harbour authority. The activity of fishing was one of the three divisions of the Mercantile Marine, in which his son would always serve as a Foreign or Deep Sea Trader.

Speaking of the capable men Fraserburgh has produced, one historian of the town quotes a northern newspaper editor as follows:

> I do not think Fraserburgh has any cause to hide its head on account of the youth it has sent forth. We must remember the drawbacks of a thinly populated locality, geographically cut off from the great main line of commercial and social access. . . . Naturally, as is the case with every maritime community, a large portion of its sons go to sea, and there many of them occupy positions of great responsibility, and do credit to the town that is proud to own them.[7]

One of these sons of Fraserburgh who drained away to the greater world is the Rev. James Ramsay, born there in 1733. After eighteen years ministering to parishes in the West Indies he became one of the leading agitators in the early movement to abolish the slave trade, and was influential in converting Wilberforce to the cause. His *An Essay on the Treatment and Conversion of African Slaves in the British Sugar Colonies* (1784) brought knowledge of scandalous social conditions to the British public's attention.[8] Another, born in 1838, was Thomas Blake Glover, who arrived at Nagasaki at the age of twenty-one and opened up Japan's first trade treaty with Britain. His story became the basis of Puccini's opera, *Madame Butterfly*.

Modern Fraserburgh hardly resembles the town of 1815. The ruins of the castle, converted into Scotland's first lighthouse, still stand, but every other building has subsequently been converted into the bleakest Victorian grey-stone. The existing churches post-date 1815. The Parish School, built in 1787, was demolished in 1887. There, where we may surmise Charles Maclean was a pupil, the subjects taught were English, Latin, Arithmetic, Writing and Navigation.[9]

That is all we know of Charles Maclean's origins. Born at the end of the reign of George III, when Scotland was deeply caught up in the Industrial Revolution – Glasgow at the time was the most populous city in Europe – he was also, we must remember, an heir to the Scottish Enlightenment which had made Edinburgh the 'Athens of the North'.[10] Sir Walter Scott, pioneer of the British historical novel, was the most read author of the day. From this milieu poverty-stricken review editor Thomas Pringle – whom Maclean so resembles – would also set forth, devoting his life to the interlinked causes of abolition and British expansionism.

Charles Maclean was yet another son of the maritime community of Fraserburgh who was 'sent forth' to make his career. By 1800, according to Steel, of a population of two million Scots, one tenth of them, the majority of them Highlanders, had emigrated to the new British colonies. Still to this day some educational projects in Fraserburgh are sponsored by Natal sugar interests.

To train to become a sea-captain in the British merchant marine he had to be apprenticed, which needed some basic skills: literacy in English (as opposed to the Gaelic of some of his less privileged rural countrymen) and numeracy for navigation and trade. We know in his youth he read *Robinson Crusoe* with ease (see the opening of Instalment Eleven) and that his formal English became extremely sophisticated. His Latinate constructions suggest fine training in rhetoric. His interest in mathematics is evident in all he wrote. He was not brought up to be a 'tar' or a crewman, so the notion that he pulled himself up by his own bootstraps is untenable. Also, the fact that he was small and frail suggests he made his way by intelligence rather than physical strength. Fraserburgh held no future for him.

How he became apprenticed to Mr James Saunders King, captain of the *Mary* bound for the Cape of Good Hope, is not known. King as master of the brig *Salisbury* had surveyed the lagoon at Port Natal in 1823, and himself gone to sea at the tender age of eleven. Certainly Maclean was not a runaway who stowed away on board the *Mary* at Glasgow, giving his name as 'John Ross', as the romantic legend would have us believe. Probably the arrangement was formal between his father and King. He was to acquire training as a ship's-boy, just as Ned Cameron had 'served his time' in trade before him (see the end of Instalment Eleven). The fact that the *Mary* was travelling to the Cape was really irrelevant, except insofar as it offered good opportunities for learning seamanship and commerce. It is not certain that King sailed from Glasgow nor that his destination was Port Natal.

The course and the fate of the *Mary* is dealt with in the commentary to Maclean's own account of her voyage, *Loss of the Brig 'Mary'*, which forms the bulk of this book. Without more primary sources of a member of the expedition, reconstructing her provenance, tonnage and full muster-roll is impossible today. The records of the Registrar General of Shipping and Seamen in the Public Record Office at Kew, London, are very incomplete for the 1820s, and anyway no less than a hundred British ships named *Mary* were on the seas during that period. More important to realize is that she was a trading brig. She was small, as she could be manned by a complement of only sixteen (captain, first mate, second mate and crew). She was a two-masted square-rigger with clear decks for storing cargo. She had no separate quarters for passengers (see Instalment One which gives us a vivid description). The prototype had been developed from the pirate ships of the Caribbean – easily manoeuvrable in uncharted waters, not suitably provided for a life of long hauls. Maclean gives many details of her victualling, including bread and spirits. On her arrival at the Cape the *Mary* plied the eastern seaboard of Southern Africa suitably as a coastal trader, her men being paid by shares in the profits of each haul. Maclean became familiar with the Cape to Delagoa Bay seaboard.

At all events, when the *Mary*, on her way to the Farewell party which had been deposited at Port Natal a year before, was wrecked on the notorious bar there – on 30 September 1825 – Charles Maclean was only six weeks on from his tenth birthday. In his first instalment, and again in Instalment Nine, he mentions that he was 'fourteen' throughout his landfall at Port Natal, so that age with him is more psychological than actual.

The details that emerge from his memoir reprinted here suggest he was at first very much a child. 'Such a little fellow as I was', 'I was no great burden' (Instalment Eight) – details like these indicate how boyish he was. If his first Zulu escorts were given to piggybacking him about whenever his feet gave in on their hardy, barefoot treks, he could not have been very sizeable. He wished, in the same instalment, to have become 'manful' and 'robust' like his shipmates, so we should see his determined effort to acquire stature and grow up as one of the unspoken themes of his Natal experience. Later, in Instalment Nine, he describes himself as a 'youth' – his adolescence started on schedule.

He is only ten weeks older in the action of *Loss of the Brig 'Mary'* when he first reaches King Shaka's capital at Dukuza, then situated near the modern Eshowe. There he remains based for considerable periods over the ensuing years. During 1827 the overland trading expedition to Delagoa Bay which has made him famous occurs. By then the complement of the *Mary* was so severely depleted it is not very surprising he was the one to make the trip. If his first trip from Port Natal (Durban) to Dukuza — which he gives as a distance of 150 miles — took five days, then his later expedition from Port Natal to Delagoa Bay (which is four times the distance) and back to Port Natal could hardly have taken the record-breaking month that is often given as the statistic. More likely it was, as he himself says, 'a six months' absence on a long and somewhat perilous journey' (Instalment Four). This occurred, then, when he was aged eleven/twelve. In July 1828, when the reconstructed *Mary* at last called in at Algoa Bay with the Sothobe delegation, he was still aged twelve. Thirteen had come when he finally left Port Natal at the end of 1828.[11]

For South Africans interested in the role 'John Ross' played in opening up Port Natal, these are the most salient details of his life. His self-portrait, which is not systematically given, but emerges from remarks on the side in his memoir, is as follows: diminutive in size, remarkably red-haired, susceptible to sunburn and peeling . . . and that is all. He is a master of reticence.

By 1853, when he began to record the experiences of his childhood and youth at Natal, we may tell from his style he was temperate, lived by the seafarer's code of attention to duty and order, had a deeply Protestant faith and democratic politics. He was a Britisher through and through, a man in command of his individual destiny. Such characteristics he projects back onto his early years to show how these qualities were tested by his extraordinary adventures and became the measure of his being. In Zululand, besides many other remarkable qualities, he learned self-reliance, physical endurance, trust in his own abilities and, above all, dedication to his lifelong goals.

These goals were to become skilled as a sea-captain like his father, and as a trader like his employer. He stayed in South Africa because he had no other option; indeed, he was most unfortunately stranded here. He remained loyal to Mr King to the extent of vigorously defending his reputation after his death (this is the main thrust of Instalment One). He left only when his commitment to King, on his death, was finally over and transport was available. He never returned to South Africa, because his allegiance was not to the land, but to the sailor's life. This does not mean he ever gave up his interest in Natal, however.

How he returned to the United Kingdom (from Algoa Bay to Table Bay, via Saint Helena, with ports of call in West Africa?) is not known. If he returned to

Scotland and revisited his family we will not know, either. His true base from here on for the next forty years was to be the 'floating homes' (Instalment One) of the professional mariner, the vessels of the largest merchant fleet the world had yet known.

We next pick up Maclean when he mentions in 1867 'It is now nearly thirty years since I made my first voyage to the West Indies' on a 'two-voyage ship running down the Trades.'[12] The dating means that after Natal the next part of his apprenticeship was served on the UK–West Indies run; indeed, on the *Sandwich*. When Lloyd's annual Registers of Shipping begin in 1840, we learn that the *Sandwich* was a barque of 253 tons, registered in London in 1823, employed between there and Saint Lucia island. Its owner is given as H. King (presumably no relative of the late J.S. King). He was Mr Henry King, one of the chief plantation owners of the island, at Belle Plaine above Soufriere, described by Maclean in his *Voyage to the West Indies* (p. 655).

King's next vessel was the *Susan King* (assuredly named after his wife, a woman of 'kind care and attention'). This was a brig, 132 tons, built in 1838 in Halifax, Nova Scotia. Probably Maclean went there to fetch the *Susan King*; he was certainly at Halifax once when the port froze over. At any rate, according to Lloyd's, by 1840 Charles Maclean was master of the *Susan King* on the London–Saint Lucia trade route. Thus, within little more than a decade of leaving Natal, Maclean had completed his training and by the age of twenty-five become a sea-captain operating from Saint Lucia. In this capacity he served his newfound base until he was forced from the sea.

The history of Saint Lucia is not unrelated to the way Natal Colony was to develop, with sugar their main crop. Both belonged to a chain of sugar producers stretching from Jamaica to Mauritius, dependent on common climates, soil and an abundance of cheap labour, for ever associated with African slavery and the plantation system. The sugar industry, which powered the expanding nineteenth-century economy, was also dependent on ocean transport to meet the newly-created markets of Europe,[13] and Maclean served them efficiently. His cargo was measured out in tons of hogsheads of sugar, molasses and rum.

Saint Lucia was first settled by the Dutch in 1654. It changed hands between the two great powers of France and Britain no less than six times thereafter, and was ceded to the latter in 1813. Even today, although English is the official language, the island's culture is predominantly French Creole and Catholic. With the neighbouring islands of Martinique (still French), birthplace of Napoleon's Empress Josephine, and the far larger Barbados, Saint Lucia is part of the Antilles group in the eastern Caribbean basin, off the coast of Venezuela. They are also named the Windward Isles, as on the old Trade Wind sailing routes they were reached first from Europe before a vessel entered the Gulf of Mexico. The normal transatlantic circuit continued clockwise from there to include ports between Florida and Nova Scotia, and the crossing back to Western Europe.

An idea of the extent of the trade in which Maclean was involved is given by the fact that when the West India Import and Export Docks, London's first enclosed dockyard, was opened in 1802 on the Isle of Dogs, at the loop in the Thames opposite Greenwich, berthing facilities were for no less than two hundred vessels at any one time. The Sugar Warehouse stretching alongside was throughout the nineteenth century known as the longest building in the world. As in Maclean's youth these docks had a government monopoly on the West Indiamen's trade, he could only have sailed from there (rather than a later sugar-depot like Greenock near Glasgow). Streets leading from transit sheds like 'Blood Alley', so named from the way jute sacking and sugar granules chafed the necks and shoulders of stevedores, and the Clock Gateway giving access to Limehouse, must have been very familiar to him.[14] As skipper of the *Susan King* and subsequently the *Gilbert Munro*, Maclean visited these docks up to six times a year, and when in Britain always gave his address as there.

The *Natal Almanack*, which always remained interested in rival colonies, in 1864 gave a description of Saint Lucia as part of the world where 'the ancient laws of France' remained in force, although it was governed by the Colonial Secretary under instructions from the Governor in Barbados. Saint Lucia had no representative assembly during most of Maclean's life, but its own Legislative Council was filled by the Governor's appointment. An Administrator at the capital, Castries, served as local authority. 'Population in 1858: 26 000, of which 716 are White.'[15]

In 1852 when under Victorian maritime law this first became compulsory, Maclean appeared before an examining board in London and obtained his Master's Certificate of Competence, Class: Ordinary,[16] whereby he was eligible to command any vessel of whatsoever tonnage. The entry is dated 26 August, and there he gives his birthplace as Aberdeen, county Aberdeen. The year: 1813. In the Scottish Population Rolls held in Edinburgh no birth of a Charles Rawden Maclean is recorded for Aberdeen in 1813 – but the one for Fraserburgh of 1815 certainly is. So we may assume he meant Aberdeen*shire* as his birthplace and that '1813' was given to the administrative clerk – or misrecorded by same – to mean he was approximately the suitable age of forty.

His life at Saint Lucia is slightly easier to follow for from 1839 the island gave rise to an extraordinarily colourful sequence of independent newspapers, many sufficient runs of which are preserved in the Colindale Newspaper

Library, London.[17] In many of these Maclean advertised his arrivals and departures at Castries; indeed, the comings and goings of the *Susan King* and the *Gilbert Munro* were often the settlers' main topic of attention.

The following is typical:

> For London, To Sail on 25th January, the Fine Fast Sailing Brig, A 1:
> SUSAN KING, Copper Bottomed and Copper Fitted. For Freight and
> Passage, apply to the Subscriber: Chas. R. Maclean. . . .

Since this advertisement appeared only on 26 January 1843, we may infer that as so often in the stormy Caribbean, departure was delayed.

Maclean often made the news as well. For example,

> On Tuesday morning last, the Sailors whilst employed in washing the
> decks on board the brig *Susan King*, at present loading in our Harbour
> with Colonial Produce for London, killed a large Serpent between three
> and four feet in length, of the most venimous [*sic*] kind; it is supposed the
> reptile must have been introduced on board, in taking in a cash of sugar,
> fortunately no one was injured (16 Feb. 1843).

According to the Saint Lucian papers, in the 1840s Natal, the British West Indies, Australia and New Zealand were the leading contenders for the attention of the Colonial Office. Although a small and insignificant volcanic outcrop, Saint Lucia was extraordinarily productive – by 1850 it was exporting 60 000 cwt. of sugar and its by-products were valued at £40 000 per annum. The chronic issue of sugar duties was a vexation to the Saint Lucian planters, for no preferential tariffs operated to protect the British-grown product against competition. As Martinique and other colonies were still slave-holders, the economics of trade with Britain did not act to encourage them to declare emancipation.

Saint Lucia liberated its slaves on 1 August 1838.[18] Thus Maclean witnessed the event, or at least was there for its aftermath, the transition through a labour system of apprenticeship to wage employment. In his *Voyage to the West Indies* he comments with pride:

> I have no hesitation in making this assertion that as far as my observation
> and experience enables me to form an opinion of other islands in the West
> Indies, many of which I have visited, that of all the lately emancipated
> class, the Saint Lucian Negro is the most tractable and best conducted that
> I have met with. . . . I am pretty certain that no colony has suffered less

than Saint Lucia, with the same paucity of labourers, from the transition of slavery to freedom. (p.653)

The issues of emancipation and preferential tariffs endlessly intersect in Maclean's transactions. In 1839 the Queen of Portugal had refused to ratify the slave-trade Abolition Treaty with Britain, so that neighbouring Brazil had no pressure put on it to stop importing African slaves to cut cane. In the 1840s, while Maclean steered in and out of slave territories, the Admiralty employed no less than 530 ships on a cruising system to suppress the slavers. Maclean clearly states which side he supports.

On topical issues such as these Maclean makes his first appearance in print, specifically in *The British and Foreign Anti-Slavery Reporter* of 1846. The report carried there is dealt with in the commentary to his Natal papers, because in them he recounts the sensational case which precipitated his protest. In the port of Wilmington, North Carolina, one of the Jim Crow States, Maclean caused an incident with regard to the unjust treatment of three of his free black sailors on the *Susan King*. The unequal treatment of British subjects in foreign ports of call in treaty with Britain – meted out on the basis of skin-colour – obviously enraged him. Through an account made to his Lieutenant-Governor, Maclean entered the British press as something of a liberty man and he was much praised for his courage and conviction.[19]

For the first time we learn that Maclean was a man who believed in human rights for all British subjects without regard to distinctions of race, and was willing to defend those rights from the poop of his ship, with force if necessary. On this matter of principle he was clear spoken, and the theme of liberty indeed colours everything he wrote to do with European-African affairs. Of the choices open to him of Tory, Whig or Radical, he belonged to the latter group. The Wilmington incident was one of several that built up to the American Civil War of North against South.

Yet there is no doubt that at Saint Lucia Maclean served the white settler interest. By the 1840s he was married as well, to an obviously good woman whom unfortunately we know only as 'Mrs M.' She was born in 1808. Her obituary recalls that she was

> well-known and generally beloved, as to her care – in ante-steamer times, when her husband commanded the *Susan King* and the *Gilbert Munro*, old regular traders to this Colony – were confided the children sent home for education, not a few of whom she brought back after their education was completed. We recall many acts of kindness done during those rough journeys across the Atlantic (8 Jan. 1887).

'Mrs M.' and Charles Maclean had one daughter who survived them both. Possibly she was called Sarah, because in *The Voice* of 20 September 1879, one Sarah Maclean is the respondent in a case of simple assault tried in the magistrates courts of Castries against one Durogie Maximin, who was sentenced to three months. (No other Maclean families appear in the records of the Registrar of Births and Deaths at Castries.) In which case, this Sarah may have married a man called Drake, for there is a tombstone in the Protestant Cemetery, Venice, erected to the memory of Sarah Maclean Drake and her daughter Janet, 'who perished in the steamer disaster near the Lido, 18 March 1914.' This is unconfirmed. All that is certain is that after the demise of Charles and his wife, the name Maclean does not recur in the Saint Lucian records of the nineteenth century.

Captain Maclean and his shipboard wife not only travelled together as a working partnership, but they enjoyed many pleasures. Riding expeditions up the slopes of the island's active volcano to picnic there, storms at sea, commissary inter-island runs to Saint Vincent, Martinique or Barbados – these were shared. On one trip in the *Gilbert Munro* to deliver timber at the battlefront of Balaclava during the Crimean War, 'Mrs M.' was one of the few British women there (together with Florence Nightingale). During the siege early in the New Year of 1856, Maclean and his wife strode through the 'iron tempest', through bursting shells and minefields. 'Mrs M., with the characteristic loyalty and pluck of a blue nose, stood her ground,'[20] he remarks, as they pour scorn on the Russian offensive. 'Blue nose' is an affectionate way of describing her as an upright Puritan, but it also has a secondary meaning: 'Blue-nose' was a nickname for a Nova Scotian, so that she was probably a Canadian of Scottish descent.

From the early 1850s Natal became a topic of rising interest in the London *Times* and the colonial papers. This drove Maclean into writing the first of his serials for *The Nautical Magazine and Naval Chronicle*. His title, *Loss of the Brig 'Mary' at Natal, with Early Recollections of that Settlement*, was explicit enough for his seafaring readers, interested in accumulating navigational and hydrographic information to facilitate their landings, and a bit of history besides. Since its inception in 1832, published by Simpkin, Marshall and Co. at Stationers' Hall, the monthly magazine had served as ongoing annals of matters marine, a veritable reference archive for British commanders of the great age of sail. As Maclean frequently remarked, no person in his profession could afford to be without it. In *The Nautical Magazine* he wrote for his peers, technically but also from the heart. As we know from the eleven instalments included here, the project grew far beyond his initial brief as the pressure of recollecting his childhood in Natal and Zululand took over. Finally he abandoned it.

Maclean continued to write for *The Nautical Magazine*, however, through the 1850s. Despite the editor's pique over interruptions in Maclean's delivery of instalments of the Natal recollections, the relationship must have been cordial. Indeed, from 1853 to 1857 Maclean was one of the magazine's most prolific contributors. The Natal recollections are 37 000 words in length, the Crimea account is 20 000, and the Saint Lucia description, which concludes his contributions, is also 20 000 words long. This represents quite sufficient to have filled a book of his experiences, but he must have felt himself not that kind of author. He was content to make his mark in the records of the Mercantile Marine, and to leave it at that. Unlike Isaacs, he did not publish to make a sensation over his own adventures.

At the end of the sequence of Maclean's 'excellent papers', the editor of *The Nautical Magazine* remarks that Maclean's accounts

> will be referred to by the future surveyor, the seaman, and the general reader hereafter for information and amusement, and they will each find in them what they want. Would that we could see others with the observation of our author and his pen to describe it, busy on those islands as he has been on Saint Lucia. Would they emulate his example in all respects, they might each add dignity to their profession, as he has done, an honour to the British Mercantile Marine.[21]

Maclean's unique kind of journalism − blending history and information, geography and character, observation and opinion − in the three large surveys he conducted during the 1850s, does deserve more attention than it has received to date. Victorian journalism is generally not much read today for its own interest, but Maclean became superbly good at practising it.

Since he and his editor referred to his work as the writing of 'papers', this term has been used in the title to this book. Papers were more than records or mere documentation. They were hypotheses argued out in stages, justifying a procedure and an attitude to contemporary life. Maclean's skill at arranging paper-writing in serials, so that each discrete paper of approximately 3 000 words became an instalment in the larger narrative structure, is not to be scoffed at. And he became better at it as he went along: the Crimea and the Saint Lucia papers are masterfully done.

If Maclean's authorship was not an ambitious matter, it nevertheless brought acknowledgement and honour to him during the course of his life. It also served the end he wished it to serve: enlarging the knowledge of the English-speaking people about three far-flung reaches of their sphere of influence. As a later colonial writer, Douglas Blackburn, with an ironic temperament so similar to

Maclean's, once commented, what the British people did not know about their own Empire would fill volumes. Maclean was part of this longstanding tradition of the traveller's tale, which Swift had so garbled in *Gulliver's Travels* – the tradition of bringing the news of overseas experience back Home.

Maclean's two later serials are appropriately titled: *Notes on a Voyage from England to Balaclava in the 'Gilbert Munro', late Store-ship at Hyder Pacha* by C.R. Maclean, Master (Oct. 1856–Feb. 1857) and *A Voyage to the West Indies, with Notes on Saint Lucia* by Captain C.R. Maclean (July–Dec. 1857). Unlike the Natal serial, these carry his signature as the author, which suggests that his name was being recognized. Most contributions to *The Nautical Magazine* were unsigned, so Maclean enjoyed fair – and probably gratifying – prominence.

Unfortunately for the biographer of Maclean, these pieces are not very revealing of the man. He remained throughout a type (the trusty captain), rather than an individualized personality. Nevertheless, many likeable characteristics emerge – his cool-headed sense of adventure (when touring the Crimean war zone) and his passionate fondness for the island of Saint Lucia which had become his adopted home. Maclean's description of the island is only the second ever to have been published, so that it holds a uniquely valuable place in the study of the growth of that island republic. His Natal papers are similarly unique, and hold just as valuable a position. The fact that his life anchored finally at Castries – rather than at Durban – need not sound as remote to us in South Africa as it does today. The development of both ports under Britain during the nineteenth century is remarkably similar, part of comparative imperial studies that we are seldom tempted to make. To Maclean himself their histories were virtually interchangeable, as is evident from his readiness to analyze Natal affairs.

In the commentary to Instalment Nine of *Loss of the Brig 'Mary'* details are given of the delays in its publication, and of another piece of Maclean's of the 1850s, 'The Law of Storms'. This recounts one of his many experiences of a Caribbean hurricane.

While *Loss of the Brig 'Mary'* was appearing, Maclean transferred from the *Susan King* to the *Gilbert Munro*, which doubtless upset his regular scheduling of visits to London. The latter vessel was described by Lloyd's in 1854 as a barque, built in 1828 and registered in London to serve the West India trade. It had twice the tonnage of the *Susan King*, so was a more profitable affair. This Maclean captained into the 1860s.

But by 1863 we have in the Saint Lucian press records of Captain C.R. Maclean, his wife and daughter travelling to and from Saint Lucia on someone else's vessel, the cutter *Liver* (departure 19 December 1863), and the following March the *Liver* is sold in Saint Lucia. At this time Maclean announced the formation of the Saint Lucia Steam Conveyance Co., Ltd., with himself as chairman and major shoreholder. By 1868 Maclean is not only grounded at Castries, but has made the transition to the age of steam. He is also the force behind the building of the island's first coalsheds, which made it the region's chief fuelling depot.

Now in his fifties Maclean had retired from the life at sea and also cut his direct access to London – this probably explains why he no longer felt the need to publish there. He invested in the 'tiny steamship *Penelope* to operate the coastal trade'[22] and two even smaller ones, the *Aid* and the *Creole*. They served to ferry to the *Penelope*, circuiting the leeward coast of the island to collect exports from the extremely precipitous inlets and bays, and delivering passengers to the many otherwise unconnected settlements and estates. Since the Conveyance Company's only competition was fleets of homemade 'pirogues under Negro management' (*Voyage to the West Indies*, p. 650), prospects for improvement were good. Maclean even offered a service more regular than the Royal Penny Mail.

The venture was a disaster, however. The *Aid* and the *Creole* are in and out of the shipping news as unfit for service with leaking boilers and so on. The *Creole*, after six months of scamped refitting work at Martinique, in September 1879, still leaked, and the *Aid* was finally scuttled in July 1880. But what really ruined Maclean was the event that befell the two-year-old *Penelope*. This occurred on one 'dark moonless night in June 1868', as Mr Devaux puts it (p. 74), the day after she was delivered to the company at Castries.

With only an engineer on board the *Penelope*, Maclean set off for Soufriere Bay, the landing at which he had made all his dealings with King and other plantation-owners over the previous thirty-five years. 'Having fallen asleep at the wheel,' Mr Devaux says, Skipper Maclean drove the *Penelope* onto the rocks. The coast of the west of Saint Lucia runs sheer down to the ocean bed. To this day there is a monument on shore near the site of where the *Penelope* was lost. Whether Maclean was asleep or not, he and his engineer survived the wreck somehow. Maclean was held legally responsible for this disaster, and he was never to recover financially.

In the Saint Lucian records, never very complete, scraps of information follow about Maclean in a succession of trials over his debts – two examples are given in the second part of Mr Devaux's paper. In order to pay off these debts, Maclean had to turn to wage-earning as a colonial official.

Ten years later, still not in the clear financially, according to the Saint Lucia Blue Book of 1879,[23] he held the following staggering list of posts with these annual salaries:

Stipendiary Magistrate and Judge	
District Court, 1st District	£130
Visiting Justice, Royal Gaol	£184
Member, Executive Council	£ 80
" , Legislative Council	£ 82
" , Road Committee	£146
" , Poor Law Committee and Chairman,	
1st District	£156
Coroner	£162
Member, Board of Education	£142
" , Board of Health	£148

In addition, his Magistrate's office, as an offshoot of the Poor Law Committee, ran the General Hospital and the Lunatic and Yaws Establishment (14 Oct. 1876). It seems that almost nothing could occur in the interior of the island without having first to go through Maclean's office. Second only to the Administrator, he was in charge of the island's daily affairs. Only the harbour-master rivalled him in importance.

Apparently he tackled this workload with vigour and good sense. Snippets of information give us glimpses of him out at all hours to investigate a drowning in a sugar-vat or a brutal murder of a husband by a wife on a palm-fringed beach. No one could die on Saint Lucia without his knowing why. He also remained Chairman of the Board of his ailing company (11 July 1874).

In *The Saint Lucia Observer* of 6 October 1874, there is adverse criticism of Maclean – in an editorial where it is suggested that as a magistrate he is presumptuous in his interpretation of certain laws. It is also pointed out that he had no legal training. Maclean's reply is that, since the Attorney-General himself is often sometimes uncertain of legal interpretations as a result of the pre-Napoleonic legal system still pertaining on the island, where not confusingly modified by the British system, he may be entitled to ask forgiveness of the paper.

His role as 'stipendiary magistrate' is an important one in the Caribbean context, different from what we think of as an ordinary magistrate's. In the British West Indian colonies this was a post created and funded directly by the Crown to regulate fair dealings in the post-abolition society. As is recorded by the Governor of Jamaica in 1839:

The conduct of the labouring populations is represented by the stipendiary magistrates, whose reports are the most frequent channels of official

information possessed by the government, as being orderly and ir-
reproachable. . . . The stipendiary magistrates are a class . . . offensive
to the proprietary interest.[24]

The post was created to mediate between plantocrats and their workers, and its
independence intended to ensure that abuses in labour practices did not occur
or, if they did, were rectified. Maclean was, in effect, the island's 'protector' of
the majority of the population.

With the post went a title. On 1 December 1874, we read of the Honourable
Charles R. Maclean making a donation of $5.00 to the Catholic church for the
erection of a public clock. As the vast majority of Saint Lucians were Catholics,
this gesture from a member of the Presbyterian Educational Committee should
have contributed to goodwill within the capital. Such gestures were appreciat-
ively noted in *The Saint Lucia Observer*.

Through the paper's summaries of the 'colonial sheets' Maclean must first
have come to hear of further events in Natal, prominently in the news as a result
of the 'Langalibalele affair'. This provoked him to open up all the issues of his
youth in Natal and revive the call he made for British justice in Zululand in his
Loss of the Brig 'Mary' of twenty years before. From Castries he wrote a letter,
dated 30 June 1875, to *The Times*, which appeared on 3 August. This letter is
included here as Maclean's twelfth 'paper', and is dealt with in the
commentary. The tone of the letter is distinctly different from that of his earlier
account: firmly done, succinct and – except for the fact that it is in no way
pompous – it may be described as truly magisterial.

On 28 August Maclean's letter was reprinted in *The Saint Lucia Observer*
with the following editorial leader attached: 'Entertaining and instructive as it
must have been to the English reader it will be peculiarly interesting to our
readers on account of the signature attached to it.' It was a matter of pride to the
paper to have Maclean 'throw fresh light on the whole affair' in Zululand, 'from
experience gathered in a most romantic way.' We may detect an element of
surprised delight on the part of the Saint Lucians.

That they were well informed about Natal and that the injustices committed
against Langalibalele were of concern even to such a distant society is evident
in the editor's firm conclusion: 'Justice cannot have been administered in Natal
according to English notions when such panics could be possible.' Maclean's
intervention in the scandalous debacle is entirely consistent with the role
he played on Saint Lucia. There he was paid to uphold these 'English
notions'.

A few weeks later Maclean appears again in *The Saint Lucia Observer*, this
time on his other topic of expertise, the unruly sea which twice had cost him so
dearly. His brief letter to the editor begins:

> For many years my vocation led me to study with some earnestness the various changes of the weather in both temperate and tropical latitudes, and in a certain way thus to form an opinion from a series of regularly recurring facts . . . (18 Sept 1875).

Although he admits he has not reduced climatology to a 'system', he does forewarn the masters of island traders on certain dates to keep 'a good pot under their lee'. Speaks the now elderly man who had made the sea and all its moods the object of 'study' of his 'vocation', one whose career at sea was bracketed by the violent shipwrecks of the *Mary* and the *Penelope*. To Charles Maclean the sea had been a dour providence. His admonitory tone to younger riders of the storm (to paraphrase his favourite Cowper) indicates he had become a grand old man, indeed.

By this September 1875, Maclean was sixty years old. It appears that his desk was filled with a paper backlog with which he could not cope, for he worked without an assistant. By 15 April 1876, the local rag seems to be nudging him: 'We cannot reliably inform our readers as to the rumour entertained in some quarters that the Honourable Mr Maclean will shortly retire from the public service on a pension.'

But the fact of the matter is that he cound not retire, because he was still deeply in debt over the *Penelope*, and the *Aid* and the *Creole* were not recuperating his losses. Maclean is there on the quayside in his official capacities to welcome the Governor-in-Chief of the Windward Islands on his state visit, later in 1879. There this run of the weekly *Saint Lucia Observer* comes to an end.

When *The Voice* is launched to take its place on 30 August 1879, the major reports are to do with the progress of the Anglo-Zulu War against Cetshwayo and his warriors. On 20 September Sir Garnet Wolseley's telegram advising that 'remaining chiefs have surrendered' is given in full. Even more attention is devoted to the funeral of the Prince Imperial of France who had 'perished in a Zulu mealie garden by the spear of a savage foe.' The name Napoleon remains in Zululand applied to a fort. The desolation of the Empress Eugenie is also reported in full. We have no reaction by Maclean recorded. But in his lifetime he had witnessed the rise of the Zulus under King Shaka, and now they were 'melted' before the British sun.

By 13 March 1880, something is amiss with Maclean, because someone else is appearing as the island's coroner. On 20 March 'Mr Maclean's illness' is mentioned; on 3 April he has 'completely recovered from his late attack, and has taken up his duties'; on 24 April that he has been granted two months' leave of absence. Then the paper becomes silent on the subject.

The Blue Books take up the story. One letter of the Acting Administrator of Saint Lucia to the Governor-General in Barbados requests 'an extra payment of £25 to the Hon. C.R. Maclean to avail himself of the leave of absence granted.'[25] In Despatch number 134 of 8 September this is indeed awarded. But Maclean has died by then. This is noted in the Colonial Despatch of 13 September (pp. 183–4).

Because an obituary of Maclean seemed not to have been printed in any source retrievable in a library, for a long time during the course of this research I was convinced only a search of tombstones on the island would reveal the final details. I had only Mrs M.'s obituary, previously quoted, to go by:

> Happy and prosperous while her husband lived, his death brought MRS MACLEAN and her only daughter a most cruel reverse of fortune, which the devotedness of a few friends helped to mitigate.
>
> We lay upon her grave the offering of our sincerest respect and regret.

Before she died and was buried on Saint Lucia she would have read (in *The Voice* during March 1886) of how 5 000 defeated Zulus almost half way round the world were being impressed into service for Britain in another of Queen Victoria's 'little wars', this time in the Sudan.

Mrs M.'s death is recorded at Castries in the Office of the Registrar (under 6 January 1887), where her age is given as 71 (not the 79 of the obituary). So the Macleans were unreliable when it came to dates; or possibly she was born in 1815 and, instead of being older than her husband, was his coeval. Cause of death: senility. She lived out the last of her days on the charity of island friends. Providence had let the couple down.

There was no entry in the Registrar's Office for the death of any C.R. Maclean, so – all other avenues exhausted – the burial plot it would have to be, and the safe bet that his loyal, destitute widow would have been buried beside him. Having gone that far to unearth the true-life story of little 'John Ross', I was not to be deterred, even by the gruesome job of brushing the lichen off century-old marble. As at that time I did not yet have Maclean's date and place of birth, either, I hoped the elusive facts that traditionally open and close a biography might at least be engraved on some forlorn stone.

Then I hit a macabre setback and a scandalous Saint Lucian story. In one Protestant cemetery at Soufriere only two tablets survived, neither of them of the 1880s. These were in the shelter of the tormented volcano, next to a deserted church long taken over by squatters and their pigs. The only other place where the magistrate and his spouse could have been laid to rest was in the cemetery of the Holy Trinity Anglican Church, Trinity Church Street, Castries, which I had already combed. This is a tumbledown triangular graveyard on a steep slope, where goats graze, the roots of royal palms and breadfruit – the imported source of slave-fodder – bore through the coffins, and old umbrella frames and rum bottles are disposed of. Marie Monplaisir, Paulina Polland, dearly beloved, were just decipherable as contemporaries of the Macleans.

But the scandal of that churchyard is that, as land on the level is scarce in Saint Lucia, its flat lower portion was sold off to the municipality in the 1980s, levelled and concreted over. To the local population this was a monumental outrage; there is a calypso still sung in Saint Lucia in protest. Its title is 'Don' Make Bread on the Dead.' That part of the cemetery, once firmed up, became the foundation of a new branch of Barclay's Bank.

I was disheartened that I would have to return to South Africa – where 'John Ross' is a national hero, where books are written about his exploits and exemplary TV serials made about his youthful daring – to report that his mortal remains were under a vault of Eastern Caribbean dollars. . . . Like Mr Hutton's and Dommana's, the resting place of the Macleans was lost to us. So are the bones of so many other characters in the ill-fated 'John Ross' story: King Shaka's (bundled into a corn-bin), Norton and his men's (lost at sea), Francis Farewell's (eaten by scavengers in Pondoland). 'Don' Make Bread on the Dead' – I thought I would have to report that 'John Ross', in the mouths of the liberated slaves he served so well, had been turned into a raucous calypso, and his mysteries would never be solved.

But, by a fortunate twist of fate, at the Colindale Newspaper Library of the British Museum some missing microfilm rolls had come to light by the time I returned to the UK. This is the generous tribute carried by Saint Lucia's *The Voice* in their commemoration of Charles Maclean (on 18 September 1880):

> We regret to have to record the death of the Honourable C.R. Maclean, who died on 13 August. . . . The deceased gentleman at the time of his death held numerous public offices in the colony. . . . To all these offices he brought unwearied activity and a strict sense of duty. Mr Maclean was one of the few public officers who believed that his duties to the public consisted of something beyond the mere drawing of a monthly salary from the Treasury. Neither bad weather nor bad roads, nor in fact any excuse ever kept the deceased Magistrate from his work; and in him the Colony has lost a most conscientious officer.

Maclean was not buried under the bank where his wife subsequently was. The reason why knowledge of his death was so delayed in Saint Lucia was that he had taken to the sea once again. When he left Saint Lucia on board RMS *Larne*, 'on his passage home in search of health', that was the last his wife and daughter saw of him. He died at sea in the Solent, before the *Larne* could put in at Southampton.

That is to say Maclean died close to where, on 23 February 1917, the troopship *Mendi* would go down in the icy waters, taking with it its cargo of 615 blacks and 10 officers of the South African Native Labour Contingent, recruited to serve Britain in the First World War.[26]

The *Larne* was captained by yet another King (Captain H. King). Its movements were as follows: on the evening of Wednesday 11 March 1880, it arrived from the West Indies at Le Havre and waited to dock until noon on the Thursday. On the Saturday morning 'she was hourly expected at Southampton'. Maclean died on Friday 13. The *Larne* arrived at Southampton on schedule 'with mail and co. from the West Indies, bringing a general cargo for England and the Continent; also passengers, and $11,400 in specie for London.'[27] The *Larne* also offloaded the body of Charles Maclean. He was buried on land on the Monday at 1.00 p.m.

On that same Monday Southampton was stirred by another arrival: the Empress Eugenie disembarked at Portsmouth 'where she was met by Princess Beatrice on behalf of the Queen, who had invited her to visit at Osborne. The Empress, who was received by the naval and military authorities, at once embarked in the *Alberta*, Royal yacht' (18 August). Princess Beatrice had encountered the Zulus in her childhood, at the private showing of the Zulu exhibition in Her Majesty's stables in 1853. So now Victoria had the last of her former French enemies, the Napoleons, as a guest at her summer retreat on the Isle of Wight to console her over her loss in Zululand.

On 21 August *The Hampshire Advertiser* carries an item, 'Rifle Shooting at the Cape' [*sic*]: 'Lady Colley, wife of the Governor, fired the first shot at the Natal Wimbledon shooting at Maritzburg, and made a bull's-eye.'

Maclean lies buried in what is now named the Old Cemetery, Hill Lane, Southampton.[28] Around him are Johanna, the wife of Samuel Ruffell, Charles Yeoman 'who fell asleep', Eliza Burgan and Celia Goldstone, and Richard Bell, husband of Mary Snook. Recently the site has been cleared by the Parks Department of waist-high brambles and grass, mown down to let the dandelions and thistle have access to light. Maclean's plot is covered in lilies of the valley and wild bluebells.

It is unmarked.

Legend

As has already been mentioned, the legend of 'John Ross' in Natal differs in several significant ways from the real life of Charles Maclean.

Although Maclean's own version of his Natal years has been available to English readers since the 1850s – and readily accessible in library collections in South Africa since the 1950s – it is fair to say that the many writers who have felt themselves capable of writing his biography – who have come to be considered authoritative on the man – have not felt the need to consult these sources. Rather, with a self-generating will of its own, and in a state of blissful unawareness, an entire sub-literature has accumulated around 'John Ross' without reference to the primary facts.

Research procedures, in other words, have been content to let secondary and subsequent renderings perpetuate themselves without the check of empirical verification. The fact is that not one published work on Natal history, including even the admirable collection of revisionary essays of 1989 (Duminy and Guest's *Natal and Zululand from Earliest Times to 1910*), has yet cited the seminal work of Charles Maclean. Can local landlubbers be that distrustful of foreign seafarers? We may indict the thoroughness of past historical researchers, and remark on the lack of curiosity of their contemporary descendants so keen to find sources to overturn them. Since only three extensive eye-witness records of life in Natal in the 1820s have come down to us, Isaacs', Fynn's and Maclean's, disregarding one of them is an oversight.

Like Fynn's and Isaacs' records, Maclean's is a meeting place of several intersecting issues: a climactic coming together of processes of transformation in south-east Africa in Shakan Zululand; the arrival there of merchant capital in the form of rather desperate and under-equipped parties; and above all the relationships of trade developed in this first contact phase. All three writers are at the interface – indeed, Maclean steps over it – between potential colonizer and colonized as well, at the very moment this huge historical action is initiated. Furthermore, Fynn's, Isaacs' and Maclean's experiences were very different in important ways, and on many fundamental issues they disagree. All three need careful and systematic sifting *vis-a-vis* one another before any possibility of a reliably adjusted picture may emerge.

Thus, at the very roots of history in Natal – be they reconstructions of the Zulu sociopolity, studies of the nature of the first white encroachment at Port Natal, or in the popular imagination in the stories of the two characters who symbolize this period most, the biographies of Shaka and 'John Ross' – a complicated and necessary process has failed to occur. Merely because he got into print first, the history has followed Isaacs, avoiding any more intricate and demanding debate. Thus, also, all of Natal history as it is today is loaded with a

Fraserburgh in the early 1800s. The parish school, built in 1787, can clearly be seen in the centre middle ground.

Fraserburgh in 1822. The picture shows Kinneard Head Castle which later became Scotland's first lighthouse. Engraving by Wm. Daniell.

The West India Docks, London, in the 1830s.   *Museum in Docklands*

A contemporary engraving of the town of Castries, Saint Lucia, in the 1830s.

Francis Farewell.

from Isaacs
by J.S. King

Shaka kaSenzangakhona.

National Museum, Bloemfon

Farewell's camp, sketched by J.P. Hoffman shortly after the wreck of the
***Julia* in 1824, prior to the arrival of King's party.**

certain bias that over the years has served the interests of its historians well enough. Naturally, to pull that trajectory back on track at this stage of its development is nigh impossible. Yet that is the challenge that Maclean's Natal papers represent for us today: beginning again.

This is not the place to make the attempt. Let it be sufficient here to give some notes towards a redefinition of 'history' in Natal that the Maclean documents provoke, with illustrations from this particular small – but crucial – case.

The evidence shows that historical myths are constructed by an accumulating process of selection and omission. Anyone reading Maclean's thick stew of data will be shocked at the thinness of the gruel we are usually served. Isaacs' own account of 'John Ross' is far more detailed and complex than he is usually given credit for, running to 1 000 words (in his Chapter 12). Half of this is summary of 'Ross's' own verbal account to King and Isaacs of the trading delegation to Delagoa Bay (see Commentary: Four). The dramatic setting is important: Maclean's seniors intercept the boy on his return leg, obviously anxious to have the massive load of 'necessaries' he and his staggering porters have brought with them. Because he has also brought them information about the far interior which at that moment they are attempting to survey, the boy is an asset indeed: the remoter tribes between them and Delagoa Bay are tractable, there is abundance of game, water hazards may be forded by native canoe, the Portuguese, by charging him next to nothing, encourage the expansion of this overland route – these are the points Isaacs makes.

Most important of all, the spindly boy has succeeded where most adult whites have failed. This is entirely thanks to the co-operation of Shaka and his armed escort, who obviously knew the route and had been using it through tributary territory for years, and so the boy has made his breakthrough. The network of trade, the great opener of the way – this is Isaacs' grand theme – has developed in alliance with the Zulus one more route to their mutual benefit.

Maclean would certainly agree with that assessment of his delegation. See his own account in the last item here, and passim in the fourth instalment of his *Loss of the Brig 'Mary'*. But while Maclean shrugs the feat off as 'somewhat perilous', Isaacs is determined to valorize him for his youth and 'enterprise', the two characteristics he most admires in himself. These are the germs of the 'John Ross' legend, which in spirit is more about Isaacs than Maclean. In Isaacs the bulk of Maclean's message – his abundant and enduring gratitude to his Zulu companions of the march for getting him through (piggybacking him?) – is getting lost. Isaacs is appallingly discourteous about Zulus and, although they kept him alive for years on end, never once acknowledges their help. Such dedicated and efficient partners in trade are the Zulus, Maclean wishes to say, that no Britisher or any other European dare lay a hand on them. Isaacs is more grudging; he already sees the Zulus as slaves. The snares of slavery set all about Zululand are joked away. Maclean replies, in the story of how the delegation ducked the Portuguese and French dealers, that Zulus, like Britishers, never will be slaves. Of all issues, for him this is the cutting edge – *his* grand theme. Isaacs' report is not true to his original.

From this nexus of information later commentators select the boy's adventurousness and economic skill. His blazing love of liberty, which is the entire point of his story, is left out. Under the label of Isaacs' casual misnomer – 'John Ross' – a legend is poised to take off. We must follow the warp it takes, if only sketchily, for it explains many things about historians and precious little about Maclean. Similar warps are taken in far larger stories – that of Shaka the Napoleon/Attila/Caesar/Nero, for example, which following Maclean needs drastically and urgently to be rewritten as well.

John Bird's *Annals of Natal* (1888), one of the first great sorting-houses of Natal documentation, selects from the records of only Farewell, King, Fynn and Isaacs as regards the 1820s at Port Natal, also in effect to legitimize British claims on Zulu-controlled territory. Maclean – who gives no grounds for such claims – is omitted. We have a classic example of the historian finding only that which he wishes to find.

By 1930 Graham Mackeurtan is his *Cradle Days of Natal* has discovered the usefulness of Maclean, but only as interpreted by Isaacs:

> . . . the party ran short of medicines, and John Ross, King's apprentice, a boy of fifteen, 'acute, shrewd, and active', was sent, with a few natives, to walk to Delagoa Bay and back. This meant a journey of nearly six hundred miles on foot. The mission was entirely successful, but John must have had many an anxious moment at night in the Lebombo mountains. . . . At the bay itself he fell in with the captain of a French slaver, who furnished him with so much of his needs without payment that John spent only two dollars. . . . The ravages of Tshaka and their repercussions had reduced the neighbourhood tribes to such a state of despair that numbers of them sold themselves to escape starvation. . . . It needed a brave heart and a wise head to complete the journey. As a physical effort alone it is worth recording; as the triumph of a mere child over the well-nigh invincible it is immortal. John Ross may, for all one knows, have died the undistinguished master of a leaky ship, but he sleeps in the Halls of Courage.[29]

Mackeurtan's discovery of the 'John Ross' story is interesting for a number of reasons. From Isaacs he takes over and extends an incipient polarization between blacks and whites: the hospitality of the Zulus, Tsongas and Shangaans which ensured the success of the 'mission' is now turned around to look as if their territories were actually the enemies', while the actual rivals of the British – the Portuguese and French – are recast as their allies and generous friends. The issue of slavery is dexterously manipulated, so that it appears Shaka's 'ravages' actually justified the trade. The status of Shaka's impi is now furiously cut back to a 'few natives', implying our hero led the 'boys'.

Macmillan in his *Durban Past and Present* of 1936 retells Mackeurtan, putting an even greater spin onto the story:

> . . . when it was found necessary to despatch a messenger to Delagoa Bay to procure much needed supplies, the person chosen for the enterprise was Farewell's young apprentice, John Ross, a lad of fifteen years of age, and it was thought politic that he should go entirely alone in order that Chaka's suspicions should not be aroused.[30]

Maclean is here entirely stripped of his Zulus and achieves apotheosis as the lone embodiment of white ingeniousness and daring. Now he undertakes the journey to outsmart the 'suspicious' Shaka. Why, one wishes to ask Macmillan, if the Zulus were so hostile, did 'John Ross' not go to Algoa Bay instead – half the distance away and in British hands? The answer is that without the Zulus he could not carry his load.

A lull in retellings of the 'John Ross' escapade follows, but when the business is revived it is the basic premise of Macmillan's version – Shaka's antipathy to the venture – which prevails.

When in 1950 the long awaited, third extensive eye-witness source of evidence about Shakan Zululand was at last published – *The Diary of Henry Francis Fynn* – writing about early Natal was given fresh impetus. The editing of these documents by James Stuart and his successor, D. McK. Malcolm, presents problems needing thorough review. Suffice it to say here that when 'John Ross' makes an appearance in Fynn's *Diary*, he only does so thanks to an interpolation by Fynn's editors, which summarizes – not Fynn himself – but Isaacs. Thus to enable this 15-year-old lad to make the journey:

> it was necessary for Isaacs to appeal to Shaka for an escort to protect Ross as well as provide him with food on his 330-mile journey there and back. Shaka supplied the escort and after a few weeks Ross returned safely.[31]

Stuart and Malcolm's logistics are inaccurate, even from a careful reading of Isaacs, who gives twenty-three days as the time taken by 'Ross' to have covered only the distance from Dukuza to Maputo. (See Maclean's own estimate in his letter.) So here we have fantasy statistics about a fantasy character whom Fynn himself, as far as we are able to tell, never mentioned.

The first of many monuments to commemorate 'John Ross', a tiled tablet, was laid (at children's eye-level) in the gardens of Durban's Old Fort in January 1954. [32] The wording is curious:

> . . . a lad of 15 years of age, who in 1827, braving the perils of an unexplored land inhabited by an unknown people and abounding in wild animals, walked with great courage from Port Natal to Delagoa Bay and back (a distance of 600 miles) in order to obtain medicines and other necessaries for the handful of pioneers at the Bay of Natal.

He is solo once more, against a hinterland of 'unknown people', an extraordinary erasure on the part of the Historical Monuments Commission. A newspaper report covering the unveiling remarks that this appealing story of an 'unknown, unsung boy' seems far too little known, and the 'John Ross' legend, boosted by the monument, really takes off from here.

Almost immediately E. A. Ritter's ever-selling *Shaka Zulu* of 1955 sees the light. Great and elaborated prominence is given in this to the 'John Ross' story:

> Arriving at Shaka's capital on his march to Delagoa Bay, young Ross called on the King, who received him kindly. Great was Shaka's astonishment on hearing that this mere child contemplated so hazardous a journey, accompanied only by two native servants, who even then had acquired an abounding faith in the protective powers of a European, even though he was but a boy! . . . The Zulus salute John Ross as *I-Qawu* – The Hero. [33]

Now the superiority of the white is explicit, the dramatic situation turned around to include even the Zulus paying homage to our subject.

Out of Ritter's fiction in 1958 the first book devoted wholly to 'John Ross' appears: Rex Gutridge's *Thunder over Africa*, a novel for children. Now 'John Ross' sets off barefoot, passes a slaver's ship at anchor off Mngeni without batting an eyelid, and continues on his lone flight without a word of Zulu. . . .

A far better novel follows hot on its heels: Elizabeth Paris Watt's *Febana: The True Story of Francis George Farewell, Explorer, Pioneer and Founder of Natal* (1962). Although he is not one of the main protagonists, in this powerful work 'John Ross' plays a substantial role. Here for the first time an author reveals the dilemma of the 'Ross'/Maclean situation. Indeed, Watt had previously made news out of the revelation of the boy's true identity and her finding of the *Loss of the Brig 'Mary'* narrative.[34] The report on her biographical evidence, sometimes inaccurate (or inaccurately reported) becomes frequently recycled hereafter.

In 1965 another Maclean finding is announced – the letter to the *Times* – in Donald R. Morris' *The Washing of the Spears*. His eccentric interpretation of it is dealt with in the Commentary. Both Watt and Morris, however, tend in effect to dispute Maclean, contorting his evidence back into the established Isaacs model, so that an unimpeded development of the 'John Ross' story may continue without upsetting any of the rest of the picture.

In 1966, having contradictory sources at his disposal, T.V. Bulpin in his *Natal and the Zulu Country* at least went back and read Isaacs more thoroughly. The Shakan escort is reinstated. J.L. Smail, on the other hand, in *With Shield and Assegai* in 1969, while fully aware of both new sources, comes up with the following in order to vindicate Isaacs:

> One of the reasons why John Ross was chosen was that he had resided with Shaka for some time and therefore there would be no possibility of Shaka giving any thought to suspect treason and a request for an escort to accompany the lad was granted.[35]

This extraordinary hoodwink shows the lengths to which commentators will go to conceal obvious truths, and how accordingly they reveal their own beliefs.

Perhaps the worst case of distortion is K. Schroeder's in a chapter devoted to 'Ross' in *Bravery in South Africa: Stories from our Heroic Past* (1972). On behalf of South Africa's white children the author expresses great sympathy for 'John Ross' for having had to spend so much time at Shaka's stinking kraal!

Although she uses the Maclean sources (not cited in her bibliography), R.E. Gordon is not much more insightful in her biography of 'John Ross' published in *Natalia* in 1974 to commemorate the 150th anniversary of Natal. This begins: 'His real name, he said, was Charles Rawden Maclean and he had run away to sea at the age of 12. . . .' From the wreck of the *Mary* at Port Natal 'Ross was saved by a Newfoundland dog. . . .' Isaacs apparently 'accounts for the popular name thus: being a sailor the lad was called Jack (or by Isaacs, John) and Ross because of his ginger hair . . .' although no detail in Isaacs substantiates this. His whole trip takes 'three weeks'. Any amount of misreading is permitted to tie in with the known facts.

In the same year Brian Roberts published his *The Zulu Kings*. Of the trip to Delagoa he writes:

King's choice for this hazardous mission was extraordinary. Knowing full well the dangers involved, he sent a fifteen-year-old apprentice known as John Ross (his name was actually Charles Rawden Maclean; he changed it to Ross when he ran away to sea as a child). . . . Shaka provided an escort and, to everyone's amazement, the plucky youngster returned in less than a month with the much needed medicines. . . . On his way back he had carefully avoided Shaka's kraal for fear that his medicines would be commandeered.[36]

Over twenty years the discovery of *Loss of the Brig 'Mary'* and the *Times* letter has made no impact at all. The Isaacs version, in a wilfully biased form, prevails.

Another work of reference, Tabler's *Pioneers of Natal and South-East Africa (1552–1878)* of 1977, serves only to obfuscate the situation further. Citing only Isaacs and the Stuart-Malcolm insert in Fynn, the entry on 'John Ross' now classes him as a ship's boy, assistant and an explorer (aged 16), and the initial point of his extreme youth is now lost as well.

Not so in 1987, however, when the youthful 'John Ross' version of Maclean reached what is probably its ultimate statement: the TV serial, *John Ross: An African Adventure*, produced by the SABC for family viewing. Suffice it to say that, glorious and persuasive as it was and purportedly based on truth, the serial was only tangentially to do with events as they actually occurred in Natal in the 1820s. It had, however, everything to do with how South Africans viewed themselves at the time. The mind-set of the movie was ours, not Maclean's. No shade of revisionist historiography had worked its way down to the market-place to darken any of the movie's light certainties.

Probably the reason why no scholar-historian bothers to investigate the 'John Ross' legend very far (apart from the enormous drain on time and money that biographical research demands) is that for South Africans 'John Ross' is frozen perpetually in the memory as a rather hyperactive, obedient child. He is not expected to have anything of interest to say for himself, since the authority of his elders and betters is unshakable, and they have done the talking for him. He is considered to have been instrumental, not influential. The spinners of legend merely insist that he be educated into what he must have been. That the Zululand experience gave him an alternative education is not anticipated, so this history from below is kept underfoot. No one imagines that John Ross might have grown up. Indeed, many comment that they do not know what happened to him after Port Natal, as if that ignorance were a virtue.

What he did once he had grown up is the substance of this book. It would be sheer parochialism to say now that this book is not relevant to the history of Natal.

Beyond selection and omission, which establishes the outline and parameters of a historical story, there is another technique which we must see as operative: replication. It takes only one repetition for a story to become fixed. Further repetitions, despite minor variations, serve to entrench the story, lending it an aura of gospel veracity. But this kind of story is legendary rather than factual; it answers to deep-felt needs in the writer's imagination that, even when the real evidence is at hand, preclude checking. The story itself is too good and too socially stirring to lose. The legend of 'John Ross' is important as a justificatory myth, validating the white English-speaking control of the coastline from Port Natal up to those foreign-speaking parts. It has detached itself from history as such; its essence is fictional. It is a national property with a life of its own.

Maclean himself knew how 'history' is made. This is clear in his main motivation for writing *Loss of the Brig 'Mary'*, the argument he chose to conduct with Kay. Quoting Kay's account of the traders at Port Natal, he comments:

> As these remarks of Mr Kay will be handed down to posterity as a matter of history, it is no less justice to the party assailed than a love of truth to refute them, seeing that from several discrepancies in Mr Kay's book in his account of Natal, relating at least to that in which I was an inferior actor (but eye-witness), is replete with error (Instalment Four).

Maclean's essential project is corrective, then. If he had written Isaacs' history into *his* account, we would probably have a fabulous story of a unicorn-hunter.

But Kay writes of Natal as an evaluator, using selective telling, omission, analysis and extrapolation to arrive at a kind of history which to Maclean is based on false assumptions. Maclean counters this process as a revaluator, widening the selection, filling in omissions, and where he finds untruths in a polemical way analysing the motives behind them. His technique is to expose and to demystify in order to reduce history back to a few basic statements of belief and event. The corrective impetus in Maclean's project keeps him on the go – it is his means of trying to understand what history itself is. This gives *Loss of the Brig 'Mary'* its appealing and compelling dialectic.

Maclean is also well aware of how dangerous history can be if it is not based upon foundations of justice and truth. Hence the occasional bitterness in his attacks on Kay, his defensiveness on his own behalf and his extreme reticence.

But what later historians have done to Maclean would surely be unimaginable to him. They have not let the court-room of history admit his evidence. His testimony has been prevented from being heard. Instead, out of the spindly details, later historians have constructed another persona for him, complete with low-class genealogy – the legendary 'John Ross' – to ventriloquise back to them what they want us to hear. And the possibility of argumentation – of dialogue – that he initiated has been ruled out of court.

There are signs, however, of a reverse flow in the celebration of the 'John Ross' legend, even if they do not lead back decisively to the source. In his entry in the latest volume of the *Dictionary of South African Biography* (Vol.5, p.659, 1987), J. Laband settles for leaving Maclean under 'John Ross', probably a wise decision. Laband acknowledges the name holds only for the youthful Natal legend, and identifies Charles Rawden Maclean as the original. For the first time he points out that there is a third version of the same: the child known as Jackabo to the Zulu people. This new character – the one who needs to be worked up as the 'Jackabo' legend of the future – is the focal one in the present collection, for it is 'Jackabo's' Natal which needs to be recreated. Although it contains many slips of minor significance, Laband's profile is the closest to accurate that South African history has produced in a cycle that has lasted over a century and a half.

The publication of this collection of Maclean's material – never used before to any significant extent as a pure source for writers – may serve to redirect that cycle back to its take-off point, and initiate the different direction Maclean intended us to find and interpret.

In the days of the formation of that historical drama Maclean cast himself, realistically enough, as an 'inferior actor'. He was never partial to the personality cult which has so flourished about his fictional alternative. As a child he had no leverage on the course of affairs, or at least not until he was later positioned to exercise a minimal amount at the Shakan court. An extra among the protagonists, he spectated . . . and later recorded. Unlike Isaacs, who knew which side he was on, young 'Jackabo' was profoundly muddled in his allegiances. In choosing the middle way he became a unique example in the Zululand of that time.

But whom did he serve – Mr King or King Shaka? Whichever way he chose, he was a traitor. His terror in the last paragraphs of *Loss of the Brig 'Mary'* is about this dilemma. He claimed he had no choice, that events abandoned him in that pivotal position. He learned, however, to transcend that falsely binary situation, emerged from it, somehow, equipped for a future that none of the other players could foresee: the liberation of his spirit, as a man of deeper justice and truth. This is how the play of history in Natal read for Maclean. This is his message.

The possibility of this being the new core of the story is far too noble and inspiring for us to keep pretending we do not know it is there to be found.

Notes

1 Held on microfiche at the Aberdeen and North-East Scotland Family History Society, Aberdeen, p. FR 309. All the information in this section is derived from their resources.

2 See his Chart of Port Natal, 1854, reproduced at the end of this book.

3 See respective entries in the *Dictionary of South African Biography*, which are listed in the Bibliography.

4 See, for example, J.P. Maclean, *Renaissance of the Clan MacLean* (Columbus, Ohio, 1913), which includes a 'Maclean Bibliography'. The secretary's reports of the London and District branch of the Clan Maclean Association of the 1950s are unhelpful, as are those of the Glasgow branch. The Maclean Museum in Greenock, near Glasgow, has no further information. See also John Robert Ross, *The Great Clan Ross, with Highland Notes and Genealogies of the Cadet Branches in Scotland and the New World* (printed in Canada, 1968).

5 For these details see the British Library catalogue under Ross, John.

6 See R.H.W. Shepherd, *Lovedale, South Africa: The Story of a Century (1841–1941)* (Lovedale: Lovedale Press, 1941).

7 John Cranna, *Fraserburgh: Past and Present* (Aberdeen: Rosemount Press, 1914), p. 398.

8 See Folarin Shyllon, *James Ramsay: The Unknown Abolitionist* (Edinburgh: Canongate, 1977).

9 Information from Mr George Dey, Fraserburgh (20 April 1990).

10 See T.C. Smout, *A History of the Scottish People (1580–1830)* (London: Fontana, 1972) and Tom Steel, *Scotland's Story* (London: Collins, 1984) generally.

11 A chronology of the 1825–28 events at Port Natal is most conveniently established from Isaacs.

12 *A Voyage to the West Indies* (July 1857), pp. 358–9. Full details of works by Maclean are given in the Bibliography. These are all held in the Killie Campbell Library.

13 See Sidney W. Mintz, *Sweetness and Power: The Place of Sugar in Modern History* (London: Penguin, 1985).

14 Information from the Library of the London Museum in Docklands Project, London E 14. Also see *Nicholson's Guide to London Docklands*.

15 *Natal Almanack and Register for AD 1864* (Pietermaritzburg: Davis, 1863), p. 95.

16 Public Record Office, Kew, BT 122: Certificate No. 6835.

17   These are *The Palladium and Saint Lucia Free Press* (Apr. 1839–Apr. 1840); *The Independent Press* (4 Sept. 1839, Jan, 1843–Dec. 1844); *The Saint Lucian* (1863–1873) with considerable gaps; *The Saint Lucia Observer* (July 1874–1876), continued as *The Observer* (Dec. 1876); *The Voice* (Aug. 1879–May, 1882); and *The Voice of Saint Lucia* (1885–1887), all published at Castries, Saint Lucia. As changes of title are of no significance to Maclean's story, only dates of publication of items are given.

18   See Henry H. Breen, *Saint Lucia: Historical, Statistical, and Descriptive* (London: Longman, 1844) and C. Jesse, *Outlines of Saint Lucia's History* (Castries: The Voice, 1956).

19   See the editor's comments in 'The Liberty of British Subjects Invaded in the United States', p. 68.

20   *Notes on a Voyage from England to Balaclava* (Dec. 1856), p. 671.

21   Editor's note, *The Nautical Magazine* (Dec. 1857), p. 659.

22   See Robert J. Devaux, 'Saint Lucia Steam Conveyance Co., Ltd. – Locals', *British Caribbean Philatelic Journal*, Vol. 27, No. 3 (Sept. 1987), p. 74. This source is heavily used in what follows.

23   Held in the archives of the Saint Lucia National Trust, Castries.

24   Quoted in J.H. Parry, Philip Sherlock and Anthony Maingot, *A Short History of the West Indies* (4th ed.) (London: Macmillan, 1987), p. 167.

25   Sir William Robinson to the Earl of Kimberley (26 June 1880), Letterbook, p. 183. Saint Lucia National Trust.

26   See Norman Clothier, *Black Valour: The South African Native Labour Contingent (1916–1918) and the Sinking of the 'Mendi'* (Pietermaritzburg: University of Natal Press, 1987).

27   These items from *The Hampshire Advertiser County Newspaper*, library of *The Southern Echo*, Southampton.

28   The plot number is 259, in Section 163. According to the Cemeteries Office, Bush Street, Southampton, Maclean died aged 67 years (which would make him born in 1813). The burial ceremony was performed by Revd Keble. The deceased's address was given as Oxford Street, Saint James Parish (this means the local mortuary). Because he died at sea, his death certificate is kept in the overseas registry section at Saint Katherine's House, London. I am grateful to Dr Robert Green of the University of Southampton for tracing this information on Maclean's gravesite.

29   Graham Mackeurtan, *The Cradle Days of Natal (1497–1845)* (London: Longmans, Green, 1930), pp. 137–9.

30   Allister Macmillan, *Durban Past and Present: Historical, Descriptive, Commercial, Industrial* (Durban: William Brown and Davis, 1936), p. 15.

31 *The Diary of Henry Francis Fynn* (Pietermaritzburg: Shuter and Shooter, 1969), p. 131.

32 See 'Forgotten Boy Hero Remembered', *Natal Mercury* (22 Jan. 1954).

33 E. A. Ritter, *Shaka Zulu* (London: Longmans, Green, 1955), pp. 253–5.

34 See 'Identity of Young Natal Pioneer Hero Solved', *Natal Mercury* (11 Dec. 1957). Watt (Mrs Gooderham) researched the story thoroughly, establishing for the first time the basic outline of the Maclean biography up to 1861, which this book confirms and elaborates. I am grateful and indebted to her. Maclean's *Loss of the Brig 'Mary'* and his letter to the *Times* have been available in the Killie Campbell Africana collection and other libraries since Mrs Gooderham's research.

35 J. L. Smail, *With Shield and Assegai* (Cape Town: Timmins, 1969), p. 35.

36 Brian Roberts, *The Zulu Kings* (London: Hamish Hamilton, 1974), pp. 118–9.

Note on the text

Maclean's work in this collection has been edited to conform to modern orthography. There is one exception – his use of the word 'Caffre' to mean indigenous peoples of South-East Africa distinct from 'Zulus' has been retained. Similarly 'Hutton' has been retained although later writers use 'Hatton'; Maclean's version is probably correct. The spelling of many South African words in his original varies: for example, for 'Bulawayo', there is 'Umboltalilo', 'Umbollali', 'Umbalallo', 'Umbalilos' and 'Cembalillo', indicating a typesetter's difficulty in deciphering manuscript. As variant spellings are of no significance to the meaning of the text, they have been standardized.

The following list is of the complete editorial changes:

amaMpondo – Amonponda
assegai – assagai
Boer – boor
Bulawayo – Umboltalilo, Umbollali, Umbalallo, Umbalilos, Cembalillo
Dingane – Dingan
Dukuza – Toogoosa, Toogosa
Farewell – consistently Farwell until the *Times* letter
Hlambamanzi – Slamla Manzie
imbongi – izebonkar
impi – impee
indaba – indabo
induna – umdoona
inkomo – inkoma
inkosikazi – incasagass
inyanga – enguager, ingangen
isangoma – eveyonga
isigodlo – izekoshlee
isilwane – sillwana
ithanga – etanger
kraal – crawl, occasionally kroll
Manyos – also Moagos
Maphisi – Mapeesee
Mathubane – Matanabanahs, Mattabana, Mottoban
Mbopha – Boper
Mhlathuze – Umslatus
Mlungu – Molongo, Moolongo, Moolonga
Mngeni – Umgainih, Amgani, Umganie
mpaka – Impaka
Nandi – Um Nauta, Umnante
Nezinwele bomvu – Nuelizebomfoo

Ngangezwe – Kanggesevie, ganggaswiee
Nkosi – inkosse
Nkosi kakhulu – Inkosiqa koola
phesheya kolwandle – pizeah illuanshla
phezulu – pizoola
Quashie – Quachee
Rachel – sometimes given as Rachael
Sakubona wethu – Saga bona wintoo
Shaka – once Chaka, once Chaker
Sikhunyana – Izee-can-yon'a, Izeecanyana
Sothobe – Satoby, Sotobie
Thukela – Zootagoola, Umtoologalie
ufudu – lafoota
umfokazana – umfogasann
umkhumbi – uncombie
umntwana/abantwana – untwane
umnumzana – etumgan
umphakati – umpagate
umthakati – umtagatie
umutsha – muchu
yayize – izee
yebo – yeabo
Zulu – invariably Zoola.

As the variant spellings (Rachael/Rachel) indicate, it is virtually certain that Maclean could never have gone back and adjusted material that had already appeared in print, especially not as his serial proceeded. Thus we must assume that any later or more frequent spelling was his preferred one, and the texts have been standardised accordingly.

More generally, it is almost certain that he had no opportunity to proof-read any of his material, so that in a very few cases uncharacteristic syntactical inexactitudes occur (for example, being for having been) – these are silently corrected here. Particularly at the start of his serial paragraphing is infrequent; where for a modern reader the text is simply too dense or impenetrable, paragraphs have been introduced in conformity with his later style. In facilitating the modern reader, nevertheless, no corrections have been made that in any way could be construed as distorting or revising the clear expression of the originals. A complete record of all sub-editorial changes has been deposited in the 'John Ross' holdings of the Killie Campbell Africana Library, from which the texts were first copied.

In what follows when an editorial change to the text first occurs the original is indicated in square brackets.

THE NATAL PAPERS

Loss of the Brig *Mary* at Natal
with Early Recollections of that Settlement

and

Among the Caffres

Loss of the Brig Mary at Natal with Early Recollections of that Settlement

ONE

The Nautical Magazine, January 1853, pp. 29–36

The recent events that have drawn public attention to Natal have recalled to my memory scenes of that now interesting place, as it was in the years 1824 and 1825. In those days it was little known to Europeans; the native Zulus [Zoolas] were then ruled by the brother of the present Chief Dingane [Dingan], the invincible Shaka [Chaker], when his sway extended from the frontier tribes of the amaMpondo [Amonpondas] on the west to the Portuguese settlement of Delagoa Bay on the east.

To relate the many interesting and tragical scenes witnessed by me during a three years' residence amongst those savages, at an early period of my life (being but a boy thirteen years old), would be beyond my power. They pass in review before me like a painted and romantic dream, yet with all the force of reality that early impressions are calculated to produce on the mind. Little connection, therefore, can be expected when narrating those events on which I now look back through a long vista of years; and had not great events agitated this portion of Eastern Africa recently, bringing my old friends the Zulus to my recollection in a most interesting light, they would have passed away 'as a tale that is told'.

I may here remark that many of my old native friends will yet recollect the little Mlungu [Molongo] who told them with all the eloquence of their language of the power and greatness of his king, the truth of which they have lived to see wonderfully verified. Little did they then dream that the successors of that king would rule over the destiny of the Zulu nation. They may remember that I told them though our king was great he was also merciful, kind and benevolent – the protector of the stranger and the weak from the violence of the strong. This I trust they have also experienced at the hands of those who have gone amongst them, and that they have been enabled to distinguish the servants of our king from the rude and lawless Boers [boors] by whom they have been assailed. I owe them a debt of gratitude that leads me to wish and to hope my countrymen, whosoever they be, will exercise that mercy and kindness toward them which I experienced at their hands in the day of their rule. Those are yet living to whom I am indirectly indebted for my life, and I trust their goodness will meet a just reward by kindness and forbearance at the white man's hands.

While I rejoice to contemplate the faint ideas that I endeavoured to impress them with of the great King of Kings, my Baba Phezulu [Pizoola], to whom I looked up for protection, I know they will in time be more fully impressed on them by the pious exertions of those worthy missionaries, who with unwearied zeal and labour are devoting their time and talents to the great work of their salvation.

Of the country I need take little notice, as it is now known from the later and better description of recent intelligent travellers that would render superfluous any attempt of mine to describe its beauty or resources. But I shall ever retain a vivid recollection of its 'woods and wilds and solitary glens', the beautiful ever-verdant and luxuriant valleys of the Mngeni [Umgainih], the towering forest-clad heights of the Bulawayo [Umboltalilo] and the peaceful serenity of the profound silent depths beneath them.

Oft have I wandered with weary foot where nature reigned in solemn, silent majesty; where the patriarch of the forest raised his majestic form that had withstood the storms of a thousand years, affording a home and shelter to many a happy family, while his wide extended arms, scarred by the blasts of time, stretched affectionately over the heads of a young and rising generation, among whose peaceful foliage they would one day fall to repose in peace. When I recall to mind my frequent solitary wanderings through the mazes of their silent gloom – a silence how pleasing to contemplate! for man had not then assumed dominion to disturb its primitive repose – a feeling of regret comes over me. Those scenes have lost their sublime and peaceful charm, that hallowed repose with which they are associated in my mind.

I mourn the change. I lament the fate of that great menagerie which lived in quiet and uninterrupted security, now alas invaded by the destroying hand of the Boer, armed with the destructive implements of death devised by civilised man, to wage a deadly and exterminating war among those once happy families of the creation. How often have I seen them disporting and gambolling before me, happy in the security of their natural and never disputed home, provided by a wise and beneficent creator; abounding in all the beauties and grandeur of a land over-shadowed with forests as a 'Land of Promise'.

The following extract from the journal of Mr James King, our lamented Commander, will better describe some of the casualties which led to the unfortunate loss of our vessel than any account from memory:

Sept. 1825. Nothing of the least consequence happened until making the land, except the usual change of wind, &c., which we observed on the 29th about noon, near Saint Lucia. Our motive for making so far to the eastward was to enable us to visit Natal at discretion. Had we made only a few miles to the northward and eastward, and no opportunity of landing, with the wind eastwardly, together with the current, we should in all probability have been swept to leeward of our port.

We experienced this daylight light baffling winds; however, with the assistance of the current, we were the next morning in a good position, Natal Head bearing S.W. by W. three leagues distant. On my former voyage I ascertained the depth and nature of the bar, time of high water, &c., &c., which by calculation had by this time arrived. However, having no wish to enter the harbour with the vessel, we lowered the whaleboat, which had been previously prepared with a few days' provisions for myself and others, with instructions for the vessel to lay off and on shore, until we had some tidings of those we had come in quest of. The bar proved too heavy to be attempted in the boat, and previous to her return the vessel was anchored in a good position, to enable her to stand out of the bay if required. Unhappily, however, she drove with an increasing gale.

The object was now to get the boat on board, as there was no other alternative, and with difficulty she succeeded in reaching the vessel, which had now brought up with nearly a whole cable. Veered the boat astern, and employed in getting all clear for making sail, to stand out until a more favourable opportunity offered; but alas! our attempts were by this time evidently fruitless, the vessel scudding forward in a most turbulent sea, and the rocks off the point extending too far to weather, and on the opposite tack we could do nothing.

One opportunity presented itself, which must speedily be seized, otherwise I knew the tide would not admit of success. The harbour was now my object, although if we failed in getting over the bar, the chances were that every soul might have perished, or otherwise left destitute and at the mercy of the natives. Not a living soul to be seen on shore added much to our distressed situation. Had the natives come boldly out of the bushes, we should have been under no apprehension in landing, having only the violence of the sea to contend with, which might have been surmounted. But to experience all the fatigue of shipwreck and at last be obliged to give ourselves up as their prey was by no means a pleasant idea. However, it fortunately happened that we were so much engaged with the vessel that our thoughts, I may venture to say, were seldom devoted to anything else.

I now consulted with the officers and people, as their lives and the safety of the vessel entitled them. They readily agreed that my proposition was the best and only method. We therefore turned to with one heart, got a spring on our cable from the port quarters and the head sails, foretopsail and foresail ready for casting and setting. We cut our cable, and in less than three minutes after getting before the wind (all anxiety), she settled between two heavy seas on the bar, and struck fore and aft with a most awful surge. The next sea almost overwhelmed us.

She again and repeatedly struck with the same violence, which broke off the rudder and started her floors; at this time she made a considerable quantity of water. The ebb tide making out strong caught her on the port bow, which was in deep water, and directed her head to starboard out of the proper channel. All our attempts to prevent this by bracing the head sails to, and setting after sail, proved ineffectual. The tide had now considerably left her, with her head settling into deep water and rolling desperately; the sea too heavy to risk a boat, therefore the only hope now remaining was to get a hawser to the beach, and have it conveyed to the rocks on our port beam, which on the flowing tide might assist the vessel's head to port to get into a better position (although at this time almost a perfect wreck), where we might be able to save such necessaries as would prove useful, for in her present situation on the bar the sea would in a very short time break her to pieces.

The whaleboat had been previously stove and sunk, jollyboat too small, and the longboat, on examining her, we found that in consequence of the sea displacing her from the chocks, a plank in the bottom was much broken, but was soon repaired and chanced. In the interim, and at intervals, succeeded in cutting away the sails from the yards, as also lightening the vessel with everything that was likely to find its way to the beach, having already observed many parts of the wreck washing up in executing this duty. The conduct of the crew was admirable. Our boat being ready, we succeeded in launching her, but was almost immediately filled alongside by the heavy surges, which continued throughout making a fair sweep over us. She was veered under the bows, and bailed out for the purpose of carrying a hawser to the rocks, which we could not succeed in doing, the boat having swamped several times. Our smallest bower anchor was carried off to the port quarter with the cable, and a purchase in the main boom-end to carry it clear of the vessel, and let go, which had a trifling good effect, but the scope was too short. The object of doing this was to prevent her forcing upon a bank directly ahead, between which and our present situation was a deep channel.

We succeeded at length in coiling a quantity of new and small line in the boat, for the purpose of conveying the hawser to the shore. Myself and four of the crew lowered ourselves from the bowsprit, and accomplished this part so far as to reach the beach, but owing to the strong current, and the line getting entangled with the rocks, produced no good effect. We were not only disheartened by this unfortunate circumstance, but had our dismal wreck and shipmates to view in the distance. To return again to them at this moment appeared almost an impossibility, but to attempt it we determined on, and after much difficulty, having shipped several heavy seas, we providentially succeeded. Previous to our arrival on board, everything had been done to lighten the vessel by throwing overboard such things that were most likely to reach the shore, and our wishes in this particular were gratified in part, which gave us fresh vigour.

The tide was now half-flood, and every article moving about in the hold, when a fortunate sea forced her from the bar to the inner bank. I say fortunate, because all our former attempts to remove to a more eligible situation proved fruitless. By having the wreck on this bank, it appeared we should have a prospect of saving some articles of consequence, at least the pieces from the wreck, in which hope we may thank God we were not disappointed to a great extent under all circumstances. Eleven hours having now elapsed since first striking, we naturally expected the party we came to assist had been murdered.

The vessel kept still gaining to the beach, but we could not attempt to land anything, and not a most distant hope remained of ever getting her again afloat. To save the carpenter's tools was now the principle object, to enable us to build a little craft as the only prospect of getting to the civilized world. But how often does it happen that those articles which are most anxiously sought to be preserved in cases of shipwreck are the first to give disappointment. This happened in the present unfortunate instance; the vessel having been thrown on her beam ends by a heavy sea, almost every movable article was washed overboard. Among others of consequence were part of the carpenter's tools.

Some of the crew succeeded in saving their clothes in part, others were not so fortunate and lost their all: and I have much pleasure in acknowledging my entire gratitude for the indefatigable exertions of Mr Hutton and crew during this unfortunate catastrophe, with but one exception. Never did I witness men more ready to obey, some at the imminent peril of their lives. A few only composed the crew of our ill-fated vessel, and few, I may venture to assert, could excel them, though I never had the misfortune to be shipwrecked before during eighteen years' service at sea, and Heaven forbid I ever should again. To the merciful goodness of Providence we all acknowledged our gratitude in thus preserving us through this disastrous adventure.

On the morning after our vessel was stranded on the bar we were obliged to abandon her, a heavy sea during the night having struck her and thrown her on her beam ends, which compelled us to take shelter, with great difficulty, on the broadside of the ship. where we passed a most miserable and anxious night. Tremendous seas were dashing against her with the deafening report of cannon, which every moment we expected would wash us off the wreck.

Threatened as we were by the raging sea and the unabated fury of the storm, little hope could be entertained of reaching land. And then we might only have escaped being swallowed by the waves to be devoured by wild beasts or cruelly murdered by the savages. Daylight was not even looked forward to with hope, for it would but reveal to us more awfully our perilous condition, and but tantalize us with the flattering and delusive prospect of a shore which, if reached in safety, would be but a change of horror. But still on passed the hours of this painful night: sixteen human beings clinging to the channels and dead eyes on the broadside of the ship, balancing in their thoughts the chances of being swallowed up by the waves or to be mutilated and devoured on reaching the shore by cruel and bloodthirsty savages.

How little then in such circumstances would a sight of the glorious sun minister to the relief of my distressed mind. No language could express the feelings I experienced in those awful hours, when a watery grave, or a thousand deaths too fearful to contemplate, awaited us. Death has no power, no horrors, beyond this. What words can describe the inward wild emotions at such a moment, and the terrible conflict that passes there, when time is about to close on us, and an unknown eternity is about to dawn. Alas! what a bubble does then appear the great and absorbing interest of this world, which has engrossed so much of our thoughts and has given us so much disquiet. To me, although so young, how evanescent did life appear when at that moment, standing meditating on its close, all those feelings rose in review before me.

When I look back and contemplate these moments of despair I trust that this early lesson of God's providence will ever stimulate my gratitude to Him for my deliverance. That providence so signally manifested in that hour of peril taught me the truth of those lines,

> Judge not the Lord by feeble sense,
>   But trust him for his grace;
> Behind a frowning providence
>   He hides a smiling face.

Night with all our fearful forebodings passed away, and never did the sun rise on a more helpless and dejected being than I was. Indeed, I cannot say that any of my companions in misfortune appeared to be much better. The only one who seemed to smile on our misfortunes was the captain: he indeed bore the appearance of that cool and unsubdued calmness of mind, so essential in the hour of peril, when our vessel was thrown on her beam ends, which happened about midnight. Her masts were all cut away to relieve the hull, and as the sun rose a wild scene of ruin and destruction was presented to our view.

Before us lay the smooth and even strand on which the waves of the angry South Indian lashed in vain, while, further on, the green hills covered with large stately trees now bending to the storm. Behind us, in endless succession rolled on the mountains of accumulated waters with white foaming crests, bursting over our devoted bark, while the whole line of strand abreast of our position and as far as it extended was strewn with wreck – masts, yards, sails, cordage, all lay scattered in endless confusion amidst the angry billows. The whole presented a scene of grandeur and desolation more easily imagined than described.

Such must ever be associated with my recollections of Natal. This day, indeed, presented to us a melancholy spectacle. Our proud floating home that had but a few short hours before been gaily dancing on the waves, with a dozen light and buoyant spirits enjoying the comforts and security of their wooden walls, now lay shattered and mutilated, a mere wreck on which there was no longer shelter. It is a sad spectacle at any time or place to contemplate the wreck of a noble vessel, but sadder still to those who from it can see no friendly shore of refuge, and the fate of their bark, in all human probability, involved that of her crew.

Towards noon the gale had abated, and the waves having forged the vessel on a sand bank, at low water the sea had become comparatively smooth, which enabled us to look to our boats, which having been washed overboard and swamped under the lee of the brig, had fortunately been protected by the hull. One was useless, but the longboat, which was fortunately uninjured, was cleared of water and loaded with provisions and despatched for the shore. On reaching it we had the mortification of seeing her turned bottom up the moment she touched the beach, and our provisions were soon scattered along the strand, among which were two or three bags of bread. Fortunately none of the boat's crew were lost, and but one man received a slight injury.

The boat having been got up and launched again returned on board, and the sea continuing to subside, we resumed the landing of provisions and anything come-atable that was likely to become of use.

Fearing to remain another night on the wreck, in case of her breaking up or of being washed off into the sea on the flowing of the tide, it was resolved that we should take up our quarters on terra firma. A place was accordingly selected for pitching our tents. By sunset, with great exertion, we had succeeded, by picking up spars and sails from the wreck on the beach, in completing a shelter sufficiently capacious for the accommodation of our whole party, at least to protect us from the night rains. We collected sufficient fuel to preserve a blazing fire to keep off the wild animals, with which the neighbouring woods abounded. Having duly arranged our tents and secured within them what provisions were landed from the wreck, we made our fires around them. Setting a watch, the rest lay down to repose after the fatigue of this day.

But, notwithstanding the vigilance of the watch in keeping up the fires, besides occasionally discharging fire-arms in the direction of the woods, about midnight one of our finest men was snatched away and carried off by a tiger! This was sufficient to arouse us, but the noise occasioned by the howling of these animals had become so appalling that all further sleep was out of the question. We had all to stand until daylight dawned with muskets presented in all directions, expecting every moment to be attacked by these ferocious beasts, whose howling had become literally deafening from their approaching to within a few paces of our tent. Thus was passed the first night of my residence at Port Natal.

On the following day the weather was fine, the sea smooth and our vessel lay in the same position as when abandoned the previous evening. We therefore resolved to take advantage of the fine weather and smoothness of the sea to land the remainder of the materials and stores that were left between decks. There being six feet water in the lower hold at low water, the tide flowing in and out of the vessel obliged us to confine our operations to what could be got at between decks, when at low water we could fish up articles from the lower hold. We launched our boats and pushed off to the wreck, which could now be reached with perfect safety in the smallest boat, and commenced removing everything into the boats that they could carry. By noon we had succeeded in landing two six-pounder carronades with which to fortify our position in case of need.

In the afternoon several of the natives made their appearance. They were males, perfectly naked, jet black, and had a singular bright shining appearance from their skins being rubbed with grease. They seemed to keep aloof as if afraid to venture near our tent, and appeared to look on with much astonishment and made many singular gestures, which we could not comprehend as to whether they were friendly or hostile.

Towards evening, while on our last trip to the wreck, we observed another party of natives who had made more bold than the preceding, having assembled close to our tents. Shortly, however, we perceived a tattered rag hoisted on a pole, supported by what appeared to be either a man or a woman in European garments. On our landing we found the person to be a Hottentot woman of Mr Farewell's [Farwell's] party, who spoke to us in good English, and gave us some pleasing and interesting information.

Loss of the Brig Mary *at Natal*
with Early Recollections of that Settlement

Two

The Nautical Magazine, February 1853, pp. 74–80

Rachel [Rachael], the Hottentot woman, informed us that she was left in charge of Mr Farewell's establishment at the head of Natal Harbour, called Fort Farewell;[1] that Mr Farewell and the male portion of the party were absent, with the chief of the country's forces, against a neighbouring tribe in the north-east, called the Sikhunyana [Izee-can-yon'a]; that the chief in whose dominions we then were was called Shaka, King of the Zulus; that the Zulus were a powerful tribe, and Shaka, the King, a great conqueror. But what proved to us the most pleasing part of Rachel's narrative was that this King Shaka was very friendly disposed towards the white people, and that we might rest assured of his protection; that Mr Farewell and his party had been called on to assist the Zulus in the contest with the Sikhunyana, for their safety depended on the Zulus being victorious, as the hostile chief was not considered friendly to the white man, but no compulsory measures had been adopted to enforce the white men to join the impi [Impee] (war or army).

Rachel wound up her account with a kind invitation to Fort Farewell, which was accepted by Mr Isaacs, a passenger, who accompanied her to the latter place. The pleasing part of Rachel's narrative, respecting the friendliness of King Shaka with the white men, infused a degree of cheerfulness among us, and the truth of her tale was evinced by the respect shown to her and us by the natives who accompanied her from Fort Farewell. She seemed to possess complete control over them, ordering them about at her pleasure, and chastising them with a cane if

---

1 Ruins of Farewell's house and fort, and also of the wreck of the *Mary*, appear on the plan of Port Natal by W. T. Haddon, Master of the brig *Dove*, in 1835, published by the Admiralty, and which differs sadly from another of the same port, published also by the Admiralty, done in 1831 by Commander E. Hawes, showing how little we know of that harbour, for they are both little better than sketches. (Editor, *Nautical Magazine*)

they did not give prompt obedience to her orders. She told us they were the servants at Fort Farewell, and that the lower order of natives were great thieves, and cautioned us to watch them closely.

Port Natal lies in lat. 29° 53′ S., and long. 31° 2′ E.; is bounded on the West by the Cape, of which there are three, called the Points of Natal, first, second and third, the latter of which bounds the western entrance to the harbour of Natal, being a bold promontory and rising to a considerable elevation above the neighbouring coast to the eastward, and on the whole presents a remarkable headland, by which Port Natal may be readily distinguished. On the East side the entrance to Natal is formed by a low sandy point, which, as it trends eastward, rises in detached and conical shaped sandhills, but as the sand composing these hills is very loose they occasionally undergo changes in appearance from the effect of the wind; while some entirely disappear, others are thrown up in their neighbourhood, varying in size and shape in proportion to the force of the wind. Indeed, the whole strand on the eastern side of the harbour appears (as also the Bar) to be a moving mass of sand, and is perpetually undergoing change. The eastern point terminates a thick wood on its interior side; a fine sandy beach thence bends to the N.E., forming a somewhat deep bay, in which there is anchorage off the bar.

Cape Natal bears S.S.W. from the mouth of the Mngeni and Mhlathuze [Umslatus] rivers, the latter now called river Saint Lucia. For about twenty miles the land is moderately high, and declining gradually towards the sea coast, with a fine sandy beach, until passing the river Saint Lucia in an E.S.E. direction, it then becomes rocky and precipitous. The land about Natal harbour is high and generally mountainous, but contains fertile valleys. On the western boundary of the harbour the soil is mostly composed of a red clay, while that on the eastern side is of a light sandy nature, and has the appearance of having been at some remote period submerged by the waters of the ocean.

The land around Natal is favourable for the production of guinea-corn and maize, as was evinced by the extensive gardens cultivated by the natives. This tribe of Mathubane [Mattabana], the amaThuli, occupy the western shore of the port, and pay to Shaka fifty bushels of each of the above-mentioned produce annually in their agricultural operations.

These poor natives in the vicinity of Port Natal were dreadfully annoyed by bands of predatory monkeys, which in their marauding expeditions committed the most dreadful havoc in their gardens and cornfields. Even while they were planting, these mischievous animals would make their incursions to the fields, and pick the corn out of the ground with such dexterity, that it required the greatest vigilance on the part of the sowers to prevent them from completely robbing an acre of land of its seed corn in a very short time. Their cunning also almost surpasses belief; in fact, they often outwit the natives by their ingenuity in carrying on their depredations, and oblige them to be constantly on the alert to counteract their work of devastation on the gardens.

When a troop of these animals meditate an attack on a field of corn (for it appears to be done by consent of numbers), their first object is to send an old experienced party of their race to reconnoitre, and if the coast is clear, which is speedily communicated by the reconnoitring party, down sallies the whole herd in the quietest manner possible, selecting the most hidden road to the field of operation, which gained, sentinels are placed in every commanding position to warn the spoilers of an approaching enemy. In this manner they first gorge themselves, and in addition carry off armfuls to secrete in the bush, and they will again return, if not warned by danger, to increase their store, where it is hoarded up for less fortunate times. In this way a whole field of corn has been literally carried off, and it very rarely happens that any is ever after recovered, unless a timely pursuit is made, when the booty is regained; but when pursued by women, they have been known to show fight for it.

The county is well watered about Natal by numerous rivulets, besides several large rivers, as the Mngeni, the Thukela [Zootagoola] and Mhlathuze to the N.E., while there are several large rivers on the N.W. towards the frontiers of the Cape Colony. The only drawback to the Natal country (if it shall ever become peopled by a civilised race) is its want of harbours, the Port Natal being the only navigable creek on the whole of this extensive coast eastward to the Portuguese settlement of Delagoa Bay at the mouth of the Mozambique Channel. The entrance of Port Natal is impeded by a sandbar extending across it, but to vessels inside it affords the most perfect security. There are many sandy flats inside that dry at low water, but the channels are deep, and vessels of a larger draught than could come over the bar might lay afloat at all times of the tide, by mooring head and stern in the stream during the lowest tides. At the head of the harbour are several small islands, well wooded, and on an average it contains an area of 150 acres.

From these islands large sandy flats extend, dry at low water, when they frequently present a beautiful and interesting sight in hundreds of flamingoes ranged over them, their scarlet colour presenting to the spectators at a distance the appearance of a grand parade of soldiers. To the N.E. and S.W. of these islands are channels in which vessels may ride in deep water.

These channels abound with the hippopotamus, which frequents the islets to produce their young, when it is dangerous to land on them. The sea-cow, as the hippopotamus is called, though timid and inoffensive, with the young ones in company are as fierce as they are at other times timid, and will not abandon them while they have life to defend them. At the head of the harbour, in secluded spots, midst long and thick growth of water weeds, were their landing places, and from thence beaten tracks to rich savannahs, the resort of these huge animals at night to graze. Always they returned to the water at the dawn of day, and but occasionally making their appearance on the sandbanks, basking in the noonday sun, resembling rocks rising out of water to a spectator off the entrance of the harbour.

Varieties of fish abounded in the harbour, particularly at a high or spring tide, when such quantities would come in from the sea as to leave the sands literally covered with fish at low water. Turtle were occasionally caught in the native fish kraals, which are constructed by fixing a framework of reeds to posts driven into the sands at low water, forming a square enclosure, in one corner of which, on the lower line of the enclosure, level with the low water mark, a semicircular pen or enclosed space is run out into two or three feet water. The kraal or pen being thus completed (the whole being erected and secured in the course of one tide), bait is thrown in the middle of the kraal, where it is anchored, to entice the fish in at high water. In this manner the natives in the neighbourhood of Natal caught cartloads of fish at low water in their kraals.

It may be well to observe that the Zulus do not eat fish, or any kind of flesh save that of oxen; but the Caffre [Kaffir] tribe of Mathubane, whom we found located at Port Natal, do eat fish, and every kind of flesh, not excepting that of monkeys, wolves, cats and tigers. This tribe was conquered by Shaka, to whom (as before stated) they paid an annual tribute in corn, and they appear to have long been the original possessors of Natal. But they have a singular prejudice and abhorrence of the turtle, and when it has happened to be caught in their fish kraals, the whole of the other fish are thrown away as being polluted by the presence of the turtle. It is with great reluctance they even handle it, and they were quite disgusted when they found the Mlungus [Moolongas] (white men) eat it. Whether this arises from some traditional prejudice is not certain, but the ufudu [lafoota] (turtle) is associated in their ideas with everything that is nasty and abominable. They say its stench is so great that it destroys the purity of the waters of the harbour, and they can smell it the moment it comes in from the sea. This was of course new to us, but this prejudice of the Mathubanes [Matanabanahs] was to our advantage, for thereby we had all the turtle.

The promontory of Cape Natal was remarkable for the myriads of monkeys with which it abounded. A singular adventure occurred to me with a troop of these animals. The shore of this headland on the harbour side is densely clothed with large trees, their branches drooping in many places below the level of high water. When the tide is up they are washed by the water, but when the tide is out these branches allow a delightful shady walk along the margin of the harbour.

One day while sauntering along the smooth sandy beach, soft and grateful to my bare feet, and enjoying the shade of this walk, I was startled by a sudden rustling of the branches of a very large tree, part of which stretched over my head, while another part bent down before me as if sinking under a weight. I was fairly taken by surprise, and at the moment the idea occurred to me that a tiger was there, as all our dogs had been devoured by them. On the instant I made a rush for the water, which was at its lowest ebb, and about ten yards distant from me, when my ears were deafened by a simultaneous rush after me, and a deafening hurrah, as it sounded to me, when I thought a legion of tigers was at my heels. I rushed into the water up to my neck, and on facing about, to my great astonishment the whole beach for several yards was literally covered with monkeys of all ages, sex and sizes. Foremost in the ranks, and standing erect on his hind feet, was a very large monkey, who appeared to be the leader. His old weather-beaten visage was screwed up into the most ludicrous shape, and he stood uttering an incessant hoo-hoo-hoo, in which he was joined by the whole troop, apparently exulting in their triumph. As for myself, I was in truth utterly confounded.

The whole scene seemed to have been conjured up by magic, such a legion of monkeys was new to me, and on turning to reconnoitre my enemy it was some time before I could distinguish more than a grey moving mass. However, I soon discovered the real character of my foe, but I was not perfectly sure as to the safety of my position, although these animals do not take the water. They appeared quite satisfied at having driven me into my present position, while the old patriarch of the tribe stood facing me in his erect position, his mouth contracted like a button-hole and continuing his hoo-hoo-hoo, though in a feeble tone, while the smaller branches of the family had commenced a quadrille on the beach. There were mothers with their young clinging on their backs and others to their bellies and all evidently pleased at my discomfiture, the whole presenting a scene which, to an observer, would have been highly amusing.

But not so to me, as the tide was beginning to flow, and being no swimmer, it became expedient for me to make some demonstration in my turn on the offensive. So picking up a handful of small pebbles from under my feet, I saluted Father Abraham with a shower, which took effect among the crowd, and in the twinkling of an eye the whole mass disappeared, with a tremendous chattering, hoo-hooing and rustling in the bush. I found, on examining the scene of this adventure, that the tree abounded with a fruit resembling the cherry in colour, though much longer, on which these animals had been feeding, and I had suddenly disturbed them.

Port Natal, as is well known, was first discovered by the early Portuguese, and is reported subsequently to have been purchased of the natives by the Dutch East India Company, and became a harbour for slave ships, a factory being established there by the company about the year 1721. This, however, is very doubtful with regard to Natal, and it may have been confounded with the trade carried on at Delagoa Bay and English River. It does not appear that this diabolical trade ever obtained among the natives about Natal, for no traditions existed among them of their forefathers ever having any traffic or intercourse with Europeans. It was, however, regarded as a point of considerable importance, and one of the most fertile regions upon earth, according to a MS copy of Maxwell's *Narrative of the Cape of Good Hope*, 1706, in the British Museum.

The first communication ever held with the Zulus was, in my belief, by Mr James S. King, master of the brig *Salisbury* of Liverpool. This gentleman surveyed the harbour and coast of Natal, as also the mouth of the river Saint Lucia, in the year 1823, and this survey was the first ever made by any English navigator of this part of the coast of Eastern Africa, although the credit of this has since been disputed by Captain Owen, R.N. Lord James Townsend, Mr King's friend and patron, on presenting the chart of Captain King's survey for indemnity for his services, was informed that this chart was compiled from documents borrowed by the author from Captain Owen. To whomsoever the precedence in making the survey in question might belong, it is but justice to the memory of a strictly honourable man to state, from my own personal knowledge of Captain James King, that I believe him incapable of committing so base an action as to produce a chart to Lord James Townsend founded on other than his own labours and research. If any such statement as the above was made by Captain Owen, he must either have known very little of the high and honourable sentiments that always guided Mr King or been led into error by some wrong information. I have myself but recently seen this chart and other documents, now in the possession of Mrs King, that fully authenticate the survey of Natal having been made by her son when in command of the *Salisbury*.

On Captain King's return to the Cape Colony, after having made the survey above alluded to of the harbour and coast of Natal, he gave so favourable a report on the position and advantages offered by Natal for commercial enterprise – the forests abounding in elephants and the rivers with hippopotami, and that friendly disposition evinced by the natives towards Europeans, by which a very profitable traffic might be carried on for ivory, &c. – that ultimately induced Mr Farewell to turn his attention and enterprise towards Natal. Consequently he embarked, with several Europeans and Hottentots, for this place, landed there in safety and commenced their pursuits, having been received by King Shaka on the most friendly terms, and his free permission granted to trade with his subjects.

On Captain King's subsequent return to the Cape of Good Hope in the brig *Mary*, the wreck of which is above described, it was rumoured abroad that Mr Farewell and his party had not been heard of since their first landing in Natal, and it was conjectured they were murdered by the natives. Captain King, actuated by the dictates of humanity, resolved while pursuing his course to the eastward to call at Natal, and ascertain for certainty the fate of his old friend Mr Farewell and party, in the prosecution of which resulted the catastrophe above related in the wreck of his vessel. This calamity was only softened by the gratification he had on being informed by the Hottentot woman, Rachel, of the safety of his friend and party.

Loss of the Brig Mary *at Natal*
with Early Recollections of that Settlement

THREE

The Nautical Magazine, March 1853, pp. 140–144

A continuance of fine weather and a smooth sea had enabled us to employ our time successfully in landing provisions and stores from the wreck, which was now fast filling with and sinking into the sand. We had succeeded in fishing out of the hold several barrels of beef and pork, but unfortunately the principal part of our bread and flour, being stowed in the after lower hold, was totally destroyed by salt water, besides the three bags of the former damaged by the swamping of the boat on the first attempt at landing. We had not remaining more than one hundred pounds of bread saved in good condition.

When the first excitement occasioned by the danger and uncertainty of our position with the natives had passed away, unfortunately symptoms of disaffection and insubordination began to manifest themselves among our party. Instead of harmony and concert, for the common benefit, scenes of riot and intemperance commenced. The wines and spirits, that in the more urgent moments of danger and exertion had been unheeded or entirely neglected, were eagerly sought after and plundered by two or three of the crew who were known to be of dissipated habits. In despite of the strict injunctions of the captain and the vigilance of the officers, daily scenes of disorder and drunkenness occurred.

To put a stop to this Captain King resolved that every drop of spirits saved or that thenceforth might be saved from the wreck should be destroyed. The disgusting scenes of riot and intoxication which had begun could not fail to degrade us, even in the estimation of the natives. That sailors in such a condition as ours should be so imprudent as to lose sight not only of their common safety, but give way to a reckless thirst for ardent spirits, would hardly be credited by persons of reflection who are strangers to this mad propensity, which does not prevail to such an extent among any other class of men.

In consequence of our captain having put his salutary resolution in force, our little band was broken up. Three of our number, headed by Norton the second mate, took offence at this measure, occasioned by their own bad conduct, seized the long boat and determined, rather than live without their *grog*, to trust themselves in an open boat to the mercy of the sea. No doubt anxiety to escape such a dreary prospect as we had before us had some influence on the decision of these daring men to undertake the perilous adventure of making the voyage from Port Natal to Algoa Bay in an open boat only 16 feet long, but I have no hesitation in saying the first was the primary reason of their adventure.

Captain King's intentions were, that as the carpenter's tools had been saved from the wreck, to have lengthened and proportionably enlarged the long boat to have taken all hands, and by decking her over and otherwise strengthening her, to make her more secure for performing the voyage to the Cape Colony. And it was mutually agreed on by the more orderly of the crew, seeing that the boat in her present condition was totally unfit to perform the voyage with any portion of the crew with safety, to give her up to these disaffected men, and to take our chance of getting away by constructing a vessel for ourselves. Fifteen days after the wreck of the brig, the party sailed in the long boat with our united prayers for their success, but they bade us adieu at Natal for ever.

Having saved everything moveable that could be got from the wreck, our attention was now turned to selecting a more eligible spot for a residence, and one at the same time suited for our design of constructing a vessel, and the erection of a more substantial residence than our tents afforded from the inclemency of the weather, and the intrusion of wolves and tigers, which were constantly annoying us by their descent at night upon our tents.

They kept us constantly on the watch, and disturbed us by their hungry howling for more dogs, for by this time they had succeeded in carrying off these our faithful attendants. The last of these was a fine Newfoundland, a most sagacious animal, who had been a most active and useful member of the community in saving many small articles washed overboard from the wreck. This faithful animal was regretted by all of us, but by no one more than myself for, having fallen overboard at sea on the passage out from England, when on the Equator, the noble animal by jumping over after me saved my life. I could not swim a stroke, but by holding on to him he swam with me alongside of the ship, it being a calm, and the vessel hardly moving through the water. I got hold of a rope, and by this means both myself and my saviour were hauled on board the brig.

The loss of this fine favourite dog drew down vengeance on these marauding persecutors. The ingenuity of Mr Hutton suggested a method of ultimately ridding ourselves of these nocturnal visitors. This was effected by fixing a musket in the ground, doubly charged with powder and ball, with the butt end depressed and the muzzle rather elevated, so that a piece of meat would lay sufficiently below it as to admit the head of a tiger or a wolf to come in contact with the muzzle. To this bait was attached a cord, which passing round the butt end of the gun was fastened to the trigger. A fence was made round the gun, so that an approach could not be made to the bait in any direction but point blank to the muzzle, so that by taking the bait the gun was discharged into the very teeth of the thief. In this way, though it was in a manner locking the stable when the horse was stolen, Mr Hutton succeeded in clearing our tents from these ferocious intruders. I have seen several tigers with their jaws literally shattered to pieces in this manner, for we found it was necessary to charge the guns with three or four balls to secure the beasts, as several had got away when severely wounded, having traced them in the morning by the track of blood on the ground until lost in the thicket and jungles, where farther search would have been dangerous. Our shot seldom failed to take effect in some part of their carcase, but so tenacious of life are these animals that they would keep the whole of us at bay, armed with bludgeons, and could not be overcome until absolutely riddled with shot.

Our party had been reduced to eight in number by the sailing of the long boat from Natal, and many were the conjectures hazarded whether or not they would ever reach their destination in so frail a bark. These reflections were frequently uppermost among us. The moment of their departure had buried all angry feelings occasioned by their disorderly conduct, and mutual sympathy and good wishes predominated on either side. The thoughts of old associations and companionship, about to be broken up for ever, softened the hearts of those departing and those remaining in the bonds of good wishes for each other. In fact, our mutual safety and deliverance naturally possessed our minds, the doubt and uncertainty of our respective prospects of the future adding still more to the interest of the occasion. When the moment of parting had arrived, manly feelings gave way. The stubborn breast which had been proof against the voice of reason and authority was subdued, and in that moment an appeal to those feelings would have sufficed to alter their purpose.

Men may become the slaves of degrading and destructive passions, but they have hearts endued with generous feelings, latent though they may be until roused by the touch of some tender string, which vibrates in unison with them in the dark hour of adversity. Companions in adversity can only share in that pure and self-denying love and interest for those on whom the mantle of misfortune has fallen. It is theirs to know the inexpressible delight which fills the heart that truly adorns human nature and brings man nearer to his God, levels all worldly distinctions but that of nobleness and generosity of soul. It is when trembling beneath the chilling blast of adversity that hearts are softened towards our fellow creatures, when man feels for his fellow man, and feelings are engendered by its effect that are unknown in the general sunshine of prosperity. Hence the many noble instances of self-sacrifice made by the poor in assisting each other.

Our labours having terminated at the wreck, and having collected all the scattered materials from the beach, we now employed our time in cutting timber and collecting thatch for the building of a house. Captain King, with Mr Hutton the chief officer, having made a survey of the locality, had determined on a spot on the S.W. side of the harbour as being the most eligible for the construction of a vessel. The headland called Cape Natal was well wooded and the side towards the harbour steep. The timber, after being cut, it remained only to launch it down the face of the hill into the channel on the S.W. side of the harbour. Having cleared away the spot selected, and on the foundation of the first house being laid, or rather when sinking the first post into the ground, Captain King, in honour of his friend and patron, named it Townsend, by which name we shall hereafter speak of it, and the remains of which may perhaps be visible to this day.

In the course of a week's steady perseverance at our labours we had succeeded in getting sufficient materials collected to commence the building of our house, when the labour was interrupted by the arrival of Mr Farewell and his party. They were accompanied by a messenger from the King who, having heard of the arrival of an umkhumbi [uncombie] (vessel) with Mlungus, requested their attendance at his royal residence Bulawayo [Umbollalili]. It was in consequence of this summons resolved to suspend our labours for the present, and as many as could be spared of our party to accompany Captain King on the journey to the King's residence.

Captain King made up a suitable present for his Majesty, consisting of beads, bugles and a few blankets. He was accompanied by Mr Hutton and three of the seamen, with two of Mr Farewell's Hottentots as guides. When the greetings with his old friend, Mr Farewell, were mutually exchanged, they started early in the morning on their interesting journey to King Shaka's residence. The distance was represented as being about fifty miles, in a north-easterly direction from Port Natal.

It was truly an amusing scene to look upon, which the starting of our party presented. Mr F. had an old stumbling, broken Rosinante, which he kindly lent Mr King to assist him over the journey and on which this gentleman was mounted. The saddle consisted of a goat's skin stuffed with old rags and a portion of the rider's wardrobe, evident by a stray shirt sleeve dangling out at the after part, the whole being firmly girted on the animal's back by a broad cowhide thong, set up, as Jack said, at the starboard gangway with a heaver – a stout piece of wood, which answered the double capacity of a buckle and stirrup.

The three tars were mounted on as many pack oxen, their broad and plump backs rendering anything in the shape of a saddle superfluous, and with only a thong passed through the nose for the purpose of steering. On this elevation Jack was chucking and whipping his stubborn steed, his arms and legs exhibiting the identical convulsive motions of those wooden men-toys which are acted on by pulling a string in the centre, and whipping away with might and main, though to very little purpose, the motion of the animal being only increased in eccentricity and, as Jack said, tacking and making stern boards.

The whole at last was got under way in a straight line, by a driver being appointed to each beast, which, after affording much amusement, passed on with three hearty cheers from those remaining at Fort Farewell. Myself and Mr Isaacs were left in charge of our premises and effects. While Captain King and the rest of my shipmates are on their journey to the King's, I will give the reader a brief description of Fort Farewell and its inhabitants.

Loss of the Brig Mary at Natal with Early Recollections of that Settlement

FOUR

The Nautical Magazine, April 1853, pp. 196–202

Fort Farewell presented anything but what its name implied, appearing, in truth, a very primitive, rude looking structure. It consisted of a quadrangular enclosure, composed of palisades driven in the ground, and about ten feet high, at each angle of which was a circular tower or turret, with a platform and embrasure intended for heavy guns which never were there.

Two pieces of ordnance lay within the walls of the fort, dismounted and neglected, from which it might be inferred that the inhabitants lived in peace and security. In the midst of this quadrangle stood a large edifice like a barn, the walls composed of what is technically called wattling daub, which is really wicker work, plastered with mud to fill up the interstices; a very expeditious, and at the same time an economical, mode of building in common use among Hottentots. Two or three other buildings on a small scale, offshoots of the parent one, being identically alike in constitution, completed the interior of this original fortification.

Outside of it, and at small distances around the walls of posts, were numerous native huts, presenting the appearance of gigantic beehives, and at a distance more like anthills. These were generally composed of a slight wicker work, of circular form and covered with thatch, seldom exceeding six feet in height. As the natives never on any occasion require to stand upright, the aperture for entrance is seldom more than eighteen inches in height, and the same in breadth, so that crawling in through this doorway the native seldom or never assumes the erect position when within his hut. The whole presented a picture of semi-civilization, blended with barbarism.

Nothing in my youth and inexperience could reconcile this wretched looking place with the name it bore. I was grievously disappointed with Fort Farewell, expecting to see something that presented the means of acting either on the defensive or offensive, as occasion might require, and afford a secure retreat in case of necessity. It might be naturally supposed that a feeling of security and confidence had not yet taken place in my mind as to the good will of our sable friends, which time and intercourse had established in those who had resided long amongst them.

The inhabitants, or rather I should say the proprietors, of Fort Farewell, were a motley group of human beings; a mixture of whites, Hottentots and native blacks, the latter in a perfect state of nudity, and the former in such a tattered condition as rendered it difficult to say in what costume they were, or whether they were clothed or not. Of the three parties the natives had certainly the advantage in appearance.

The government of Fort Farewell appeared to partake of the democratic, so far as the white men were concerned, while as respected the natives it was of the patriarch. Each one of Mr Farewell's party had a number of native retainers, over whom he exercised the most absolute control. All disputes that arose between these people were referred to and settled by their respective masters, the latter generally satisfying the aggrieved party by chastising the offender, while the only authority possessed by Mr Farewell was that of a magisterial capacity of settling quarrels arising amongst his party, and to his decision all in general acquiesced. The whole aspect of men and materials in this singular place partook, in fact, of the character of the semi-civilized and semi-barbarous state, which to a stranger presented a highly curious and interesting scene.

Behind the Fort lay the extensive and gently undulating valley of the Mngeni with here and there scattered clumps of stately trees, giving it a park-like appearance. The dark and well defined outline of the wooded heights, which bounded this extensive plain as far as the eye could trace, the flocks of roebuck or fallow deer, grazing quietly here and there, or gambolling in the distance, presented a beauty and grandeur of scenery that quieted the gloomy thoughts of our forlorn condition. Often at the morning's dawn have I watched the first golden rays of the clear rising sun stretching far over the wide expanse of this beautiful valley, resembling pillars of gold abutting on the distant hills, when its death-like stillness would be suddenly broken by the tuneful voices of a thousand little feathered songsters in the adjoining groves, all uniting to complete a picture of nature which shed a soft and cheering influence over the mind, and in the midst of adversity raised the drooping spirits, and rendered the endurance of our lot comparatively happy.

While on the subject of Fort Farewell and its proprietors, I must observe that Mr Stephen Kay, in his book entitled *Travels and Researches in Eastern Africa*, has dealt some severe and unmerited reproof on the white people who first opened a trade with the Zulus. This of course more particularly applies to Mr Farewell and his party, and subsequently the shipwrecked crew of the brig *Mary*. As these remarks of Mr Kay will be handed down to posterity as matter of history, it is no less justice to the party assailed than a love of truth to refute them, seeing that from several discrepancies in Mr Kay's book in his account of Natal, relating at least to that in which I was an inferior actor (but eye-witness), is replete with error. I am disposed to think that Mr Kay wrote from mere report, as I could not reconcile the idea of a man professing and teaching the Christian faith being guilty of so gratuitous and malignant an attack on a party who claimed his Christian compassion rather than slander.

Mr Kay says in his *Caffrarian Researches*, Chapter XVI, page 401:

> It is almost superfluous to add, that the life of a black has in the estimation of such degraded wretches become quite common, and that the hope of gain, or a desire to secure the favour of chieftains, has not unfrequently proved a sufficient incentive to deeds the most base and sanguinary. Twenty or thirty of the natives having one day fled from the presence of Shaka, and taking refuge in the rocks where his spear was not able to reach them, the enraged savage, bent on making them the victims of his vengeance, called in the aid of these fire-armed men, who, horrid to relate, by means of their guns brought down the poor creatures like birds from a tree. The reader will not be surprised to learn that some of his band speedily afterwards fell by the hand of violence, and that others of the party were soon also called to the bar of the Almighty.

This is the character which Mr Kay gives of the white people at Natal in 1826. Certainly it is but true, to go so far with Mr Kay, as to his account of the living here. In reference to bed and board we had of necessity to submit to much. Long habits of association with the natives, and seclusion from civilized society, even from that of each other, as their trading journeys to the interior kept us long and often separated from each other, had stamped their manners with a degree of uncouthness that was obvious to us on our first landing at Natal. And the same remark might have, and assuredly would have, applied to myself if, after three years and a half of residence among savages, I had been criticized in my air and gait by one who had never been without the comforts and style of a drawing-room.

Indeed, I feel no shame in confessing that after six months' absence on a long and somewhat perilous journey from Natal to Delagoa Bay, with occasionally three and four months' residence with the king, during which I never saw nor had converse with a white man or woman, my constant and only companions being my rude native attendants, I had become so heathenish, as this pious missionary would say, that I had absolutely forgotten some words of my mother tongue. A Caffre word for an English one would drop in my conversation when meeting my shipmates after these long seclusions from their society. Certainly I was very young, but the same cause was productive of proportionate effects on the adults. Nevertheless, they possessed the open and generous hearts of Englishmen. Although their manners had been thus somewhat distorted, their hearts retained their natural impulse of feeling and humanity, which had produced their effect on those natives who were under their guidance when contrasted with those who had not the benefit of this civilizing influence.

It is true that the object of Mr Farewell and his party in visiting Port Natal was not the spiritual reformation of the natives, nor had the shipwrecked crew of the *Mary* either the opportunity or the means of devoting their time or their labours in preaching the gospel to these rude and barbarous people. But their conduct was such as not only to inspire them with confidence and esteem, but exercised a salutary influence on all who had the benefit of their advice and example. Therefore the paragraph which I have quoted from Mr Kay is as unjust as it is uncharitable.

Whether in the wise counsel of Omnipotence commercial enterprise, conquest or missionary labour shall prove the fittest and most successful medium through which to effect the civilization and conversion of the heathen to Christianity is a problem which the history of the past and the experience of the future only can solve. But while hundreds of souls of our own kindred, nation and tongue are sunk in ignorance deep and dark as the African heathen, without even the knowledge of their having an immortal soul or the name of Him who redeemed them with his blood; while such a state of things is well known and widespread throughout our own land, every true and sincere Christian must deplore the time and means that are spent by the latter on any distant field, when those of our own present the same barren and uncultivated waste.

Perhaps, indeed, the difference may consist in this, that our domestic heathenism does not afford so loud an echo for the voice of fame as that of the deserts and wilds of Africa. It cannot supply a harrowing tale of some zealous pioneer of the gospel being devoured by a wild beast in the jungle, or cruelly butchered by the bloody hand of a savage in the deserts of Africa, and thus a demand on the sympathy and drawing of the purse-strings of the Christian public in behalf of these martyrs for the propagation of the gospel is lost. Or why is it that the quiet and tranquil field at home should be overlooked and forgotten and left yet far and near to want the good tidings of the gospel?

In the course of these recollections there will be occasion to notice the cold-blooded massacres of these fire-armed men. A simple statement of the truth needs no embellishment, nor requires that I should stop now to refute so flagrant an assertion as that of shooting the natives, who, as Mr Kay says, got out of reach of Shaka's spear. Mr Kay, I again repeat, wrote from hearsay. Having myself been an eye-witness on the scene of these cruelties, now at an advanced period of life, I do not, to my knowledge and belief, hazard a statement which is otherwise than true. The modes of living and the manners of the party at the time alluded to were their misfortune, not their fault. On our landing at Natal we found Mr Farewell and his people destitute of every article even essential to civilized life. Time and habit, which always sooth down the ruggedness of the highways and byways of life, reconciled them to their many privations. But the want of them was not the less severely felt.

Fort Farewell was rich in cattle, obtained by bartering with the natives and as presents at various times from the king, a cow and calf or a fat ox being given readily in exchange for a blanket, or five to six pounds of glass beads, more or less, according to colour and size. The smallest beads were preferred, blue, red and green being more highly prized than those of other colours, white and black being considered the commonest, while green and yellow were only permitted to be worn by chiefs and persons in high authority, or by attendants on the royal household.

On our visit to Fort Farewell we were regaled with sweet milk fresh from the cow, and sufficient to our heart's content. While the distance from our tents on Sandy Point to Fort Farewell was but two and a half to three miles distant, I availed myself night and morning of the opportunity of gratifying my appetite with refreshing draughts of this wholesome beverage. Besides which, the good hearted Hottentot woman, Rachel, was in the habit every day of sending us a large calabash of sour curds, somewhat resembling new cheese, this being the manner in which the natives invariably use it, and which, with Indian corn, constitutes the principal part of their food.

The corn is first boiled and bruised between two stones; the milk is prepared first, being thrown into calabashes or gourds made of skins, or compact basket-made vessels, similar in size and shape to the French demijohns, and it is left to stand until it becomes sour, which it soon does from the acidity retained in the vessel. Perhaps the process is accelerated by the state of these vessels, as they are never on any occasion washed. Indeed, it would be considered highly improper to do so at each milking of the cows, which is done with great regularity night and morning. The watery portion of the curdled milk is then drawn off by a small spill at the bottom of the vessel. It is then filled with fresh milk, and the same process gone through until the whole contents of the calabash is one solid mass of curds, which are then fit for use, and the same process is repeated. And thus every village where there are cattle (and what Caffre settlement is without them) has a constant supply of this kind of milk kept ready for consumption.

Returning to our position at the departure of the Captain on his visit to the King, we were entertained for some days during his absence with a description of the war from which Mr Farewell's party had returned. It appears that the battle was fought in the night, so that the services of the fire-armed men on that occasion were not called into requisition. The enemy fought with great obstinacy and bravery, equal in every respect to the Zulus, but the superior discipline and practice of the latter in war prevailed over the more uninitiated forces of the Sikhunyana

[Izeecanyana]. The latter were beaten and almost totally annihilated, no quarter being given or received. The brave fellows, even when wholly discomfited, scorned to seek safety in flight, and even the women stepped into the ranks and filled up the gaps occasioned by their falling husbands; the old chief alone, at the earnest persuasion of a handful of devoted followers, saved himself when the field was irretrievably lost.

It was thought that if this battle had been fought by daylight the result might have been very doubtful, as great numbers of the enemy had fallen by the hands of their own people, the darkness preventing them from distinguishing friend from foe. On the other hand, this was effectually guarded against by the superior generalship and intelligence of Shaka, his forces being guided from falling into the same error by having a countersign. Three thousand men and women of the enemy lay dead on the field, and of more than five thousand Zulu warriors, about half survived to witness the rising sun. To the credit of Shaka, be it said, that on hearing of the gallant defence made by the enemy, he departed from the general rules in Caffrarian warfare by proclaiming that all of the enemy who had survived and made their escape should be spared and received as his children, and worthy of becoming the companions of Zulu warriors.

The policy of adding these brave men to his band of warriors, to strengthen and promote his success in future schemes of conquest, might be considered as the primary and only motive in the savage chief for exercising this act of mercy, were it not known that courage always had been a sure passport to Shaka's favour and esteem. Indeed, this fact will be illustrated by many other instances in these recollections in the memoir which I have attempted to give of the life of this extraordinary savage chief.

About 1 500 head of cattle were captured in this battle, and the unfortunate tribe of Sikhunyana entirely annihilated, with the few exceptions I have before mentioned. This tribe inhabited the rich and fertile country on the N.E. of, and nearly midway between, Port Natal and Delagoa Bay. Their pursuits appeared to partake more of the agricultural than pastoral habits of the Caffre generally. They were represented as a powerful, well proportioned, robust, active race of people. The men joined in the labours of the field, contrary to the practice of the Zulus and the Caffre tribes generally on the S.W. of Natal and towards the frontiers of the Cape Colony, where all this hard work and every species of drudgery is performed by the women. Their extensive gardens of Indian corn and Guinea grain were laid waste and devastated by the enemy, who to complete the ruin of their fallen adversaries left not the vestige of a habitation for shelter, or a blade of corn for their subsistence, throughout the land. There it remains a barren and desolate wilderness, there the bleaching bones of the slain now blanch the plains, and present to the traveller the painful evidence of a field where one of the most fearful conflicts that ever took place between savage hosts was decided.

This then was the first instance that the fire-arms of the party at Port Natal were brought into use. But from the above brief notice of the battle (which is really the truth) it is needless to state the party assailed were not, as Mr Kay has it, a few fugitives that had fled from the vengeance of Shaka, nor that they were brought down by the deadly aim of fire-armed miscreants like birds from a tree.

But for the sake of truth, it has occurred to my recollection at the moment of writing this, that a solitary case of one native being shot occurred thus. In the mingling of the engaged in the darkness of the night, a Caffre had mistaken one of the Hottentots for an enemy, rushed on him, and was in the act of raising his spear to run him through, when the Hottentot shot him dead on the spot. This man, on examining the body, proved to be a Zulu soldier, and it was conjectured that the attack proceeded from design to kill the Hottentot, owing to an old standing grievance that existed between them.

Loss of the Brig Mary at Natal with Early Recollections of that Settlement

FIVE

The Nautical Magazine, June 1853, pp. 298–303

After a month's absence we had the pleasure of greeting our captain and shipmates on their safe return from King Shaka's residence at Bulawayo [Umbellilo]. They represented the journey as very fatiguing, more particularly that of the first day, being for the most part along the sea beach, on a soft sand, tiresome both for man and beast. But after this first day's travel, on striking off the beach into the interior, the journey became interesting, the beautiful scenery through which they now passed alternatively changing from hill to dale, and on ascending a somewhat steep mountain side it amply compensated them for their fatigue. Flocks of cattle widely scattered over the immense fields of rich pasturage, with the strange and novel appearance of the large circular ithangas [etangers] (cattle-folds) interspersed throughout the country, gave the whole journey a degree of interest unexpected by the travellers.

They arrived at the royal residence on the tenth day from their setting out from Natal, but having travelled by very easy stages the distance, as they thought, did not exceed what it was represented to be, 150 to 180 miles. The native villages through which they passed, and wherever they halted, all vied with each other in supplying the wants of the travellers, and showing marked respect and attention. The largest and most commodious and comfortable apartments in the village were voluntarily and invariably given up to the king's white men. This attention and respect I have since had reason to suspect proceeded more from the fear of incurring the king's displeasure by any neglect, or complaint being made of their want of hospitality, than from any good feeling in general on their own part towards us. Yet among the Zulus hospitality to the stranger and wayfarer is very strikingly marked and predominant. Such a thing as the purchasing of meat and drink on the way is utterly unknown, and it would be considered as inhuman and barbarous for anyone to exact payment for food from a hungry traveller or a stranger who might happen to be on a visit in the neighbourhood. Hence the Zulu in travelling has no concern as to what he shall eat or drink on the way, knowing that he has an equal right with the invited guests to sit down and partake of the same banquet.

Our party were received by King Shaka in a friendly manner, but with that air of haughty indifference which might be expected from the Napoleon of Eastern Africa, before whom everyone was prostrated. A hundred thousand warriors, whose victories had annihilated nations, who had fought in fields saturated with the blood of their slain comrades, knelt at his feet, and to them his words were as the mandate of their deity. Our present excited neither pleasure nor curiosity. He received it with listless indifference, causing it to be thrown aside, and commenced a desultory conversation, asking questions of King George's dominions, if he had as many cattle and as many warriors as he had, expressing his wish to be on friendly terms with King George, and would give his white people every attention; repeating that if any of them gave them any offence or insult, he would kill them all, men, women and child.

'Yes,' said he, turning to the chiefs around him, 'do you hear me – Nandi [UmNauta] (the name of his mother, by which he often swore), I will kill, as sure as I am the son of a king'; to which the whole responded simultaneously, 'Yebo [Yeabo], Baba' (Yes, Father).

'I wish,' he added, 'that there should be only two great kings in the world; that King George should be king of the whites, and I king of the blacks.'

Captain King here met with a man named Jacob, who had deserted him on a former visit to the coast at the mouth of the Saint Lucia river. He had attached himself to one of the Caffre tribes on the frontier of the Cape Colony, and like many others of his countrymen, in their marauding expeditions on the colonists, had been captured and transported to Robben Island. At the intercession of Captain King and his friends, aided in a measure by his own good conduct and contrition, he had been liberated by the authorities at the Cape, and joined the *Salisbury* as Interpreter, proceeding to the coast of Natal in that vessel with Captain King in 1823. While on shore, as I have before stated, at the River Saint Lucia a quarrel arose between him and one of the boat's crew, who cast up to him his former position as a convict. The man made his escape from the boat, and all search for him proving ineffectual, he was left on the sailing of the *Salisbury* on the coast of Natal. But being a cunning fellow, he succeeded in getting into favour with Shaka, having previously however suffered many vicissitudes and hair-breadth escapes, and from him there is no doubt the Zulu chief first learnt the white men's strength and numbers at the Cape Colony.

Jacob could yet speak a little English, and evinced his joy at meeting his old master by much kind attention to him and his crew. He impressed Shaka of his obligation to Captain King in delivering him from the white men's bondage, but carefully concealed his real crime from Shaka of stealing the white men's cattle, telling him that he had been made a prisoner of war, his countrymen having been vanquished by the whites, and that the latter never killed the enemy that fell into their hands, but shut them up in dungeons or in some solitary island, where they were detained for life; and it was through Captain King's intercession with a great chief (by which he meant the Governor) that he was liberated, but that many of his countrymen still lived in hopeless captivity.

This account of Jacob's to the king, though mostly false and incorrect, had the best effect. For with such a man as Shaka at the head of a nation, though himself a merciless tyrant, he was not blind to this virtue when exercised by others. The same measure that he observed others to give, the same was invariably given by him to them. Indeed, I have remarked this to be the great rule on which Shaka founded his ideas of justice, and the many bloody sacrifices he made of his own people, strange as it may appear, proceeded from this mistaken barbarous notion. Jacob had therefore unconsciously given him a favourable opinion of the white men, and in Shaka's reasoning, if they spared the lives of their enemies, how much more then ought he to protect them as friendly and unfortunate strangers.

As a proof of Shaka's sentiments and concern for us, I recollect his saying very seriously to me one day, 'Jackabo (the name he always called me), if it was not for me I fear that there is scarcely an umfokazana [umfogasann] (a common man, or an expression for the lower order of the natives) but would rejoice of having the opportunity to kill all my white people. Oh!' he continued, 'they are a bad people; I am obliged to kill a few to gratify the rest; and if I were not to do it, they would think me an old woman, a coward, and kill me themselves. I have been often told by my Indaba (Council) to kill you wild beasts of Mlungus. How happy King George must be, as king of the white men, to me. I see and feel that you are a good and a superior people; a strange, a wonderful people. If I understood writing, I would write to King George, and tell him all that I feel, and what I think of the Mlungus.'

Jacob had, besides obtaining Shaka's friendship, received many head of cattle, and Shaka having changed his name to Hlambamanzi [Slama Manzie] (Swim the Sea or Great Swimmer) made him a petty chief, and the head of a considerable village through which Captain King passed on his journey to Shaka.

Captain King took occasion to represent to Shaka the loss of his vessel, and of his intentions to set to work with his people and build another, soliciting at the same time his permission and assistance in the work, by allowing him to hire people to haul timber to the yard, &c. Shaka immediately gave his consent, and said, 'I will send for Mathubane [Mottoban], who is the chief of the people about Natal, and I will tell him that you are building an umkhumbi for me, to negotiate with my friend King George, and that I require him to send you all his people to bring the largest trees in the wood to your workshop for my umkhumbi, at any time that you may send and let him know you want them.'

It was evident our party had made a favourable impression on the savage monarch. From the moment of their intimating the intention of building a vessel, he continued to evince a lively interest in the work, and from that moment he determined on and planned the embassy to the Cape Colony, which was ultimately effected by our taking to Port Elizabeth Sothobe [Satoby] and suite, which, as will appear in the progress of these recollections, through the parsimony or indifference of the Colonial Government, was a shameful failure.

Shaka seemed to entertain an absorbing interest in this mission, and appeared anxious and solicitous to have some certain and tangible proof from the British government of its friendly alliance. I feel assured he would have made a sacrifice of any minor consideration for this. His penetration convinced him of the vast superiority of the white man's mode of warfare in the use of fire-arms, and though his military genius had effected great improvement in the Caffrarian mode practised by his predecessors, he saw with all his improvements its disparity when brought in contrast with the musket.

One day in haranguing his warriors, in the presence of Captain King and the sailors, on the subject of a contest with the white men, his warriors affected to despise the izibamu [izeebann] (musket), stating that when they heard it go off they could fall flat on the ground, and the missile would fly harmlessly over their heads; 'and before they could load again,' said they, 'we should be upon them, and cut them to pieces.' However, on a bayonet being fixed on our people's carbines, they confessed that it now presented a more formidable implement of war. To test their boasting of courage to face the white men's izibamu [izeebanns] Shaka had privately arranged that three of our men should be posted behind a group of the most daring and loud declaimers of fire-arms, and at a signal given by the king the pieces were fired immediately behind their ears. The surprise and fear occasioned by the report caused the magnanimous warriors to fall prostrate on the ground, and terrified as they were they presented the immovable appearance of men actually shot. Nor were they on their feet again until another party of attendants on the king, aware of the ruse, fell upon them with bludgeons to chastise them for their vaunting and cowardice.

The many sanguinary conflicts carried on between the Colonists and the Caffres on the frontiers, in which the latter were constantly and signally defeated, had no doubt been described to Shaka by Jacob, and perhaps exaggerated. The thought that his countrymen had often been mown down by European artillery like grass before the scythe had no doubt induced Shaka to seek a secure and friendly understanding with the Cape Colony. He wisely and truly foresaw that the time was not far distant when they would visit his country with their powerful and formidable engines of destruction. The cruel and bloody aggressions of the Boers on the Caffres, under cover either of defence or recovery of plunder, but really from malice and hatred, have engendered feelings of hatred and retaliation in the breasts of the simple and untutored natives, and have led to barbarities reciprocal and terrific, and raised feelings in the minds of the Caffres that will in all probability be long remembered and go down to posterity. At any rate, many years of kind treatment will be required to blot out the atrocities perpetrated by people professing the doctrines of Christianity, that are not paralleled in the records of the most barbarous nations.

It is worthy the attention, and the strictest surveillance of the British

Government, to prevent the same abuses from being introduced into Natal, and no aggression or infringement of the native rights and interest in the soil should be tolerated. Otherwise the same feelings will be engendered, which will lead to perpetual strife, and scenes of rapine and murder will follow in endless succession, until the whole of the Aborigines become exterminated.

The subtle arguments that have been adduced by civilized plunderers in defence of their aggressions and expulsions of the Aborigines from the land of their forefathers have, it is to be regretted, hitherto proved a specious cloak for carrying on these cruel and unjust practices. The argument that obtains in defence of these intrusions on the homes of the natives is held to be this, that as they employ little or no labour on the land, they have no property therein; therefore as labour constitutes the first and only unalienable right to the soil, and the natives not having invested this capital or right in the land, but leaving it in a measure a barren unproductive wilderness, we had a right to step in at our pleasure, and by investing the capital of our labour in this unproductive soil drive out the original idle proprietors.

This argument, looking at it from any side and with all its logical conclusions is, after all, neither more or less than might against right. It is very certain had we not the power of assuming all the argument on our own side, and of putting it in force on the other, it would wear a very different aspect. Suppose these barbarians in their turn were in a position not only to argue, but physically to dispute or retaliate on these civilized robbers.

It would be an easy matter to show that the soil produced in abundance all that their necessities demanded, and to which they and their forefathers had been accustomed. While the mountain forest was their preserve, and the valley and the savannahs their grazing fields, the intrusions of a stranger into the former is as the poacher on the manor of a nobleman, and claiming the latter as identical with robbing the farmer of his right to the use of his field. As before stated, the woods and pasturage supply to the full extent the wants of the whole mass of people; the cultivated fields of the most civilized country do little more. The artificial wants of the one have created an additional demand on them for labour to extort from the soil to supply them; the other wants, being little more than nature demands, are supplied profusely by her hand.

After little more than a week's stay at Shaka's residence, Capt. King and his party obtained his permission to return to Natal, desiring him on his arrival to send on the rest of his ship's crew, that the king might see and know them, and not to lose any time in commencing the building of the umkhumbi. The pompous manner in which he always behaved towards our party while in the presence of his chief captains and warriors to our amusement was altogether thrown aside in the retirement of his residence, where he conversed familiarly with Capt. King through Jacob the interpreter and sent for the present, condescending to thank the captain for it. While minutely examining the texture of a blanket, he held it to his face, and expressed his admiration of its warmth and softness. A looking-glass among the articles presented appeared to please him very much, and he asked many shrewd questions as to the material from which it was manufactured, and appeared greatly surprised when informed of the simple article from which he was told it was produced. While closely surveying his person in this mirror for the first time in his life, he detected some grey hairs in his beard, which caused him great uneasiness, indicating he was getting old. He anxiously inquired of Capt. King if the Mlungus had any medicine that could prevent such effects of increasing years. The captain replied in the affirmative, that the Mlungus could do such things, which pleased his majesty so much that he declared when his vessel was finished he should send it to his friend King George for the valuable preparation.

Our party were well supplied with food daily by the king's attendants, consisting principally of boiled and roast beef, of rich and excellent quality, with occasionally huge calabashes of curdled milk, accompanied by boiled Indian corn as a substitute for bread; whilst every evening a large earthen vessel, containing from three to four gallons of beer, was sent them from the king's private brewery. This latter beverage is, when carefully made, exceedingly pleasant and agreeable. It is prepared from malt of the Guinea corn. The grain is first steeped in water, then laid out on mats in the sun and kept constantly turned; it is then laid aside until it germinates, when it is prepared for brewing in the usual way, but in place of hops a species of herb is used by them, which gives it a somewhat intoxicating quality when drunk to excess.

Besides this abundant supply of provision, when our captain and his crew had taken their leave of his majesty, they had not proceeded far on their journey homeward when overtaken by a servant of the king, driving before him some fifteen head of cattle, part of which consisted of five good milch cows with young calves. The man drove the cattle at a quick pace about fifty yards in advance of our party, and squatting himself down on the ground, said in a loud tone of voice, 'See the inkomo (cattle) the Ngangezwe (Great as the World), my master, King of the Zulus gives, that you may neither hunger nor thirst in the country of our Great King.' Having said this, he commenced begging on his own account in the most imploring manner a few beads from the king's wild beasts, a term which the Zulu warriors called us by way of compliment.

Capt. King presented him with a few, with which he was greatly delighted, and he immediately returned, leaving however two of his party to drive and tend the cattle on the journey to Natal.

These two lads, on arriving at our quarters, appeared determined on remaining with me. Fearing that the king's displeasure might be incurred by not sending them back, we used every means to prevail on them to leave us, but to no effect. They were determined to stay by us, and did so until we left Port Natal.

Loss of the Brig Mary at Natal with Early Recollections of that Settlement

SIX

The Nautical Magazine, July 1853, pp. 349–357

Being now all collected together, we diligently set to work erecting our houses at Townsend, and making the necessary preparation for building a vessel. Numbers of the natives now began to collect about our little settlement, and evinced great astonishment at the rapid progress we made in our operations, and at the ease and expedition with which we felled the largest trees, and reduced them to the size and shape required.

The native artisans display much mechanical skill and ingenuity in the manufacture of various articles in wood and iron, producing many curious and even elegant articles of use, when the simple nature of the tools employed in their manufacture is considered. These chiefly consist of iron hoes, assegais (spears) and elaborately carved wooden bowls and spoons; also ivory rings, worn as ornaments on their arms, and snuff spoons. These manufactures, though generally well executed, employ much time, patience and labour, and indicate much mechanical genius.

They must also possess a knowledge of smelting metals, as their persons were frequently seen adorned with brass and iron balls of native manufacture, evidently cast in moulds. For this purpose they employ stone crucibles, and a very simple contrivance for bellows, composed of two leathern bags; at the bottom of each is inserted a tube, generally a bullock's horn, while the bags are raised and depressed by hand, causing a strong current of air to be forced through the horns, by which means a very powerful heat is kept up in their rude furnace, which is simply a hole made in the ground and filled with charcoal.

Many of the natives now frequently visited us. They would collect in groups on the beach opposite our stranded vessel, which each high tide had successively surged nearer the shore, until she was now within twenty yards of low water mark. They seemed to look on her huge mass with apparent awe and wonder; many and amusing were their speculations about her hull. Some said it was not the work of men's hands, but an isilwane [sillwana] (wild beast) that lived in the ocean, considering us a species of amphibious animals that lived within it. At first they imagined our clothes grew on our backs, that our flesh was soft and pulpy like that of any oyster or shell-fish, until they had convinced themselves by pinching it between their fingers and thumb that it was flesh and blood like their own, differing only in colour.

Their attention was particularly excited by the figurehead of the wreck, a well finished female bust painted in colours. Their wonder and astonishment on seeing it was great, particuarly of those who had the courage to venture on board to survey it more closely. But we could not on any account prevail on one of them to touch it, nor could we at first persuade them of its being made from a piece of wood such as grew in their own forests. They have not the remotest idea of painting or sculpture beyond that of staining their wooden vessels black or red with a species of vegetable dye. Seeing that the figurehead of the *Mary* excited such a lively interest in the natives, Captain King resolved to have it carefully unshipped, securely packed and forwarded as a present to his Majesty, to give him some idea of the *beauty of our fair sex*, as he had made some curious inquiries as to the character and condition of our countrywomen.

Many of the Mathubane people voluntarily came and assisted in the thatching of our houses, and at this work proved very expert and able assistants. When we manifested our appreciation of their services by distributing among them some beads and trinkets, they were delighted and redoubled their energy. By this valuable assistance we were enabled to complete our little village much sooner than we expected.

It consisted of one large building, about twenty-five feet long by fifteen broad, divided into several compartments for dormitories, two smaller buildings and two native huts. The two smaller buildings in the European style were set apart for storing the sails and cordage saved from the wreck. These, having already sustained considerable damage from washing in the surf and exposure to the weather, had become objects of our solicitude and preservation as the only material with which to fit out our new vessel, should we be so fortunate as to see this accomplished. The two native huts were erected for the accommodation of the natives who had attached themselves to our service, in preference (as I have before mentioned) to returning to their native masters, and for the lodging of messengers or visitors from the King.

Our habitations thus completed, it only remained to remove our effects from the tents at Sandy Point. As this work had to be done by our boats, these on being launched were found to be so leaky that considerable delay was occasioned until they could be caulked and otherwise repaired so as to be in a fit condition for the transport of our stores across the channel of the harbour.

The general appearance of the natives on this part of the coast of Eastern Africa is so favourable, and particularly of the Zulus, who are a well made, robust, muscular and powerful race of men, perfectly devoid of the characteristic features that distinguish the African negro, that really with the exception of the colour of the skin they might justly rank with the most perfect European. Their well proportioned figures and prepossessing features, with the high expansive forehead, denote much physical as well as intellectual capacity. They are capable of enduring great fatigue and privation, and while the young lead an active, temperate, even life, their physical capacity becomes fully developed, and it is seldom or never that any deformity is to be met with. Bold and manly in their bearing, and evincing much candour and openness in their countenance and deportment in their social relations, there is also much kindness, affection and generosity in their character, and even gratitude to those from whom they have received kindness or attention, and they seldom fail to return it when the opportunity offers for doing so.

Faithful and obedient to his superior, the Zulu manifests no cringing servility in his manner, maintaining a bold and manly independence even in the presence of an enraged chief, awaiting the sentence of death from his lips. He will maintain a dignified and manly bearing with an apparent fearlessness of confronting death that claims admiration, and is seldom to be witnessed in other than the true Zulu character. When accused the Zulu will boldly defend himself with an animated manly eloquence, devoid of all cringing or humiliating supplications for mercy, for these are deemed cowardly and unbecoming to a Zulu soldier.

But the most peculiar trait in the Zulu is a passionate fondness for cattle, and in blending together the herdsman and warrior. His riches consist in the number of his flock, and his whole ambition and energies are turned to the study of its increase and preservation. No miser is more wedded to his gold, or derives more pleasure from contemplating his hoarded store, than the Zulu when he is surveying his flock as it passes before him, or is quietly contemplating the animals as they browse on the choicest pasturage. Whilst he is in possession of a flock the Zulu has all his wants supplied and all his heart desires, as from them he derives his food and clothing, and indeed every comfort and luxury that he knows or wishes for. When not attending his chief in war, most of his leisure hours are passed in herding his flock. There is nothing degrading to the character of the greatest chief to be thus employed, and no matter however numerous his possessions may be, each one of his flock is as well known to him as his children. So familiar is he with every little mark and spot on the skin, or the turn and bend of the horns, that one out of a thousand or two would be immediately missed. This says much for their power of observation, and it is a standing measure of the great wealth and affluence of a chief when it can be said of him that he does not know all his own cattle.

Every man, being both herdsman and warrior, is trained to the use of the spear and shield from his youth. They lead an indolent kind of life, particularly during the summer months, when the weather is generally very hot, and they sleep away their time in listless apathy while the females perform all the drudgery, being literally the hewers of wood and drawers of water. In time of peace the men employ themselves either in herding the cattle or journeying to the king to present themselves at headquarters, their principal object being to feast on the royal bounty, when tired of the milk and vegetable diet at their homes, for it is a rare occurrence that a Zulu can find it in his heart to kill one of his own flock, however he may be pressed by the wants of himself and family. The soldier has thus the privilege of removing at pleasure to headquarters, where he is fed as long as he chooses to remain, his only employment being feasting, dancing or sham fighting. It is the duty of a certain class of officers to report to the head Captain, or his Majesty, the number of warriors in attendance at the King's residence and a proportionate number of oxen are slaughtered daily for their maintenance.

It, however, occasionally happens that his Majesty, when tired of the pomp and parade of military display, and to enjoy his ease and quiet, is desirous of reducing the number of his warriors in attendance. In no case, however, does he issue any public orders to this effect, but adopts a very effectual means of ridding himself of the burthen of superfluous numbers, either by reducing or entirely stopping the supplies, so that the garrison becomes shortly starved out, and whole companies of these attendants are soon seen wending their way homewards. In the course of my long residence with the King I have had frequent opportunities of seeing these clearings out of the garrison, and many distressing scenes occasioned by hunger have come under my observation among some who have persevered in staying with the anxious hope of reaping a harvest when the King (as they said) opened his heart.

Though the Zulu country abounds with game of almost every description, hunting forms no part of the native pursuits, either as a source of pleasure or profit. This can only be accounted for by the aversion which the Zulu has for all animal food excepting that of oxen. In this respect he differs from all other Caffre tribes around him, the pursuit of game with a great number of those tribes being not only followed as an amusement but as means of subsistence.

The King occasionally indulges in hunting the elephant and the hyena, with which the country about Natal is much infested. On one of these occasions I had an opportunity of being present, and came off with a very narrow escape of my life. An ailing ox had been slaughtered and left in the thicket of a ravine close by the royal village as a bait to attract these midnight prowlers. This is speedily known to the natives by the loud chattering and laughing of the animals when they meet with food, which never fails to attract to the spot a large concourse. But often also the tiger and panther is drawn to it, the latter often appropriating to himself the booty to which the hyena's merriment attracted him. The resemblance to the human voice in the time of merriment of this animal's noise over its prey, and particularly when eating, has indeed justly obtained for it the name of the laughing hyena.

But the affair to which I alluded was this. Knowing the preparations that had been made for the evening's sport, I determined to avail myself of the opportunity to witness it. The night was calm and serene, not a breath of wind moved the still leaves of the forest, while a bright full moon reigned in the cloudless sky, and nature seemed hushed to a death-like repose. Everything seemed propitious for the huntsmen, and I was impatiently waiting and listening for the order to move. About midnight I had just fallen into a doze, and a confused dream of wolves and Caffre warriors had taken possession of my thoughts. I was suddenly woke by one of my native companions telling me he thought the parties were on the move toward our ravine. Up I started, soon rubbed the sleep from my eyes, and seizing a stout club and a couple of assegais, followed by my two companions sallied forth in the direction of the sport. Here and there I could perceive dark moving masses stealing noiselessly along, and though consisting of upwards of a thousand to fifteen hundred Zulus, they moved on with the silence of shadows, producing an effect on my mind in the stillness of the night that I can never forget. It was a time when the falling or rustling of a leaf might have been heard on every side.

On approaching the ravine the laughing and chattering of the hyena became more audible, on which my native companions fell back and entreated me to do the same. But I was too much engrossed with the scene and bent on seeing the sport, and to throw the assegai myself, to listen to their salutary advice. So on I went, and took up my position on an eminence looking down on the ravine whence the noise proceeded. Here and there around me, at yet considerable distances, I could observe approaching masses of the natives. But soon I heard a bark of consternation from the ravine. The approaching squadrons on the windward side had been scented by the wily hyena, and the change of their tone, with an occasional dead pause, intimated their sense of an approaching enemy.

I was all excitement and anxiety to see the game started, and little dreaming of the perilous position in which I had placed myself, when the loud yell of the Zulu war-whoop displayed the object of my solicitude and the danger of my position. A stricken hyena came bounding past me so close as almost to brush me with his tail, the eyes starting from his head like balls of fire, and his tongue nearly dragging on the ground. I had scarcely time to get on my feet and raise my assegai to have a throw at the animal, when a shower of these missiles fell thick as hail around me. The animal was surrounded on every side, and the spot on which I was posted was becoming the centre of the fray, so that I was in as perilous a position as he was.

Indeed, it was a miraculous interposition of Providence that I escaped unhurt midst the shower of spears that flew over and around me, being of course aimed at the pursued wolf. Fortunately my foot tripped and I fell flat on my face to the ground, by which the missiles passed over me. The result of the hunt, however, was the destruction of three hyenas and several men severely wounded by being like myself too far in advance of the chase.

The mode of attacking these animals is that of surrounding them and approaching on them simultaneously in every direction, by which, as may be expected, others suffer from the spears thrown besides the chase. The King enjoys the sport, and generally directs the movements of the hunters, remaining himself a distant spectator with his bodyguard.

The ingenuity of these people is evident in their villages, although their huts are anything but comfortable. The building and repairing of the hut and the erection and repairs of the cattle-fold next constitute the employment of the men. The huts are of a compact wicker work, circular in form, and much in the shape of a beehive, averaging from ten to twenty feet in diameter, the latter being the size more generally of those occupied by chiefs, while the former is the average size. They are very neatly covered with thatch of a long tough grass, and the floor, composed of a mixture of mingled clay and cowdung, is of glossy smoothness, having even a bright polish. The fire is in the centre of the dwelling, on a circular elevation above the surface of the floor, but there is no chimney or any aperture for the smoke to escape, so that it finds its way through the roof and thatch of the huts, or out by the door, which is a small aperture of about eighteen inches through which one has to crawl on hands and knees. There is generally a dense cloud of smoke floating within a foot or two of the floor that renders it impossible to sit up, and the only remedy against suffocation is to lay flat on the floor.

The cattle-fold is a circular enclosure, varying in size according to the wealth or possessions of the proprietor, as this is not exactly determined altogether by the actual number of cattle belonging to the chief of the village or his dependants, but frequently by the number of its inhabitants, arising from the manner in which the village is constructed. Considerable attention is paid to the warmth and comfort of the herd. The sloping faces of hills, and a dry, porous soil is generally selected for the site of the fold. When this has been determined on, the working commences by sinking a double row of posts into the ground, generally of five to six feet in height. The space between the posts is then compactly filled up with branches and boughs, generally of a species of thorn, forming a close and solid fencework, which when neatly arranged and evenly cropped has a very pretty appearance, very like a natural hedge. Outside of this fence the huts are then built, completing the entire circuit of the cattle-fold, while outside of the huts another fence or hedge, similar to the first, is thrown round, by which contrivance the cattle are doubly protected from the attacks of wild beasts, the huts and two fences being their defence. This constitutes the whole external economy of a Zulu village. As it often happens that either by long droughts and the failing of pasturage they have to remove and seek a more fertile spot for the preservation of their flock, this simple mode of erecting their habitations has been found most suitable to their wandering life.

The Zulu is even courteous in his manners, and on meeting his countryman on the road never fails to salute him in a friendly way with 'Sakubona wethu' (I am glad to see you, friend) and they partake with each other a friendly pinch of snuff. This is an article which every Zulu adult, male or female, is passionately fond of, and with which they invariably provide themselves for a journey, the box being either carried in the lobe of the ear or suspended round the neck. When meeting his superior or a chief, the Zulu respectfully turns aside, and stands erect like a soldier presenting arms until his superior has passed on. He salutes him with 'Umnumzana' [Etumgan], a word of which the nearest import translated into English would be, 'Your servant, master.'

Every Zulu when travelling is armed with a miniature shield and two or more sticks with knobs at the end of the size of a man's fist. These in the hands of the Zulu are formidable weapons. He can throw the short knob-stick with such precision as to bring down the smallest bird on the wing, and with it he can defend himself against any assault. They are great adepts at single-stick, and can so admirably defend themselves as to render it almost impossible to get a blow to reach their person. They have often put a stick into my hand and given me permission to hit them as hard as I could, but although having some proficiency I hardly ever succeeded.

As no written records exist among the Zulus, the history of the past is lost in the mist of ages, or only preserved by a vague, uncertain and confused tradition, which only leaves us to fill up the blank by conjecture. Their fondness for their herds, and the great anxiety and solicitude evinced for augmenting this stock, together with the respectable feeling with which herding is regarded among them, would argue that they have been long a pastoral race, and that warlike enterprise has only emanated from the ambition of their chiefs, not with the view of enlarging their territory by conquest, but to enrich themselves with the cattle of their neighbours. The several bloody and exterminating wars of Shaka appear to have had no object in view other than to enrich himself with cattle of the conquered tribes; to obtain these was a sufficient incentive to engage in the most daring and arduous enterprise.

The religion of the Zulus is very vague and unintelligible, and to a traveller passing through the country might seem as if they had no religion, as they generally hold the name of a great chief sacred, and swear by it. But it is now pretty generally known that there are no people, however rude or barbarous, who have not some sort of religious notion or form of worship, combined with a superstitious dread of invisible agency working secret influence on their destiny. A little acquaintance with the Zulus tends to confirm this truth, and that they are no exception. The most pernicious and baneful superstitions, however, that exist among the Zulus are their belief in witchcraft, and that human beings, through the agency of inferior animals, can work the most deadly purposes on their fellow creatures. The animal employed by the Umthakathi [Umtagatie] (Evil One) for these deadly purposes is the mpaka [Impaka] (wild cat). One of these creatures seen by any accident near their dwelling is ominous of some dreadful calamity and throws the whole village into consternation. This superstition, which too often causes the effusion of much innocent blood, is fostered by a vile set of wretches called inyangas [Enguagers] (Prophets or Soothsayers), who live by keeping up this monstrous delusion.

The Zulu believes that the disembodied spirit of his ancestors, father or grandfather, exercises a secret influence on his destiny. Hence when attacked by disease and long suffering on a sick bed, he freely sacrifices the fattest of his flock to the manes of his ancestors. The animal thus selected as an offering has to go through a special religious form, causing the poor beast a cruel and often protracted death. The morning or evening is generally the appointed time as most propitious for the occasion. The animal is then driven immediately opposite the sick man's hut; his nearest of kin then arms himself with a spear, with which he goes up to the animal and plunges it into it near the left shoulder. The blow in this case must on no account be repeated, and the poor beast often undergoes many hours of agony. The person who inflicts the wound then addresses a long prayer or appeal to the spirit in Hades for the recovery of the patient, which is generally continued until the animal expires.

It is then cut up, the gall being sent into the patient, a little of which he drinks, and then anoints himself with the remainder. The gall sack is then bound round his wrist as an amulet to prevent the progress of the disease. The four quarters of the slaughtered beast, together with the hide, hoofs and horns, are then carefully deposited and shut up in a hut set apart for its reception, and there it is kept for several days, or until it becomes quite putrid and offensive. It is then taken out and eaten by the women or lower order of the natives, or if too far gone for consumption it is carefully buried.

In going to war, or about undertaking any perilous journey, the Zulus have recourse to these sacrifices to the spirits of their ancestors. The poorer class who have not cattle to offer in their emergencies have recourse to chewing a bitter herb with which they besprinkle their breasts, arms and legs and offer up petitions, invoking the spirits to assist them or to alleviate their sufferings. After having performed all these religious ceremonies, or often repeated them without any good effect, the superstitious natives then attribute the visitation to the workings of the umthakathi and his impaka. Recourse is then had to the isangoma [Eveyonga] (Witch Finder) to point out the umthakathi when, if the patient happens to be a chief or a person of consequence, some innocent person, who is perhaps obnoxious to the inyanga, is singled out as the victim of this diabolical superstition.

Their traditions respecting the creation of the human race are simple and singular. They say the germ from which proceeded the first human being was deposited in a reed, or hollow cane, that grew on the margin of a clear and beautiful stream, by a large and splendid bird, which having accomplished its mission flew away into the immensity of space and has never again been seen upon earth. They describe this bird as the largest and most beautiful of the feathered creation, and speak of it with a degree of reverence, blended with a mysterious air, from which one might infer that at some remote period it had been an object of religious worship, but now almost obsolete. However, it is supposed this bird will again visit the earth as the herald of some great phenomena.

Such is the simple tradition now extant as relating to the origin of the human race, but there is no doubt that it has lost much of its original importance. Small as the remains now are, it presents a wide field for conjecture. Whether it may have some remote reference to the finding of the great legislator of the Jews in the bulrushes or, in contemplating the ever mutable state of mundane things that as the aggregate result of cause and effect are constantly following some cycle of vast extent, it may reasonably follow that the reactions on human beings are comprehended in the same necessary system, that all the events and phenomena we witness in the existence and condition of human beings are the successive evolutions of an extended series, which at the return of some vast period repeats its everlasting round through the endless flux of time. So we view those vague superstitious notions as the corrupted remains of a higher and more intelligible religion, already highly advanced in some distant age of the world.

The Zulu when advanced in years becomes grave and thoughtful. Indeed, in all his actions he seems guided by grave deliberation, and undertakes nothing in a hasty manner, or without giving it serious consideration. The old men take a pleasure in raking up the memory of the past, and of conversing on subjects that engrossed their attention in their youthful days. From these I obtained many amusing and interesting accounts of the early wars of Shaka, in which my communicants were actors, and of traditions that descended to them from their fathers, that by the vicissitudes of time and the revolutions effected by Shaka in the policy and government of the Zulus will in all probability be lost to the present generation. The brilliant warlike exploits of Shaka will absorb or eclipse all their traditions, and will no doubt be their wonder and admiration for ages to come.

Editor's note: We find the following in the daily prints, respecting some of these Indians, now in London:

The Zoola Caffres, now performing at the Saint George's Gallery, have had the honour of attending at Buckingham Palace, by royal command. Arrangements were made for the exhibition of the peculiar dances and evolutions of these interesting and extraordinary people in the riding school. The royal party, which consisted of her

Majesty and his Royal Highness Prince Albert, her Royal Highness the Duchess of Kent, all the royal children, and the members of the household, appeared greatly interested by the novel character of the exhibition. At the close of the performance, before the retirement of her Majesty, the chief addressed her Majesty in his native language, in a speech of which the following translation was made by the interpreter, Mr C. H. Caldecott: 'Houn Inkosi Kasi M'Angées (Oh, great Queen of the English)! This day a great honour has been conferred upon the people of Zoola. The nation great in battle, and high above the other nations of our country, have cause to rejoice, inasmuch as a chief of Zoola, with his followers, has been noticed by the great mother of the whites – a people of whom we have heard much, our kings have heard, and much has been said of the great English nation across the waters. But now the hearts of the Zoolus will be gladdened. When Manyos returns to his country, it will be in joy that we have seen and observed, and surprise has been with us: all that we have seen and heard verifies all that has been said of the M'Angées (the English). May the Inkosikazi (Queen) of such a nation live long and in happiness. Goopeleaka (we have said – and are satisfied). Great has been our satisfaction in having this day been received by the great mother of the whites. Bi it (your greatness).' On visiting the stables they were very much struck, asked the cost of the state carriages and value of the horses, and returned highly gratified. (This note is reproduced exactly as in the original text.)

Loss of the Brig Mary at Natal with Early Recollections of that Settlement

SEVEN

The Nautical Magazine, August 1853, pp. 430–434

Hitherto we have only considered the Zulu men. Let us now look to the women. These specimens of the human family, as in all barbarous nations, are looked upon as beings of an inferior order, on whom devolves the labour and drudgery.

The Zulu women, when young, are generally what would be considered good looking; many of them, indeed, are remarkably handsome. But from the custom of being early obliged to accompany their mothers to labour in the fields, the figure is spoiled and prevented from assuming the graceful development of which it is capable. The consequence is that they are generally very much below the stature of the men and their fine forms and attractive appearance are lost by premature decay.

In agricultural pursuits digging, sowing and reaping are occupations that devolve entirely on the women. The land is generally first cleared of the brushwood by the men; the women then follow, throwing the seed corn amongst the grass and herbage, and with their rude hoes they turn the seed into the ground, leaving the loose weeds on the surface to wither and decay. When the young maize begins to shoot up the loose weeds and herbage on the surface are collected together in heaps and burnt. These agricultural labours commence in October when all the women of the village go to work, even to the underwives of the chiefs, the inkosikazis [incasagass] only being excepted. It is nothing uncommon to find a Zulu woman at work in the fields with an infant on her back only three or four days old. They secure the child on their back in a skin strapped round the loins and shoulders, leaving the arms at liberty, an enjoyment which the North American Indians do not permit theirs to have.

The Zulu females are chaste in their conduct. When a Zulu warrior is about to marry, it is indicated by the shaving of the head and wearing the umutsha [muchu], a circular tuft of hair encompassing the crown of the head. This tuft of hair is then moulded closely to a slender hoop, and the whole is plastered over with gum, which gives it a jet black colour and durable property. He generally selects a young woman on whom his affections had been already placed, and the bargain is completed by making a present to the parents of the girl, consisting generally of a cow or an ox, and such other articles as the means of the husband admit. These presents, under every circumstance, are indispensable and considered in the light of indemnity to the parents for the loss of their daughter's services. Although polygamy is customary among them, yet the Zulus cannot be said to be a licentious or sensual people.

Notwithstanding the severity of their treatment, the Zulu women can hardly be excelled in cheerfulness and buoyancy of disposition. Though the order of civilized society is reversed with them, a cheerful contentment and devoted attachment particularly characterize the Zulu woman.

An incident which occurred during my residence at Natal affords a striking proof of the extent and warmth of affection and gratitude of which they are susceptible, and rarely equalled, in the history of civilized life. Our chief officer, Mr Hutton, was one day occupied in cutting timber near to a native village when his attention was arrested by the cries of a young female, reiterated to a degree that convinced him something was wrong. Leaving his occupation, he hastened in the direction whence the cries proceeded and soon found them to be caused by a man in the act of beating a young girl most unmercifully with a bludgeon. The poor girl presented a most pitiable sight, having received a severe cut on the head from which the blood flowed so copiously as to cover her from head to foot, while the enraged savage continued to inflict the murderous blows, deaf to all entreaty of mercy from his helpless victim. His ferocity seemed only to increase as the bleeding and mutilated victim of his savage cruelty was sinking beneath his blows, until the appearance of Mr Hutton for a moment arrested his arm. Even then, although the poor girl was already prostrated with the blows he had inflicted, he was again about to resume this work when Mr Hutton indignantly commanded him to desist, and followed up his intention by appealing to a broad axe which he had taken with him.

The savage, seeing that Mr H. was in earnest, made a sullen retreat towards the village, threatening he would yet have the poor creature's life; on which, Mr Hutton immediately turned his attention to the bruised and bleeding girl, humanely tearing up a portion of his linen to bind up her wounds. He then endeavoured to assist her towards the village, which was at no great distance, and left her in charge of persons whom he believed to be her friends. To this, however, she was averse and resisted all his efforts for this purpose. Believing, however, that she would think better of it after a little reflection, when she was more composed, and having carefully bound up her wounds, he left her and proceeded to resume his work.

He had not been long occupied, when, on turning round, he perceived the object of his sympathy advancing towards him with a slow and trembling step. She seated herself on a fallen tree near the place where he was working and addressed him in a low and plaintive tone of voice. Mr Hutton understood little or nothing that she said, but the language of gratitude was eloquently manifest in her blood smeared and sorrowful countenance. She seemed to say at that moment (as the whole of her existence ever after testified) you have saved my life and it shall henceforth be devoted to you in gratitude. Mr Hutton's warm heart required no interpreter to explain the meaning of this, so plainly expressed in the girl's intelligent countenance, and on his return towards Townsend thither she also followed him, and could not be again prevailed on to return to her own village.

On inquiry we found that she belonged to a family of Mathubane's tribe. She had no mother, and the man who had so cruelly beaten her was her father. Her poor mother had already fallen victim to the cruelty of this heartless savage, and there is no doubt but the unfortunate daughter would have shared her mother's fate had not the timely interposition of Mr Hutton prevented it. The conduct of this monster was condemned in severe terms by the more humane of the people to whom he belonged, and who agreed with the girl in her resolution of seeking the protection of and remaining with the Mlungus, rather than be subject to the brutal treatment of her unnatural father. This man, finding that she was determined on remaining with us, gave up his claim to her in consideration of receiving a small present in beads, as a remuneration for the loss of her services.

Her first appearance at Townsend was a painful and disgusting spectacle. She was covered with blood and, being in a state of nudity, was an object of pity and disgust. This was quickly remedied with a shirt, and her wounds were carefully dressed. She told us her name, Dommana; she appeared about eighteen years of age and had rather a prepossessing countenance and an amiable disposition.

On recovering her composure she was solicitous in finding how she could make herself useful. When Mr Hutton resumed his labours in the morning she was constantly at his side, watching for an opportunity of assisting him in turning over or hauling a piece of timber. Seeing her so anxious to make herself useful, Mr Hutton hit on an employment for her more suited to her sex. He soon provided her with a tub of water, and collecting some soiled linen, gave her a lesson in washing! Dommana was an apt scholar; she required very little instruction to become a very good laundress; her eager desire was not only to make herself useful, but to please and elicit the approbation of everyone at Townsend, but more particularly that of her benefactor, Mr Hutton. She would watch and study every gesture so as almost to be able to anticipate his wishes, and his approval of her conduct or actions seemed to be her greatest delight.

Two years afterwards, when Mr Hutton lingered on a bed of sickness that carried him to his grave, this devoted creature watched over him with all the solicitude of a mother over an only child. The sequel proved that no selfish motive had a place in the breast of this simple creature. The patient attention and anxious and incessant watching of this poor Indian was, indeed, with her a labour of love that only terminated with the last struggle of Mr Hutton's departing spirit.

Then no outburst of grief, no wailing voice, was heard from the sorrowing Dommana. A long, deep and heavy sigh alone indicated the anguish in her breast. Her grief, alas, was too poignant; no softening tear came to her relief. That sigh was a deep drawn fearful effort that snapped the chords of her grateful heart, and she left the corpse of him who had been her friend a heart-broken idiot. That simple innocent girl had lived but to discharge a debt of gratitude, and the last breath of her protector dissolved her worldly tie; reason had forsaken her mind, and all that remained of the once gay and lively Dommana was now a pitiful idiot.

The kind and soothing treatment that was administered, through the best and most judicious means, failed to reclaim this affectionate creature from the lethargic state into which she sank on the night of Mr Hutton's death. Having also myself been a favourite with her in her recent happy days, in vain were every means tried by me that concern and kindness could suggest to arouse her into a state of consciousness and to induce her to partake of food. It was truly affecting to witness the heart-broken creature as she lay extended on a mat, her eyes presenting a painful vacant stare, while a heavy breathing, with occasionally a deep drawn heavy sigh, was all that indicated the existence of the unconscious Dommana.

In this manner she lived three days, and on the fourth, being the fourth day, also, after the interment of Mr Hutton, the grateful Zulu girl was laid by his side in the same cold bed of death.

The devotedness of this African girl to her benefactor is a trait of character that commands our respect. When it is considered how many similar ties, and others perhaps more sacred, are broken by the slave trade, the Christian shudders at the thought that there are beings who are guilty of trafficking in such affections as the above. But it is too true. How many thousands of heart-broken wretches have been torn away from this same African soil, by that infamous traffic in Human Flesh, from all that was held dear to them in reality and sacred in memory, to endure, if they could, the suffering occasioned by the pestilential air in the crowded hold of the slave vessel? There, indeed, are victims interred alive; there they would almost devour each other to obtain a breath of fresh air. Fiendish and revolting to humanity as this is, what is it compared with the mental agony caused by tearing piecemeal all the holy affections of the unhappy victims? May we not believe that if aught in the catalogue of the crimes of nations or individuals ever caused the divine wrath to descend, the people of that country which is striving to annihilate the slave trade traffic in blood will stand conspicuous on that great day when the awful account of all shall be rendered? . . .

But to return from this digression to our Zulu people. Both sexes go perfectly naked until they reach the age of puberty; the female then provides herself with a prepared skin that is wrapped round the loins, sometimes reaching to the knees. They then shave their heads with the exception of a small round tuft, two or three inches in diameter, on the crown of the head, which they plaister with grease and red ochre.

They are very cleanly in their persons but invariably anoint themselves with grease or rancid butter, which gives them a very disagreeable smell.

When the women become old and infirm and, therefore, unable to work or provide for themselves, their condition is deplorable. They drag out a painful miserable existence without exciting any sympathy or compassion. The aged of both sexes are held in the utmost contempt by their friends or relatives, and are treated with cruel neglect and indifference. They are often thrust out of the hut in which they have been wasting away with the infirmity of age and want while yet the feeble lamp of life is flickering in the socket. But, to account for this, there is a religious superstition among them that a dead body pollutes the dwelling where the last breath has been drawn, and thus the sick and the aged are often left by their friends to expire in the ditch or the jungle, there to be devoured by beasts of prey.

The bodies of the dead are never interred, except in the case of a great chief. They are dragged to some distance from the village and left in the nearest jungle, where the bodies are speedily devoured by birds and wild animals.

Loss of the Brig Mary at Natal with Early Recollections of that Settlement

EIGHT

The Nautical Magazine, November 1853, pp.568–576

A messenger and escort now arrived from the King, commanding the attendance of the rest of our party for his Majesty's inspection. A present having been hastily made up, consisting of various coloured beads, and medicines, which Shaka had earnestly solicited from Captain King, and which the latter had promised should be sent on his return to Natal, we departed with the guides on our journey, but without the accompaniments of horses and pack oxen with which our shipmates had been favoured. I had looked forward to this journey both with curiosity and pleasure. It had been long known that the King must needs have a look at all of us, but now that the time had actually arrived, it was with some degree of anxiety and a heavy heart that I took leave of my shipmates at Natal, and placed myself under the guidance of the Chief of our native escort.

We travelled over the same ground as our predecessors had done; on the first day along the sandy beach, which completely knocked me up. The scorching sand soon blistered my feet, and before we got half over this stage I had to be shouldered by one of the natives. But I was no great burden to my sable friend. His shield and assegais, with the never failing bundle of bludgeons carried by the Zulus, of which he divested himself, were nearly equal to my weight, and for which I was now the substitute. Although it was not the most easy or comfortable mode of conveyance to be thus hoisted on the shoulders of a raw-boned fellow, it was a great relief to my feet, and but for his services I should have been left by the way.

We forded the Mngeni [Umganie] river, then scarcely more than knee deep, and started two or three huge alligators basking in the sun. During the rainy season, when the river is swollen with heavy rains, these reptiles make the fording very dangerous. Men and cattle are frequently carried off by them in crossing this and other streams in the Zulu country. We now halted under the shade of a tree, and after an hour's rest and refreshment I was taken up by another carrier, and we pursued our journey eastward until nightfall.

We then halted at the first kraal or native village, where our party were most hospitably entertained by the head man, who was one of Shaka's captains. We were regaled with milk to our heart's content, and were supplied also with excellent veal which had been killed expressly for us, and badly as it had been cooked, was very delicious. We were much entertained at their operations of cooking and dispatching their meals. Our guides having squatted round a large fire in the open air, in front of their sleeping apartment, commenced cutting up their beef into lengths of a fathom or more, and coiling it on the fire. When several coils had been thus disposed of, and the first had got fairly warmed through, a party got hold of each end, and commenced eating towards each other until in close proximity, when the bight was cut by one or the other, and the two would thus separate and begin afresh. Having in this manner disposed of their allowance, a few would crawl into the hut, while others slept around the festive fire. Here we resolved on remaining for another day to recruit our strength. Sailors, as is pretty well known, are no great pedestrians, even travelling on the best roads, but this hot, soft, sandy beach had literally knocked us all up.

After having enjoyed the good things and hospitality of our kind host the induna [Umdoona], we again resumed our journey, which now led us towards the interior. Our travelling became more cool and agreeable, for in traversing the sea coast the heat and glare of the sand, with the spray of the sea, combined with the powerful rays of the sun, had scorched the skin so much that my face was shedding its coat, the skin peeling off like the coat of an onion. Now the grateful shade of trees, and the carpet of green spread before and around us, was a great relief. Though my feet were still very sore and tender, I refused the aid of my good friends to carry me along, and struggled manfully to keep pace with my more robust shipmates; in fact, I must do them the justice to say, they had great consideration for my youth and weakness.

I observed as we passed along that I was an object of great curiosity to the travellers that we met, and in the villages as we passed along, and I seemed to occupy their undivided attention. A full grown white man had in a measure become familiar to them, but such a little fellow as I was at that time was a new sight for them; hence I became the lion of the party. The women and girls were particularly curious about me, and caused me often to blush from the way in which they handled and inspected me. At first I did not fancy this much, but when I became convinced of the harmlessness of their intentions, I submitted to all their curiosity with as much grace and good humour as I could command.

We pursued our journey on that and the following day without anything of interest occurring. Our track lay through a fine country, rich in wood and pasture, and well watered by numerous never failing streams, although we were now in the height of the dry season. Here and there, the nearer we approached the mountains of Bulawayo [Umbalallo], beyond which was the site of Shaka's residence, we met with large ithangas containing many hundred head of cattle, and where we were invariably regaled with a plentiful supply of rich and excellent milk. These ithangas are but temporarily constructed, for the convenience of removal, when the pasture fails, to a more favourable district. They are under the management of a number of juvenile warriors, who are enjoined by stringent regulations to a life of celibacy, no females being admitted within the precincts of these establishments, and any breach of these regulations is visited by death to the offender. The government and direction of these again are confided to a chief, who, however, seldom resides on the spot, but delegates his authority to resident officers under him, who may be considered as captains of these bands of warriors.

Each of these establishments constitutes a regiment. They live principally upon the milk from the cows, with occasional contributions of Indian and Guinea corn, levied on the inhabitants of the kraals [krolls] in their vicinity. Those we saw were certainly a fine specimen of savage warriors, all young, active, cheerful fellows, apparently from eighteen to twenty years of age. They appeared to consider themselves much above the common herd, and a somewhat privileged class. Being, moreover, trained to arms, they seemed to despise their more humble brethren whose pursuits were those of peace and utility; a very foolish notion, indeed, that I have marked also in many juvenile sons of Mars of a more civilized description, and in countries boasting the highest state of civilization, in whose favour the same amount of ignorance could hardly be brought forward in extenuation.

On the fourth day of our journey we crossed the large river Thukela which I take to be that called Saint Lucia on Captain King's chart of the coast of Natal, but as we were a long way from the embouchure this was uncertain. It was very low where we forded it, only having about three feet water, but from the steepness of its banks there is ample evidence that it is a formidable stream during the rainy season. Here in a deep basin some distance below the fording place we saw several hippopotami, their heads appearing like rocks dotted over the surface. We should assuredly have taken them for such had the natives not convinced us to the contrary by throwing some missiles at them, when they immediately disappeared under water. At night these huge animals (between an ox and a hog) leave their river haunts to graze on the rich pasturage along the banks of the river, and as regularly again, at dawn of day, they retreat to their oozy beds in the deepest pools.

There is a class of natives called Maphisi who make it their special business to hunt these animals, as well as the elephant, for the means of subsistence. As these people, I observed, differed in their habits from the Zulus, I concluded them to be a conquered race. Indeed, the whole of the country we had traversed from Natal I subsequently found had been inhabited by separate independent tribes that had been conquered by Shaka, a few of which had escaped the general destruction of their race. There was, in fact, no evidence wanting in our travels by the wayside to show what the fate of the many had been. The heaps of human skulls and bones blanching the plains were sad monuments of the fearful conflicts that had annihilated whole tribes, while these Maphisi were but the wretched remnants.

Their mode of attack, and the manner of capture of these huge animals, require great agility, with considerable strength and adroitness in the use of the spear, which is their only weapon. They lay wait for the animal on his midnight excursions to the savannahs for food, and watch him until he is sufficiently advanced from his retreat in the river to cut him off from it. The attack is then made simultaneously on him on all sides. Some of them, as they told me, often leapt on the animal's back, and plunging the spear into the back and neck, would cause the beast to throw himself down, when he would become a more easy prey to the huntsman.

I had occasion on one of my journeys in the interior to witness a moonlight attack on the sea-cow by a dozen huntsmen. The animal's legs are so short that his movements on land are slow and awkward, and he fell an easy prey to his pursuers. It nevertheless requires a good deal of activity and courage to effect the conquest. The expansion of his enormous jaws, opening two feet wide at least, armed with four formidable tusks, some two feet long, has a somewhat unpleasant appearance, and requires a firm nerve to approach and attack in a hand to hand or, rather, a hand to tusk, combat. The hide is exceedingly thick and tough, and requires great force to penetrate it, but the Maphisi have their spears very sharp for the work and have a quick and unerring eye.

There is another mode of killing these amphibious animals practised by some of the natives, but not by the Maphisi or professional huntsmen. It consists in digging deep pits with pointed stakes set perpendicularly at the bottom, the points uppermost. The pit is then carefully covered and, as the animal invariably pursues the same path to and from his haunts in the river, he falls into the pit and is impaled.[1] The food of this singular animal is entirely grass and herbage and, though so large and unsightly, the flesh is excellent food, both good and wholesome. I have, at various times, eaten a good deal of it, and often preferred it to ox beef as an agreeable change. I never detected anything strong or unpleasant in the taste, but when the animal was old the meat was exceedingly tough with a very coarse fibre, in which case it was hardly eatable.

We halted at a village inhabited by a number of these huntsmen, and they had a few of the sea-cow tusks which they offered to exchange for beads and brass ornaments. When the beads were strung they were generally contented with the length and circumference of the tusk in beads as its value. Although not exorbitant in their demands when trading, they are great beggars. Our Zulu guides treated these poor people very unceremoniously, and we had to interpose our authority to restrain them from committing acts of cruelty on these unoffending people. However, we found that they were used to it, and did not expect anything better from Shaka's soldiers. They seemed to have nothing of what is considered wealth by the Zulus (i.e., cattle) and, apparently, no possessions in the world but the bare walls of their miserable huts. A mat

---

1 Another is that of suspending one of the stakes in a narrow part of his usual path, so that it falls and pierces the animal as he is immediately beneath it. (Editor)

to sleep on, and a few clubs and assegais, completed the whole of their stock. Perhaps it would be impossible for these people, under such a military despotism, to retain anything from the greedy and rapacious warriors who occasionally honoured them with a visit, and no doubt the property of which they may be possessed is secreted.

There was no difficulty at once in seeing that they were but the remnant of a race that had been spared from the desolating wars of the great chief before whom we had soon to appear, and that the life of one of these relicts of a conquered race was no more, in the estimation of a Zulu warrior, than the grass which he trod underfoot.

Here, too, we observed the first process in the manufacture of native cloth from the ox hide, and its preparation for conversion into blankets. A hide was stretched out on the ground and pinned down with wooden pegs, around which were three or four operatives, male and female, the former with their assegais scraping off the fleshy and mucilaginous matter, and the latter following the men with a serrated piece of iron scraping the skin and raising on it a sort of nap; after which operation it had to be well rubbed with grease to make it soft and ductile. Some skins prepared in this manner, which serve the natives in the double capacity of mantle and blanket, are exceedingly soft and pliable, having, when well prepared, a velvet-like softness, and affording a degree of warmth equal to the best blanket. But it has always an offensive smell from the quantity of grease employed in the preparation; in fact, it is always getting a fresh supply of this from the hide of the wearer, for the native who pays attention to his toilet freshens himself up every morning with a fresh coat of grease. This is, generally, rancid butter, which is churned in a calabash for the purpose; and it is a very disagreeable affair for a stranger unaccustomed to such perfumes to be in a crowded hut with a party of natives thus lubricated and polished up.

On the evening of the fourth day's travel we encamped at the foot of the mountain range of Bulawayo, on attaining the summit of which we could view the termination of our weary journey. It is needless to say that, notwithstanding the many interesting objects and the beauty and grandeur of the scenery which nature spread before us in this vast and unexplored region, we were getting tired and weary.

That our journey was nearly over was evident by numerous pedestrian warriors, decked in their full war costume, wending their way to headquarters. Hitherto, we had passed through comparatively depopulated country where nought was left us to contemplate but the perishing remnants of humanity that were, indeed, thickly strewn in the way. It now became more cheering to hold communion with, and carry out our speculations on these living specimens of inhabitants.

This mountain range which, at the time of our visit, was the boundary of the Zulu territory proper, was celebrated for abounding with elephants, the roebuck and various kinds of game which the Zulu monarch occasionally engaged in hunting. The elephant hunt, in particular, was a most exciting and interesting spectacle. The extraordinary sagacity of this powerful yet harmless animal (when unmolested) to evade his enemies, his pitiful cries and supplications for mercy when he sees every door for escape shut against him, would subdue the most cruel and hardened heart.

A little before reaching our halting place one of the native guides had procured some wild honey, which, to me, was a great treat, and we were not a little astonished to find that for this little luxury we were, in a great measure, indebted to a little bird. These singular little creatures are numerous and common in this part of the country and, I believe, are pretty well known through all Southern Africa. In its plumage this bird has no recommendation to notice, being of a darkish colour, and it is about the size of the common sparrow, but it has secured for itself protection from harm by man and his respect from its peculiar faculty of discovering the hives of the wild bee, and the instinct it possesses for calling in his aid and piloting him to the spot where the treasure of the industrious bee is concealed, that he may get a share of the spoil. The nest of the bee, being generally in a hollow tree or the cleft of rocks, is out of his reach, unaided by man.

The natives, who are accustomed to follow these little guides, can by their actions and chirping pretty nearly calculate the distance they are likely to have to follow. The nearer the nest the shorter are the stages in his flight and the more earnest are his calls, until he flutters awhile over the spot which he wishes to show. He then perches himself in a neighbouring tree or bush and patiently awaits his share of the plunder, which the natives never fail to reward him with. I have been told by some of the natives that it was not always safe to follow these little guides, as they were sometimes incautious. Instances have occurred of their conducting them into the lair of the lion and tiger. But the little honey bird must not be blamed for this; in a country infested with these dangerous animals, it could hardly be considered safe to traverse the jungle when instances are of common occurrence of persons being snatched away, beyond rescue, from their very huts.

Sunrise the following morning found us scrambling up the western verge of this mountain range. Our party was here joined by a large concourse of warriors, bound to the same point, that by noon amounted to several hundred, and by which hour we had attained the summit. Though the ascent was fatiguing from the steepness of the way, we were agreeably shaded from the heat by the canopy of foliage ever stretched overhead, magnificent forest trees, of immense size and value, growing in great luxuriance to the very top of these fertile mountains.

At this hour we halted for a little rest and refreshment. We found the air cool and agreeable at this elevation, which might be two thousand feet above the sea level. While thus occupied we were entertained by our new friends with a war song, which our guides informed us was executed in the first style. Though we could not appreciate or understand the perfection of the performance, seeing very little grace or beauty in the movements of the dancers, it certainly was not wanting in novelty to attract and secure our attention, and it possessed a degree of romantic wildness in perfect harmony with everything around.

Here, also, I was the great object of attraction and curiosity to the natives, and many of them determined on presenting me with something as a mark of friendship and peace. These presents consisted of sticks neatly trimmed, with a knob at one end, and averaging from the size of the little finger upwards, until my stock of canes of this description almost became a load. These tokens of peace afforded me ample means (in the native fashion) of carrying on a desperate war!

One individual in this company of warriors, in particular, paid us marked attention and respect, though all of them were exceedingly civil and even respectful in their deportment to us. But this man seemed particularly anxious even to anticipate our wishes and to seek out and do little things that he thought might be pleasing to us. Evidently he endeavoured to show us how much pleasure it afforded him to be of the smallest service to us.

We soon, however, discovered that this poor fellow's anxiety to show us kindness proceeded from a grateful remembrance of an obligation he was under to the white man. It appeared that he had been indebted to the humane attentions and skill of Lieutenant Farewell some time previous, if not for his life, at least for the use of his limbs. Being out on a hunting expedition, it appears the unfortunate fellow had fallen over a fearful precipice and sustained a compound fracture of the leg and thigh; and here would have ended his mortal career so far as his own countrymen were concerned, the injuries he had sustained being far beyond the skill of the native doctors to remedy. There was nothing to be done but to leave him to be food for the beasts of prey, if, happily, one should speedily come to end the remnant of his miserable life. Fortunately for the poor fellow, Mr Farewell happened to be near the scene of the accident and at great personal risk, on hearing of it, humanely repaired to the spot, had him removed on a litter, set and splintered the fractured limbs and, by his further attentions in bleeding and administering remedial measures, brought him, by divine aid, out of a dangerous fever that subsequently set in consequent on the serious accident.

This incident, as a matter of course, tended to raise Mr Farewell high in the estimation of the Zulus as a great inyanga [ingangen] (doctor), as also respect for his care and humanity. The poor fellow himself was bent on doing all in his power to evince his own sense of gratitude to Mr Farewell, and he felt bound to extend it to the white race.

I have had occasion before, in the course of these recollections, to note the uncharitable comments of Mr Kay in his *Caffrarian Researches* on the white men at Natal, and particularly the unfortunate Lieutenant Farewell and his party. From the bitterness of his invectives against the traders with the natives on the frontiers of the Cape Colony, with whom he came immediately in contact, one would infer that some desperate rivalry must have existed between these traders and the missionary crew. Whether it was for the loaves and fishes or for the precedence with the natives, I had no opportunity or means of personally observing, but were I to judge from report and indulge in speculation from hearsay, I should put it down to the latter cause. Like Mr Kay, I too have travelled a good deal, in Africa, America and elsewhere and, though I may not possess his descriptive powers, I have not been an idle observer of what was passing around me. I have met many good and truly pious men of the class to which the Author belongs, and to which description I have no doubt he would be found to hold a prominent place. It is because his history and remarks have been carried to Natal, where it is evident at the time he wrote *Caffrarian Researches* he had never been, that I am constrained, in justice to parties on whom the grave has now long been closed, to correct one or two grievous errors into which Mr Kay has fallen.

It is not my intention to enter into controversy with the pious and talented author on the subject of his favourite theory of civilization. I shall only remark, if the question is satisfactorily settled that missionary stations are the approved and most efficient means for reclaiming the savage from his state of barbarism and for uniting him to the family of civilized and Christian men, it is certainly much to be regretted that this respectable and pious author had not, instead of myself and my unfortunate shipmates, been the pioneer into the darkness of the Zulu kingdom.

But as Mr Kay has cited Lieutenant Farewell and his party as an instance, in refuting Mr Stout (an American writer) on the subject, and because there were no missionary preachers at Natal with the first settlers and the shipwrecked seamen, he necessarily and very charitably concludes they soon became savages also.

This is evident from the following paragraph from Mr Kay's book, in chapter 16, pages 398 to 400, where he says, in speaking of Lieutenant Farewell and party at Natal:

> Here then we have a party of settlers, such we may suppose as Captain Stout of the *Hercules*, and others of his way of thinking, would, in all probability, recommend as the civilizers of Africa! Men of science, men of enterprise, men of general information, accompanied by labouring men; men who professedly went to trade and to cultivate, to introduce the plough and European manufactures, &c. Before such a force, bare morality, upright intentions, and the gentleman's high-toned principles of honour, rank and what not, are borne down like so many straws in the stream; and, instead of civilizing others, he gradually slides from one degree of corruption to another, until he at length becomes himself a savage, a perfect sensualist, a polygamist, and that of the most depraved caste!

Thus, then, it appears that a naval officer, with gentlemanly qualifications, science and general information admitted on his side, retrogrades and becomes a savage because forsooth there is no priest to remind him of his being a Christian. But what is most amusing in the argument is that the force before which the gentleman and man of science must bend can have no influence on the infallible and invulnerable missionary!

This is really too heavy a weight of absurdity to hoist in at the present day, and it may be as well to mention en passant, for the information of the well intentioned and philanthropic individuals who support these missions for the propagation of Christianity.

This argument of Mr Kay's might be applied with a little more degree of probability to some ignorant men who, in a fit of enthusiasm for the conversion of the savage, leave their homes for the jungles of Africa and, having nothing to sustain them but this religious fanaticism, forget the precepts and example of the 'great teacher' – 'that he that humbleth himself shall be exalted.' Like the impostors of old, both Christian and pagan, these men arrogate a superiority over their fellow men to which they are neither entitled by birth, education or talent. Consequently they make themselves objects of contempt to men who have no greater claim to respect than themselves. By a different course of conduct they would silently have secured that deference and respect, which their ignorance induces them to expect or aspire to as a right.

Loss of the Brig Mary at Natal with Early Recollections of that Settlement

NINE

The Nautical Magazine, January 1854, pp. 23–29

The class of traders with which the Missionaries came incidentally in contact were, I have no doubt, not a bit better than they ought to be, though not so bad as they are represented; but the conduct of a gentleman, as represented by Mr Kay, of Mr Farewell's standing in society is monstrous.

Had I not been personally well acquainted with Lieutenant Farewell, the narrative of his humane assistance to the maimed and abandoned Zulu would be sufficient alone to rescue him from this obloquy. Such reports, emanating from religious fanatics, should be received with caution, as this class of men very often assume a licence, in the name of the Great Master whom they profess – and I dare say believe – they serve, to traduce and vilify, even, at pleasure and anathematize the rest of the world who differ from them. It is possible that, in the inscrutable counsels of Infinite Wisdom, religious enthusiasm, fanaticism or even insanity may enter into the scheme for the advancement of His kingdom, but the tyranny exercised on mankind through such delusions is now, happily, becoming extinct. The days of the inquisition have passed away and the denouncements and maledictions of priestcraft, by whatever name it may be called, have been consigned to the same tomb – sad mementoes, indeed, of the abject slavery to which the human mind is capable of being reduced by trickery and the terrors of a religion, the first Great Teacher of which was the embodiment and perfection of humility and love. Nor is the sacred and saving truth of Christianity impaired by the phrensy, vice or delusions of enthusiasts.

The reflecting and sober Christian does not whine or howl over the darkness by which he sees large portions of the human family surrounded, when he knows that the Great Architect of the stupendous work of creation has not left them to perish from caprice, ignorance or oversight; that their condition is comprehended in the necessary economy and arrangement of His mighty scheme; that their minds are accommodated to the circumstances in which it has pleased Him to place them, and are thereby endowed with instincts and gratifications unknown to us. A revolution in their habits and condition is not to be effected by the work of a day, a month, a year or an age, as he sees in the dark cloud, though charged with the desolating tempest, but a mark of infinite wisdom and care in the government of the world. Knowing the effects and consequence of this elemental strife, he does not desert his post to raise a clamour about his neighbours' peril until assured his own possessions and his own flock are secured and sheltered from the storm.

I have steered thus far out of the course of my story to vindicate Mr Farewell and his party from what I conceived a gratuitous though indirect calumny. That familiarity reconciles us to many things and in the end begets indifference is a principle of human nature too well known to admit of contradiction, and that barbarous scenes of cruelty when often presented tend to deprave and harden the heart. But it is obvious that the gentleman, the man of education, rank and its accompaniments, is at least as likely to resist the force of these influences as the man who has little else to sustain him but a religious phrenzy, kindled perhaps on a sudden by a spark, fallen from a piece of impassioned eloquence in behalf of the perishing heathen, that might just be as evanescent.

Lieutenant Farewell fell a victim only to his confidence in the respect that he imagined he had secured to himself from the native; he was assassinated, on his return to Natal after visiting Cape Colony, by a revolted band of Zulu warriors, into which the nation it appears soon split up after the murder of Shaka. My own impression had always been that the white men at Natal were entirely indebted to Shaka for the forbearance and respect evinced towards them by his subjects. The fate of Lieutenant Farewell, who fell by their hands so soon after this event, tends in a measure to confirm the correctness of this conjecture.

To finish with Mr Kay's notice of Natal leads me to make another short digression. It is an ungrateful office, though no doubt a very useful one, to rake up the errors into which the writer of a history has fallen, either from ignorance of the facts or prejudice; and it is painful for one being on the spot, and a witness of the passing events, to read the

monstrous absurdities supplied either by the fertility of the writer's brain
or from exaggerated and evil report. It is hard to say whether regret or
indignation should predominate, when such agency is employed to
degrade the character and darken the follies or crimes of our fellow-
creatures, when it falls on those of whom our own experience makes us
feel it to be unmerited, and on whom we have reason to look back as
benefactors.

My intentions are far from vindicating cruelties, with many of which
Shaka can be justly charged. But presuming the notice of his life and
death in *Caffrarian Researches* rests on the same authority as the
account given of the first settlers at Natal, and there being a statement in
this notice illustrative of Shaka's cruelty which, the author says, is from
'well attested facts' that I know to be a monstrous injustice (savage
although he was), I cannot be silent.

The part in question [p. 405] says:

> The awful degree of barbarity of which this wicked chief was
> capable will appear fully evident from the following appalling and
> well-attested facts. Being one day annoyed by the playful gambols
> of a child, which happened to peep into his hut, he instantly vowed
> vengeance on it, and declared he would kill it. On perceiving his
> anger kindle, the little innocent fled with all speed, and took refuge
> amongst the crowd of its companions. Thither the monster
> pursued; but not being able immediately to identify the object of
> his rage, he issued orders for the whole company (amounting to
> seventy or eighty children) to be massacred. On another, hearing
> that one of his captains, commanding between four and five
> hundred men, had been routed by the enemy, and had lost some of
> the spears, he immediately ordered him and his soldiers to appear
> at his residence, where every man was, without ceremony, put to
> death, and the wives were added to his seraglio! This is said to have
> contained an extraordinary number of females; but, in order that it
> might not be known that he had converse with any save his own
> acknowledged concubines, the moment any of the other poor
> creatures were pronounced with child, their death warrants were
> generally sealed.

Now the atrocity of Shaka's barbarity in the above statement is only equalled by the falsehood of the whole tale! My knowledge of Shaka's history is contemporary with European intercourse with Natal, at least with regard to any knowledge we have of the Zulus as a nation and of Shaka as their chief, and his slaughter of the children is a portion of that history which was never heard of at Natal up to the death of him who is represented to have perpetrated that atrocity!

Shaka's huts were considered too sacred and well guarded from intrusion to admit the chance of a child's peeping into them; I am safe in affirming that I was the only child, or youth, who ever gained admittance within the sacred precincts of the enclosure within which Shaka's huts were placed. It was the outer court alone that was accessible even to his captains and those in high authority. As the course of our journey where I left it was bringing us near the scene of this reputed slaughter of innocents, I shall give a description of the 'palace' in its proper place.

The massacre of the discomfited captain and his band of warriors also has no place in the recollection of anyone with whom I had any acquaintance, nor did I ever hear of such an occurrence. If the report of these barbarities was propagated by any of the party of Natal of which I was a member, or from that of Mr Farewell, I emphatically declare that no atrocity of the savage chief could surpass the crime of raising the falsehood of these cruelties having been committed. Thoroughly conversant as I was with the native language, in which I was surpassed by no European at that, or I may even venture to say the present day, I must certainly have attained some knowledge of such an appalling circumstance.

In a biographical memoir which I have noted of this extraordinary Caffre chieftain, his origin and rise to power will show a very different career to that which is stated in Mr Kay's *Caffrarian Researches*. Shaka raised himself, from being a persecuted wanderer in the bush, where he and his mother had to fly from his father's vengeance (when he was but an infant), to rule the Zulu nation. It was from a thunderstorm bursting over him, at the moment of victory over the forces of his unnatural parent, that this name was derived, Zulu signifying thunder.

I have indeed witnessed many blood executions of innocent victims prompted by degrading superstitions, and I know too that many victims were immolated at the instance of a cringing and cowardly scoundrel named Mbopha, a confidential servant; so much so, that he was the only individual in the Zulu nation who was permitted to carry a spear in the presence of and within a limited distance of the king. Availing himself of this privilege, he subsequently stole behind and assassinated his master, an arrangement having been previously entered into with the murdered Shaka's brother, Dingane, whose ambition it appears became weary of waiting for the removal of his brother, Shaka, in the ordinary course of nature.

I have noted in my biographical memoir of this unfortunate chief that an arrangement was entered into with this brother Dingane that at his death he was to succeed to the head of the Zulus, and it was on account of this understanding that no doubt (indeed, I know it was so) the latter's life was spared. But as the account of Shaka's life may never meet the public eye, it may be interesting to the present and future settlers at Natal to know that such an arrangement was in actual existence, and that it was in consequence of this arrangement the story no doubt has originated that the moment any other than his acknowledged concubines were pronounced enceinte, their death warrants were signed. In fact, Shaka, though he was surrounded by women, who were the only inmates of his palace, admitted no intercourse with them. But of course everyone knew better, and when any of these women who were called umntwana (princess) showed symptoms of pregnancy, they were sent away from the court, and afterwards lived in great retirement and obscurity.

This was carrying out a part of the compact with his brother Dingane to have no heirs to interfere with his succession. The writer was in a position to know that these women were not put to death on account of being enceinte, having had the opportunity of meeting two of them after their banishment, as well as the children. But it was never hinted the latter were of the royal blood. The reader will not be disposed to doubt the correctness of this statement when I tell him that I enjoyed the extraordinary privilege of associating with these women in the very interior of the palace, where the foot of a male subject never pressed the floor, and that their habits and their history was as familiar to me as to themselves. So far from their dreading such a contingency, it was rather looked forward to with pleasure, as a relief from the dull monotony of their secluded life.

But to say that their number was recruited from the seraglios of murdered chiefs only shows how little the author knew, or how ill-informed he was of the habits and customs of the Zulus. The meanest subject in Shaka's dominions would have looked on such an acquisition as a degradation. The unfortunate wives of a doomed chief had no such hope before them, nor such mercy to expect. The fate of their lord involved their own. The barbarous practice prevailed of exterminating the whole of the family and dependents of a chief at his execution, so that nothing was left to survive him. His very kraal with the dwellings were consumed to ashes, his cattle alone being saved from the general wreck.

This barbarous custom had long obtained in the part of Africa of which we are speaking, and would appear to have originated in a necessity for the security of the community when the country then composing the Zulu nation was ruled by numerous petty chiefs. In fact every headsman of a tribe was an independent ruler acknowledging no superior; hence, when a quarrel arose, and one of them was overpowered by his neighbour's superiority, the whole of his adherents suffered with him to prevent their augmenting the force of another rival whom they might join and prevail on to take up their cause. So that in a measure it was the policy by which a balance of power was maintained by these petty tyrants. Though this necessity appeared no longer to exist, the inhuman practice was still kept up, the only reason advanced to justify it being their superstitious belief that the surviving relatives of the malefactor would be continuously plotting mischief against the rest of the community by means of witchcraft.

I have just remarked that I had extraordinary privileges. I may add more, that I had extraordinary power and influence with the savage chief. Mine, indeed, was a strange destiny. That facts are often stranger than fiction many incidents of my early adventures given in these recollections afford very striking proof. The recollections of these rise before me now, and I almost doubt their reality. That I had the influence to stay the mandate of death issued by this savage despot, and that I had the courage to plead the cause and defend the doomed victim from the rage of him before whom armies of warriors trembled and bowed to the dust, and I but a youth of fourteen years of age, seems to belong to those incidents which are classed in the catalogue of fiction.

But that I possessed that power and influence over Shaka is nevertheless true, strange as it may appear. I believe that with the exception of his mother, Nandi, I was the only living soul that dared to breathe a contradiction to his will. Ah! it is a pleasing reflection, too, that I can recall to mind the day when my feeble voice, raised in the distant wilderness of Africa, stayed the bloody hand of a relentless executioner from destroying many innocent victims. Tears of gratitude stain the page of these recollections to that Almighty and Blessed Benefactor, in whose hands are the hearts of men in the uttermost ends of the earth, where indeed could I be lost where his mercy could not reach, or where his arm could not save me. What signal manifestations have I not had of his providence when all around seemed but the darkness of despair.

But it would be wandering from our journal, and anticipating my recollections, were I to mention in this place the many strange adventures and providential escapes from a variety of dangers, with many singular conversations and confidential communications made to me by the man who was the terror of that portion of Eastern Africa from the frontier of the Cape Colony to the Portuguese settlement of Delagoa Bay.

One great end of the commandments is charity and now, having endeavoured to rescue the memory of two important characters in the early history of Natal from the infamous imputations abovementioned, I will resume my journey. . . . at that point of time and place on the summit of the Bulawayo mountains where I left it, with our band of Zulu warriors who, having finished their dance, had now commenced their toilet, and were vigorously anointing their bodies with grease, an operation which certainly gave them a fine polish, and very much improved their appearance.

They now commenced ornamenting and decorating their persons with beads and brass ornaments which, on the journey, had been carefully wrapped up in leaves and carried round the waist. The most curious part of these decorations consisted of several rows of small pieces of wood, about the size and shape of those used in playing drafts, strung together and made into necklaces and bracelets. Some of these warriors had their necks and arms ornamented with several rows of this description, and those particularly about the neck seemed to be very inconvenient to the wearer, and certainly were not very ornamental. But on inquiry we found that the Zulu warriors set great value on these apparently useless trifles, and that they were orders of merit conferred by Shaka on those who had distinguished themselves by daring deeds of bravery on the field of battle. Each row, whether round the neck or arm, was the distinguishing mark of some heroic deed, and which the wearer had received from Shaka's own hand. These were principally gained in the last amaMpondo [Amapanda] war, from which Shaka had returned with a large booty. These of course were all of the first class of warriors, high in favour with the Zulu monarch, and were now displaying their finery and decorations preparatory to presenting themselves before him.

As our next halting place would end our journey, which our guides told us would be concluded by sunset, our little party also began to set themselves in order for this grand occasion. On the strength of which I bent a clean frock and pair of ducks, which had been carefully wrapped up in paper and several folds of old canvas, and which constituted, with what I had on, my entire wardrobe.

We had not been much encumbered with luggage. A roll of mat to sleep on, and a bundle containing a change of apparel, was all that any of us could afford. These arrangements being completed, we again proceeded. Our Zulu friends being in front, and our party bringing up the rear, we commenced our descent of the Bulawayo through a continuous dense forest of timber that the sun's rays hardly anywhere penetrated. On emerging from this sylvan obscurity we saw a vast plain, but slightly undulated, like old Ocean's bosom after a breeze, and tinged by the golden rays of a setting sun with numerous herds of cattle lowing in the distance, and moving on to their fold. Within a mile of this point of observation, Dukuza [Toogosa], the great capital of the Zulu kingdom was seen. Around it in all directions bands of warriors were in motion or encamped, the blue smoke curling high up in the still air from the numerous camp fires of this dark host. Altogether this combined to present a spectacle of wild grandeur, magnificent beyond my power of description, one to which the pen of the poet or the pencil of the painter alone could do justice, could he have stood there, and 'with my brave companions of the sea,' fearless to view the wondrous scene with me.

Onward we moved, the throng increasing as we neared the capital, until the din of the multitude and lowing of hundreds of cattle became almost deafening. What contrast was this to the deathlike stillness that had hitherto pervaded our journey. Just as the shades of evening began to close on us, we entered the gates of Dukuza.

Our guide conducted us to a commodious hut, from which he very unceremoniously expelled the occupants to make room, as he termed us, for the king's wild beasts.

Loss of the Brig Mary *at Natal*
with Early Recollections of that Settlement

TEN

The Nautical Magazine, February 1855, pp. 64–71

The contrast of the deep solitude of the wilderness and the noise of the assembled host, with the novelty of the scene, tired and fatigued as I was, for a long time banished all sleep from my eyes. Besides which, I was in a state of fear and anxiety.

No sign of civilization appeared amidst the darkness of this barbarism to inspire the hope of compassion towards us, unfortunate strangers, and we might rather speculate as to how soon the caprice of this savage chief would make our lives the sport of his no less savage warriors. We were certain they were not cannibals; although it was some consolation that if killed we should not be eaten, such speculations were far from being calculated to encourage that repose so needful after the fatigue of our journey.

The darkness of the night rendered the numerous fires of the great multitude encamped around the royal kraal[1] more imposing, and the sable figures of the naked warriors lighted up in the glare of their fires suggested a picture to the imagination of the inhabitants of the region of darkness holding their orgies around us. Numerous were the visitors perpetually peeping into our huts to get a sight of the new addition to the king's wild beasts.

What a change has now come over the land of the Zulu. The white man thus designated now rules his country, and it is no great prophetic stretch to say that the whole Zulu race will soon disappear before him, as the snow melts before the sun.

People of Zulu, I leave this record of you in the day of your greatness as a nation. None of you may ever see the greatness of mine,[2] but its

---

1 Kraal [krawl], a name given by the Boers to the Caffre [Copper] villages. (Editor)
2 In the *Nautical Magazine*, Vol. 22, No. 6 [Instalment Six], in an editorial note to the notice of these 'Recollections,' I observe by an extract from the public prints, that the

influence is already surrounding you. I write this in testimony of my gratitude for the many favours I received at your hands. It is too much for me to expect that a revolution in your habits, so great and so opposite to all you have been accustomed, can be effected in your generation without doing violence to your happiness. The white man's notions and yours differ widely on this point, and I am concerned for you in the struggle. But I look forward with hope that your successors will enjoy the advantages and benefits which you cannot appreciate.

I am a decided advocate for your liberty, in common with that of the whole African race, and rejoice that my country has been the first to acknowledge that right, and has set the example of your freedom to the rest of the world. Other advantages will follow: the Genius of universal emancipation has set her foot in every land, before which slavery must be for ever trodden down. The work is begun, and the pseudo-Christianity that reduces you to the condition of the brute creation is fast losing ground. Greater and more talented minds will rise to vindicate your rights as members of the human family. I have had occasion, and done so under great disadvantages and in the very strongholds of slavery, and I trust discharged my duty with fidelity commensurate with its importance. . . .[3]

Zulu Caffres have had the honour of attending at Buckingham Palace by royal command. I am not aware that I have any recollection of the favoured Manyos [Moagas]; perhaps he was but a child when my sojourn in the Zulu country terminated.

3 When in command of a small brig at Wilmington, N.C., I had for three of my crew black men, natives of St. Lucia [in the Caribbean], where I had shipped them. The law of North Carolina required that these men should be given up to the harbour master to be put in jail until the ship was ready to sail. I entered a protest against this cruelty to these unoffending men in which I referred to our commercial treaty with the U.S. of America, and positively refused to give them up, intimating that I should repel by force any illegal attempt on the liberty of my crew. And having posted the victims of this persecution behind two 6-pound carronades, loaded to the muzzle with grape, and myself at their head, I told them:

Now, my friends, you must defend your liberty as British subjects, and unless a warrant duly issued by a magistrate or justice of the peace, by which any free citizen of the State may in like manner be arrested and sent to jail, fire on your assailants. I will stand or fall with you in the result. I wish no other white man to endanger himself. This is my quarter-deck, and I devote myself and it to your liberty.

In the morning, our arrival having been reported to the king, we were visited by a chief (Sothobe) and Jacob. They caused us to shift our quarters to the head of the kraal, more in proximity to the palace. Our distinguished visitors brought with them a large supply of food for our use, consisting of cold boiled beef, Indian corn and sour milk, on which we made a hearty breakfast. We were desired to hold ourselves in readiness to be presented as soon as his majesty should come from the palace, to which there was no admittance but by special order or invitation from the king himself. In the interval I took the opportunity of surveying our present locality — the Zulu metropolis — for which our new position, near the head of the immense enclosure, was most favourable, being situate on a gentle elevation whence a view of the whole capital was obtained.

Except in size, Dukuza, differed little in structure from other Caffre kraals, being of circular form. Including the external and internal fence-work for the protection of the dwellings and cattle, the diameter might have been about half a mile, and it contained about 1 500 huts exclusive of those immediately occupied by the king's household. These latter were of a superior description, and entirely hidden from observation by a close and compact fencing very neatly arranged. They were about forty-five or fifty in number, and were built on sufficiently elevated ground to command a view of the whole village. Around this portion of the kraal (indicating it to be headquarters) numbers of warriors had already collected and squatted on the ground, either guarding the palace or eagerly waiting to salute the Ngangezwe [ganggaswiee] (Great as the World) on his appearance from within the sacred precincts of the isigodlo [izekoshlee] (palace) into which, despite the awful consequences to children reported by Mr Kay in *Caffrarian Researches*, we will take a peep.

I have to mention to the honour of the authorities at Wilmington, who, feeling the injustice equally as myself of this persecution, made my obstinacy the excuse for not carrying the law into execution in my case. Lieutenant-Colonel Torrens, then Governor of St. Lucia, to which colony my little vessel belonged, with that high-minded zeal and sense of duty for which his government was characterised, laid this case before her Majesty's government. Whether the government of the U.S. have abolished this persecution of British seamen of colour I am not aware. For details of this transaction, see *Anti-Slavery Reporter* for 1846.

On entering the gate of the compact fencing on the interior side is a spacious square, containing half a dozen huts of unusual size and neatness in their construction. The ground is exceedingly smooth and even; everything wears an air of neatness that elsewhere we had not witnessed. The fencing, on close examination, is stronger than one would suppose when looking on it at a distance, being composed of two and sometimes three thicknesses of compact wickerwork, carefully worked with young twigs or saplings, and about eight feet high, so that it cannot be looked over from the ground. In this square, which is but the outer court of the palace, the king sometimes assembles his chiefs and councillors to hold indabas [indabos] (his war councils).

We observed before us another gateway in the side of the square, fronting the one by which we entered, that leads to another oblong enclosure, more spacious than the former, and containing a dozen or more huts, still more elegant of construction and of still larger dimensions. The floor of this enclosure is of glassy smoothness, with a polish that reflects the image like a mirror. A continuation of enclosures of this last description, with more or less huts in them, and of different shapes, some semicircular and some triangular, which together complete the internal economy – this is called the black palace, inhabited only by the abantwana nkosi [untwane inkosse] (king's women). No other class of persons being admitted to these apartments, they were as little known as their inmates, who were not allowed to hold any intercourse with the world without. Their number might amount to about 150 to 200, and here the Zulu monarch would sometimes shut himself up in this seraglio for several days together.

At such times I had the extraordinary privilege of being admitted to his presence, and made the medium of communication between him and his chiefs without. He always on these occasions reported himself sick, and I held the honourable post of first physician, which took precedence of every other post of honour! It appears that I was the first gentleman physician that ever had the honour to be consulted within the seraglio. My predecessors in that office (which in reality was that of aide-de-camp) were generally his head women for the time being, who carried his orders to Mbopha, his head servant, who communicated them to the different chiefs.

The whole extent of the enclosure compassing the palace was about

400 yards in length, and from fifty to sixty in breadth, and contained, as before mentioned, about fifty huts. The population of the kraal itself was about 3 000 inhabitants, but from the number we observed at this time encamped around it, for which there was no accommodation, was fully equal to 3 000 more, all of whom appeared to be warriors, as a very small portion of women or children was to be seen, while vast numbers continued to arrive. The cause of this immense gathering we discovered to be for the promulgation and celebrating of the agrarian law, that when the war song, the dance, and festivity were over at the capital, the warriors could return to their respective homes to reap and enjoy the ripe harvest. Until this ceremony was performed, and permission obtained, it was a capital offence to touch a blade of corn in the field.

About ten in the forenoon several messengers were observed running at full speed, calling out at the top of their voices the names of chiefs and divisions of warriors summoned by the King. This gave us notice of his being abroad, of which we were soon certified by two other running messengers approaching our quarters at full speed, and calling out 'Nango mlungu bo, nango mlungu bo' [moloongo] (now then the white men, now then the white men), this being our summons to appear. And, as we had been already in a state of preparation, we had only to pick up the present, consisting of a few beads and bangles, with a little medicine, composed of salves, blisters, plasters and salts, we sallied forth, with the messengers (who appeared very impatient of the least delay) and our friend Jacob, as interpreter and master of ceremonies, for guides.

On passing through a private gate in the outer fence of the kraal we observed a large concourse of people squatted on the ground in a very humble posture, their elbows resting on their knees. On a nearer approach in front of these we obtained a sight of his Majesty who, elevated on a large roll of matting for his throne, was in earnest conversation with a few chiefs, somewhat nearer to him in front of the kraal but in the same humble posture as the rest. At every pause in the King's conversation we heard a response, first from the chiefs, then from the whole assembly, of 'Yebo baba, yebo baba' [Yea boba] (yes father, yes father).

Let him who has entered a court to hear judgment passed on a momentous question in which he was deeply interested, or who has ever awaited an interview with a man on whose favour or on whose word depended his chance of advancement or means and prospect of subsistence, let him imagine what I felt on this occasion, who had been taught to bow the knee only to my Maker. It was no small addition to the perturbation of my spirits to behold the awful solemnity with which this mighty savage was approached. The crowd formed a semicircle in front of the throne, round the extremity to the right of which we were conducted. Moving forward in a half bent posture we took up our station near the centre and in the interior of the circle where, on looking round me, I now saw no means of escape, being completely hemmed in by the sable host.

Groundless as were my fears, I venture to say many a stouter man would have trembled in a similar position. It would be difficult to conceive oneself placed in a more trying position. The harangue with the chiefs went on without any interruption by our presence and, though we passed immediately before Shaka, he appeared not to notice us in the least, and at every pause in his conversation the everlasting response, 'Yebo baba,' reiterated by the throng, was a sound that long afterwards continued to ring in my ears.

It appeared that a grand display of military manoeuvres as well as dancing was contemplated, and the subject of this conversation of Shaka was to instruct the chiefs and generals of the different divisions of his plan and arrangements for its conduct. He sat before this council perfectly naked and was also engaged in anointing his body with grease, preparatory to investing himself with the royal war dress.

On mustering sufficient courage to look about me, my attention and that of my shipmates was arrested by a strange and ludicrous object, which at first sight appeared to be a complete nondescript. It was a kind of wild animal in an erect posture, and proved in reality to be a human being enveloped from head to foot in the skin of a tiger, so fitted on him that the skin of the hind legs served as pantaloons and that of the fore did duty as sleeves for the upper garment. Thus he was in reality the only individual in the assembly, except ourselves, that could be said to have any clothing. The skin of the tiger's head being drawn over his face served as a covering for the head, on which was mounted a pair of huge horns belonging to some animal of the deer tribe. These were decorated with several bunches of different coloured feathers, presenting altogether a most extraordinary and ludicrous appearance.

We were at a loss to conceive what this monster was intended for, and what duty he had to perform as an appendage to his Majesty's establishment. We could hardly consider him as an ornament, and were not a little surprised on being informed that he was an imbongi [izebonkar] (a priest) dedicated to the worship of the Nkosi Kakhulu [Inkosiqa koola] (great King of the Zulus). It was certainly a novel idea of Shaka's, when he assumed the power and attributes of a deity, to clothe his priests in the garb of wild beasts of prey. A very significant emblem, indeed, of the ignorant and wild extravagance of his assumption; but Shaka was worshipped as a deity, and was believed by the Zulus to have supernatural powers. No one of his subjects doubted his having these powers, but he did himself.

On his conversation with the chiefs being terminated, the latter withdrew to the rear and joined the crowd. After a pause of a few minutes duration, he motioned us to advance. On our moving forward to within a few yards of him, he again motioned us to squat.

After another pause of about ten minutes, which is the Zulu etiquette, he addressed us, through Jacob our interpreter, thus: 'You are the Mlungus that came in the umkhumbi (vessel) with Captain King.'

To which we answered in the affirmative.

'You are King George's people.'

'Yes.'

'Captain King promised to send me some medicines; has he sent me any with you?'

On which we brought forward our present, opened it out and explained the different articles, their use and description.

On which, he held up his forefinger and, while shaking it, he uttered, 'Yayizi, yayizi, yayizi' [izee, izee, izee] as a mark of approbation. He ordered the immediate removal of the present to the isigodlo and directed the greatest care to be taken, particularly of the medicines, on which he appeared to set the greatest value.

He remarked that Captain King had told him he was going to make another umkhumbi in the room of the wrecked one, and that he would return phesheya kolwandle [piz-eah illuanshla] (over the sea) and bring him a large supply of medicine.

'Don't hide yourself' [Umzeuita goo-nautee], said his Majesty, looking steadfastly at me, meaning the little Mlungu. Here he ordered me to stand up and come nearer for his inspection.

I approached very cautiously and timidly, and when he called out 'Nearer, nearer yet,' I almost lost my self-command from fear, which Shaka observing shook his forefinger as a mark of encouragement.

It appeared that the colour of my hair which, at that time, was a brilliant red, had struck him with admiration and astonishment, being no doubt the first of that colour he had ever seen. Red is a favourite colour with the Zulus, and the ladies of this portion of Eastern Africa (contrary to our countrywomen, who when they happen to have red hair endeavour to blacken it) when they arrive at the age of puberty shave the hair, all but a circular tuft on the crown of the head which they embellish with a pomatum of a deep red, made by a mixture of oil or grease with a species of red clay or ochre.

Shaka continued repeating to himself, 'Nezinwele bomvu, nezinwele bomvu' [nuel-ize-bomfoo] (red hair, red hair).

To show my agility, he caused me to run and jump, which I did with all my might and main, seeing that it pleased him, until I became quite exhausted.

While going through this exercise, he continued shaking his forefinger in token of approbation, and I heard the buzz of the assembled multitude responding the everlasting 'Yebo baba, yebo baba.'

And when informed by Jacob that this proceeded from the King, saying that I was a clever little fellow, and other encomiums on my exertions, I felt fully compensated for the fatigue occasioned by my zeal and activity.

He remarked that I was very young to come from phesheya kolwandle and could not conceive what use I would be in the umkhumbi or in a battle.

While his Majesty was thus occupied with us, a large body of warriors, in full war costume, were seen advancing from the lower part of the kraal. Their number may have been from five to six hundred, all carrying white shields spotted black. Shaka had his armies divided into regiments, distinguished by the uniformity of colour in the shields. There was a regiment of black shields, one of white with black spots, one white with brown spots, and another brown or bay colour, and lastly a regiment of pure white, which last was a favourite corps and constituted his regiment of bodyguards. The division drew up in front of the King, in form of a crescent, three deep, with Dingane, the King's brother, at their head.

Having saluted the King with a simultaneous blow on their shields with the handle of the umkhonto (a short-handled assegai or spear) and a general exclamation of, 'Great master, great King, you great as the world,' the whole squatted on the ground in the position I have represented. Their shields were laid transversely on their breasts. Behind these was another small detachment who, unarmed, were driving before them about a hundred head of cattle, and which halted in rear of the assembled warriors.

For a moment a dead silence ensued. I note this because it was such a deathlike silence that, though several thousand were present, a pin might have been heard to fall on the ground. There is a peculiar solitude and stillness pervading all around you in Africa, at least this portion of it, that I have not felt in any other part of the globe. Whether this may arise from pure imagination or a peculiar state of the atmosphere I know not, but it was very strikingly remarked by us all.

This pause in the conversation was interrupted by his majesty requesting Jacob to ask us if King George had as many warriors as we saw.

We said King George had a great many more than that.

He again asked how many, at the same time clapping his hands together and saying how many, 'Shumi, shumi, shumi,' meaning how many times ten he had beyond what we saw.

When we answered that King George had twenty times 'shumi' (tens) more than those we saw present, he shook his forefinger as usual in token of satisfaction and said, 'UmGeorge is the greatest King of the whites as I am of the blacks, is it not so, Hlambamanzi?' meaning Jacob; who replied, 'Yebo baba, you are the great King of the blacks, and King George is of the whites.'

He then motioned us away. 'Go,' he said, 'go eat,' at the same time telling Sothobe, who was at the head of the victualling department, to take care we had plenty to eat.

Amidst the barbarism, ferocity and warlike disposition that character-ized the Zulus, from the King to the meanest subject, their hospitality is unbounded. That the visitor or stranger is well provided with food is always with them a matter of first consideration and solicitude. The greatest stranger, if even but passing by a village while any of the inhabitants happen to be at their meals, sits down uninvited, holds out his hand, and it is immediately filled, even should it extend to depriving themselves.

The first law of nature and the first right of man, that no man should starve while his neighbour has abundance, is recognized by the Zulu in the fullest extent. I verily believe that were there but a handful of corn in a village it would be equally divided.

Loss of the Brig Mary at Natal with Early Recollections of that Settlement

ELEVEN
The Nautical Magazine, March 1855, pp. 127–132

Our interview having terminated, and it being evident his Majesty had important business on hand from his brevity and apparent anxiety to finish with us, we withdrew to contemplate the wild novelty of the spectacle around us.

Nothing indeed was wanting completely to manifest that we were in a new world, at least to us; that between it and the civilized there was a great gulf. I had read a little about strange lands and wild people, but the reality that now presented itself before me far surpassed the utmost stretch of my imagination. I had been greatly interested, as no doubt youths generally are, with the adventures of Robinson Crusoe, but the reality of my own were about to rival the fictions of Defoe.

Droves of cattle with bands of warriors were to be seen in every direction, altogether presenting a scene of wild grandeur and animation very different from the general solitude pervading every other portion of the country. It was now noon, and we had taken up our position under the spreading branches of a tree, the shade of which was a protection from the heat. We were looking on with great interest at the preparations, when we perceived in the distance approaching groups of white shields moving rapidly onwards, like the white crest of a wave. These were the great Umphakathis [Umpagates] or the king's bodyguard, dressed in full war costume. With his Majesty at their head, they were to lead the dance.

By the time these had come up and taken their position on the right, the king was dressed in his full uniform of war. By a glance of him through the crowd of warriors by which he was surrounded, I saw that his person was highly decorated with green, red and yellow – colours only permitted to be worn by royalty. But the war dress most attracted my attention. This was the first time we had seen the Zulus dressed in this manner.

The first portion of their dress consisted of a kilt, composed of stripes of tiger-skin made into the shape and length of the animal's tail, and closely joined on to a girdle fastened round the waist. Below the knee is bound a tuft of hair generally, and apparently that at the end of the tail of the ox. This covers the shins nearly to the ankle, but no kind of covering is used for the feet either in the shape of shoes or mocassins. The upper part of the war-dress is a cape made of the same material as the kilt, which, with a hole in it to admit the head, drops on the shoulders and covers the back and breast, leaving the arms quite free. These are generally ornamented with bracelets of beads and bangles. Round the forehead is bound a tiara of stuffed tiger-skin, about three inches in diameter at the middle, and tapering smaller at the back of the head, where it nearly meets (exactly in the shape of what sailors call a pudding, used to prevent chafing). In front of this tiara a long plume is stuck vertically, and at the sides about the ears are also appended little bunches of red feathers, very neatly put together, the whole in fact giving them a very warlike and commanding appearance. At a distance a body of these warriors bore no small resemblance to a regiment of Highlanders, but a nearer approach of course expelled this illusion.

The same style of war-dress, as worn by the king, is also worn by the warriors, differing only in the material. That composed of tiger-skins is only worn by chiefs; the rest are made up of monkey's tails, or the skin of that animal made up in imitation, while the cape or upper garment was made of the tuft of hair at the extremity of the tail. The head band also was devoid of the plume, excepting that of a chief or captain, who invariably wore this mark of distinction. We observed Dingane, who was at the head of the white and black spotted shields, to be dressed in the same manner as the king, but without so large a display of beads. The king had a long band of these thrown on his shoulder in the manner of a soldier's belt.

By the time the guards had formed, we saw, issuing from a private gate at the back of the palace, a crowd of females, numbering about two hundred or more, marching two and two, with great order and regularity towards the scene. Their sable arms and legs were profusely decorated with beads and bangles, while round their dark brows were tastefully bound several rows of different coloured beads. The ingubo or petticoat, which constitutes the entire of the Zulu lady's dress, was richly decorated with little brass and metallic balls, very highly polished, and their dark skins also splendidly polished with grease. A few had their necks choked up to the chin with these brass rings (called bangles) which one would suppose must have been very uncomfortable as well as inconvenient to the wearer, the neck being thus rigidly kept in one position. This part of the lady's toilet had of course to be performed by a blacksmith. These women were the abantwana nkosi, and were now brought forth for the dance. On arriving at the ground of operation, these women formed in line behind the king, the two regiments being drawn up in front.

Suddenly by a quick and very accurate movement the men were wheeled into a circle enclosing the women, the king being in the centre, the ladies having formed in the same manner facing the men. The dance began by the former clapping their hands and stamping their feet, at the same time singing a Zulu air at the top of their voice. This was the challenge for the men, who now approached the females, holding their spears and clubs in a threatening attitude, and singing also at the top of their voices in turn, and stamping with their feet, now advancing a few paces, and anon receding. This appeared to be the whole manoeuvre of the dance, which to us altogether presented a mass of confusion.

Nevertheless, all was conducted in their way with the greatest regularity. The most exact time being kept to the vocal music, and the rough bass of the men's voices blending with the more gentle ones of the females, altogether combined to produce an agreeable harmony. While the valley rang with the sound of this music, the ground resounded with the tremendous stamping of the many thousand feet. The spectacle itself was novel, grand and wild beyond my power of description.

Dancing is a favourite amusement with the Zulus, who were soon all excitement at this grand turn out. The perspiration soon flowed in streams to their feet, which, mixing with the unctuous matter with which their bodies were anointed, produced an odour within a considerable radius of the scene that would have required a few gallons of Eau de Cologne to overcome. Many a Zulu warrior's heart beat high on this occasion with excitement, when, advancing in the dance, they were honoured by the presence of the choicest beauty and elegance of the Zulu kingdom, as well as that contributed by conquered nations. On the other hand, it was a great treat to those handsome damsels to see the Zulu heroes in this grand display before them, and paying homage to their beauty, as it is only on such occasions that they are permitted by Shaka to move from within the bounds of the isigodlo.

The dance and song were kept up till late in the afternoon. We were tired of looking on and returned to our huts. In the meantime fifty oxen had been slaughtered, and Sothobe with a score of cooks was employed in preparing the meat in huge earthen boilers to feast the dancers. We came in for a goodly share of boiled beef, of most rich and excellent quality, with a due proportion of boiled Indian corn ground to a paste between two stones, and sourmilk in calabashes, so that we had no reason to complain for want of food. The evening was devoted by the multitude to festivity and small dancing parties.

Amidst such an assemblage of savages we could not be long without witnessing scenes of another and very different description. Early on the following morning three unfortunate victims, who the evening before had been enjoying the festive scene, were now carried forth for execution. What their crime was we could not at that time discover, but I subsequently learnt it was on complaint made against them for a breach of the corn law.

It has often excited my pity, admiration and astonishment to witness the fortitude and dignified calmness with which a Zulu will go forth to execution and receive his death blow. No fetters or cords are ever employed to bind the Zulu culprit; he is left at liberty to run for his life or to stand and meet his doom. Many do run, but few escape for, alas! every man they meet is an enemy. Many stand and meet their fate with a degree of firmness that could hardly be imagined.

The cruel and barbarous manner by which criminals are put to death is shocking to humanity. There are no regular executioners; that would be superfluous where everyone appears to have a savage gratification in the horrid and revolting employment, and all are ready to carry out the most sanguinary orders of the king or an enraged chief. The victim is first stunned by a blow on the head with a club which, when well directed, terminates his sufferings at once. But it often happens that he is merely stunned, and the moment the wretched man falls to the ground a sharp pointed stake (which is already prepared) is introduced behind and thrust up the abdomen. Being in this manner skewered, he is thrown into the nearest thicket or jungle.

Instances have happened, that after being thus impaled, the wretched creatures have recovered sufficient strength to withdraw the stake from the body and get away. I saw a man who was then living and had attained a pretty old age who, having been treated in this manner and left for dead by his executioners, recovered sufficiently to drag the stake from his body. He proceeded directly to Shaka with the bloody weapon in his hand to sue for pardon, which was granted. From henceforth he became an almost constant attendant at court, Shaka having considerably enriched him with cattle. It appears he had been a person in authority, a captain or something of the kind, and besides restoring him his former possessions, Shaka had increased his stock.

Notwithstanding the cruelty of this mode of executing criminals, not one of these savages to whom I explained the more humane method adopted by us but shuddered at the cruelty of our practice of hanging a man up by the neck. So much for the force and effect of habit, showing how different men's notions are moulded even in the matter of humanity, and how difficult it is to alter a state of things, however barbarous, that has obtained for generations. Is it a wonder that the progress of civilization is slow, and all attempts to force it only increases the obstacles and adds to the obstinacy of those who are opposed to it.

I have had favourable opportunities of observing with what tenacity the savage clings to his habits of life, and also to his superstitions, and how absurd and ridiculous the most refined domestic system appeared compared to his own. I believe it possible to be easier for an ignorant man, in fact, more properly speaking, for human nature to relapse into a state of barbarism than it is to advance a savage to a state of civilization. These opportunities have also convinced me that our sympathies for the unhappy and deplorable state of the savage are mistaken. His misery has no place but in our imagination, being unknown to him, and irrespective of a future state of existence. Were I called upon to state in which condition the most happiness existed, I should, from the knowledge I have of man in both conditions, bear testimony to the Zulus being the most cheerful and happy people of which I have had any experience. These opinions may not be orthodox, but are at any rate based upon experience.

On the other hand, if we are to deplore the darkness in which he is placed as regards his future and eternal happiness or misery, we must at the same time bear in mind 'that of him to whom much is given much will be required,' and how much we may have to answer for who have so large a share of the talents that the Lord gave to his servants, and how better it may be for the savage in that day of account than for many of us. . . .

One of our party, Ned Cameron, a seaman who had served his time in a West Indiaman in the Jamaica trade – a lively, frolicsome fellow – seeing that dancing was the order of the day and a favourite amusement with the Zulus, determined on giving his Majesty a specimen of his own performance in that way. Ned had, in the course of his nautical training, learnt a great variety of Negro songs and dances and was, moreover, an excellent mimic. His intercourse with the Niggers while on strallop duty, dragging sugar, had not been neglected, and he could imitate Quashie in all his actions most admirably, and with whom he said he was always a great favourite. He did not see why he should not hit it as well with the great King Shaka as he had done with Joe Sash, the head driver on the Amity Hall estate.

Mr Hutton, the chief of our party, was opposed to the scheme, as well as several of his shipmates, not knowing how his majesty might be inclined to take the performance. But Ned was not to be put off his old favourite project by any chimerical apprehensions of danger. He felt certain of pleasing his audience and particularly the king, and Ned set to work to prepare his instruments. All that he required was a tabor, which he said was rather awkward to have to play and dance besides. However, as none of the rest of us had acquired any of Ned's musical accomplishments, he was obliged to make his arrangements accordingly.

Having procured a large earthen pot, about the size of a five gallon keg, out of which the bottom was carefully knocked, in its place a piece of cowhide was tightly stretched over in fashion of a drum. This constituted the 'tambo' or drum which, as Ned had to beat and dance also, he now slung so as to hang on his neck. Having tightened up his tambo to his satisfaction, Ned sallied forth, determined on introducing his performance as soon as the King should be abroad. Of course none of us would volunteer to accompany him on his expedition, nor did our friend Ned seem to care much about our desertion, feeling within himself great confidence that he would meet with a favourable reception.

It was not long ere the desired opportunity offered. The King had taken up his usual post under a large tree, as was his custom in the morning. Our friend Ned advanced with great confidence and, after performing the usual ceremony and obeisance, commenced his Negro song and dance.

With a boyish curiosity, I had followed Ned so far as to keep him in sight, at the same time, as I thought, sufficiently in the rear as not to be implicated with him should any harm come of his project. Those who have seen a Negro dance, with all its fantastic movements and gestures, know it to be amusing enough.

Shaka was so highly pleased that, sending immediately for Jacob the interpreter, he presented Ned with five oxen for his excellent performance, besides making him drink about a gallon of Caffre beer, which was poured out into his tambo! Fortunately for Ned his drum was not very tight, so that it saved him from bursting, as it would have been a great want of decorum to leave or throw away anything given immediately by the King. All that Ned regretted was that it had not been old Jamaica instead of swipes.

The throng continued daily to increase around the capital. The accumulated host of warriors was now prodigious, far beyond our conception of the Zulu force. The whole day long was devoted to the war song and dance, and the night was followed up with festivity and mirth. On these occasions this mighty Zulu monarch, relaxing somewhat from the stern severity of the despot, granted indulgences that were more highly appreciated from the rarity of their occurrence and the shortness of their duration.

The novelty and wild grandeur of this vast assemblage of at least fifty thousand savage warriors, the innumerable fires brightening up the darkness around the capital, like a beleagured city, is more easy to imagine than describe. After three days' sojourn, gazing on this to us new and wonderful picture, our party made application to return again to the solitude of Natal. . . where, at that time, nothing distinguished it as the abode of humanity but the melancholy wreck of the ill-fated *Mary*, now so high on the beach as to defy the surge of angry waves.

Mr Hutton's application to return was favourably received by the

King – with the exception of myself, who, his majesty very sagaciously observed, could be of no use in the construction of the umkhumbi. I should remain with him to explain the use and administer the medicine to patients.

Though in this capacity I was as ill adapted for service as that of a carpenter or ship-builder, it was not so easy to convince the sable monarch of my unfitness for the office. He determined on keeping me with him.

On this intelligence being communicated to me, my heart sank within me, and I nearly fainted with the idea. At the horror of being left alone in the midst of this wild and terrible scene, cut off from all communion, all intercourse and even the sight of civilization, my heart sank with despair. Compared to it, my recent shipwreck, and the very waves that had threatened every moment to swallow me up, were comparatively insignificant. Great was my despair when, on the following day, my shipmates took leave of me, as I thought in all probability for ever.

Shaka very liberally supplied them with several head of cattle for our use at Natal, and assured them of every assistance in his power for the building of the vessel. To convince us of his sincerity, he full often repeated his promise.

Among the Caffres

The Times, London, Tuesday 3 August 1875, p. 3

Sir, – Having been one, and I believe now the only one living, of the small band of Europeans who first had intercourse with the Caffre tribes of Natal, I have taken a lively interest in what has been doing in that part of the world, wherein lay the field of many adventures and privations in the days of my youth.

Nearly 50 years ago I was shipwrecked at Port Natal. The object of the visit which led to this disaster was to ascertain the fate of Lieutenant Farewell and his party, who had gone to Natal on a trading expedition for the purchase of ivory, and of whom nothing had been heard at the Cape Colony for a very long time, and it was thought that they had been murdered by the natives.

The wreck of the *Mary* at Natal, on the 29th of September, 1825, cast me among the Zulu Caffres at a very early age, and I have read with an interest only equalled by regret the result of the proceedings instituted against the Caffre chief, Langalibalele.

The name of Langalibalele has long been, and is yet, cherished in my memory. When disease and death had thinned the ranks of our crew, and the chance of completing the little vessel we had commenced building, with a view to get back to the civilized world, became exceedingly doubtful, Langalibalele was the name of a chief appointed by King Shaka, who at that time ruled the Zulu nation, to command a party of 30 warriors charged with the escort of the writer to the Portuguese settlement at Delagoa Bay. Though it was at that time a perilous journey, nobly and faithfully did the chief and his men perform this duty.

My sympathy, however, with the present Langalibalele is not caused simply because he may be a descendant, or because he bears the name of one to whom I was so deeply indebted, and for whose memory I must ever entertain a grateful remembrance, but for reasons that will, sooner or later, if they have not already, become apparent to the authors of his misfortune.

During four years of my residence in Natal, three years were, with little interruption, passed at King Shaka's residence. He kept me with him, first as a sort of rare pet animal, on whom he bestowed a large amount of genuine kindness and, I must add, a large share of indulgence; and latterly as a confidential companion, as far as companionship could be held with such a mighty potentate, who could only be approached on all fours. Though very young, my observation and perception were sharpened by a sense of uneasiness, excited by a feeling of the insecurity of my position in the hands of savages. In consequence of this all-pervading feeling I was constantly watching the looks and gestures of those around me – at least, until I had sufficient knowledge of the language to reassure me that I was not to be slaughtered.

My seclusion from the rest of the party at the king's residence, about 150 miles distant from the port of Natal, gave me the opportunity of studying the native character, as also the policy that governed and the intrigues carried on at headquarters. It is by the light of that study and knowledge of the Zulu character that I feel certain of the Chief Langalibalele's innocence.

Shaka was a man of great natural ability, but he was cruel and capricious; nevertheless, it is possible he has left behind something more than the terror of his name.

One thing Shaka strongly impressed on his subjects was respect for the white man, and the impression was strong and general. What its duration has been, or whether it has entirely passed away, it would be curious to know. But whether the Zulus love the white settlers or not, there is pretty conclusive evidence that they fear them.

Shaka had one engrossing idea – that there should only be two kings in the world, King George to be king of the whites and he, Shaka, king of the blacks. So strongly had this idea laid hold of him that on the completion of our little vessel, and when leaving Natal, he sent Sothobe, a favourite Chief, as his ambassador to King George. Sothobe never got further than Port Elizabeth, where at that time there were but three or four houses; thence he got as far as Grahamstown, at that time also a very insignificant place. The Cape Government thought King Shaka and the

Zulu nation too remote from the Cape Colony to give any trouble; the Chief Sothobe and his suite were speedily embarked on board Her Majesty's sloop *Helicon*, then on the Cape Station, and carried back to Natal without even having seen Cape Town. Sothobe could not, from what he had seen, have carried back to his master any very high notions of the white men's country or the greatness of their cities.

Now, in my time, a summons issued by the King commanding a Chief to appear before him to answer a charge in which his loyalty was questioned invariably involved either death or the confiscation of his cattle and disgrace. In the former case, the wives and followers shared the fate of their master. It was the signal for the general slaughter of every soul who had the misfortune to be either the friend or dependent of the unfortunate and often innocent chief. Many innocent but timid chiefs, when thus summoned, fled with their wives and followers to the fastnesses of the forest, or allied themselves with distant tribes. There is not the shadow of doubt in my mind that the Governor's summons was disobeyed by Langalibalele from the fear that he would be confiscated and himself disgraced. The fear of their chief being killed would spread terror through the whole tribe, and thus flight would be the result.

That this would be the view of Langalibalele and his people of the Governor's summons is next to a certainty, and that Langalibalele's disobedience arose from sheer panic is equally certain, unless the character, policy and traditions of the Zulus have greatly altered since my acquaintance with them ceased.

The Governor, owing to his recent arrival in the Colony, could hardly be expected to know much about the native character, policy and tradition. There is not, however, the same excuse for the Colonists, some of whom at least, one would suppose, must have arrived at such an estimate as to guide them to a more correct view of the circumstances. Bishop Colenso seems, however, to have studied them more closely and earnestly, and his view of the case is undoubtedly the right one. I rejoice that Lord Carnarvon has, at the risk of great outcry and annoyance, taken the humane and sensible action of redressing an injustice that was done under a mere delusion.

Though Lord Carnarvon has, regardless of clamour, undertaken to do all that, in the circumstances, could be done to repair the injury and redress the wrongs inflicted on Langalibalele and his tribe, yet, if I am not mistaken, they will have caused a great mischief, which time only can repair.

In closing this letter I will show that the concern I feel for the treatment of a people to whom I owe so much is not of today's growth by quoting from my narrative of the loss of the *Mary* at Natal the following remarks, written many years back at the time when the Boers first invaded Natal:

> I owe them a debt of gratitude that leads me to wish and to hope my countrymen, whosoever they be, will exercise that mercy and kindness toward them which I experienced at their hands in the day of their rule. Those are yet living to whom I am indirectly indebted for my life, and I trust their goodness will meet a just reward by kindness and forbearance at the white man's hands.

(*Loss of the Brig 'Mary' and Recollections of Natal* in the volume of the *Nautical Magazine* for 1853.)

I am, Sir,
Your obedient servant,
CHAS. R. MACLEAN

Castries, Saint Lucia, W. I., June 30.

THIS TABLET COMMEMORATES
JOHN ROSS
(LIEUT. J. S. KING'S APPRENTICE)
A LAD OF 15 YEARS OF AGE, WHO IN 1827, BRAVING THE
PERILS OF AN UNEXPLORED LAND INHABITED BY AN
UNKNOWN PEOPLE AND ABOUNDING IN WILD ANIMALS,
WALKED WITH GREAT COURAGE FROM PORT NATAL TO
DELAGOA BAY AND BACK (A DISTANCE OF 600 MILES)
IN ORDER TO OBTAIN SORELY NEEDED MEDICINES AND
OTHER NECESSARIES FOR THE HANDFUL OF PIONEERS
AT THE BAY OF NATAL

T. Semevsky

The editor at the memorial to 'John Ross' in the gardens of the Old Fort, Durban.

138

Commentary

ONE

The 'recent events that have drawn public attention to Natal' – to which Maclean refers in the opening sentence of his recollections – provide the spur for him to commence writing about 'that now interesting place'. He seems to mean no dramatically newsworthy incidents, but rather the general opening up of Natal to British interests after it was annexed to the Cape in 1845. Brookes and Webb summarise the context as follows:

> The end of the West administration was to leave Natal with a large African population, beginning to be settled in definite Locations, a small and fast-diminishing Boer population, the beginnings of British immigration, and in a vast half-empty territory a shortage of unencumbered land on which to put immigrants. The four years 1845–9 made Natal a British, rather than an Afrikaner territory, with a large African majority. (p. 62)

So Maclean is writing for an audience becoming increasingly familiar with Natal through news items in the British press, particularly as regards its prospects as a new Crown Colony, ruled by a Lieutenant-Governor from its inland capital, Pietermaritzburg.

Throughout the course of his recollections Maclean supports the British cause in Natal; indeed, the period of his publication (1853–5) coincides with a peak of immigration to that territory. Lieutenant-Governor Pine's Commission of 1852–3 specifically encouraged 'white emigration by every legitimate means' (Brookes and Webb, p. 70), and Maclean takes the opportunity to encourage that call. 1852 also saw the publication of the *Proceedings of the Commission appointed to inquire into the Past and Present State of the Kafirs in the District of Natal*. It is doubtful that Maclean read this report – he would certainly have mentioned it – but nevertheless an interest in the origins of black-white relations in Natal had been revived as well. This, too, obviously spurred him to emerge from obscurity.

Before the Charter of Natal (of 1856), by which Natal became a separate colony with a limited form of representative government, as Brookes and Webb point out, there were basically three areas of attitude among the whites, particularly as regards 'Native' policy – the officials', the settlers' and the missionaries'. Maclean addresses himself especially to the new settler population, although he is also deferential towards authority in specific ways. While he devotes a whole early paragraph to endorsing 'the pious exertions of those worthy missionaries', he ultimately becomes somewhat antagonistic to the missionary interest in most of its aspects and sometimes outrightly hostile towards them.

One of his major themes duly emerges of a debate about whether missionary or commercial penetration of the indigenous heathen populations is more effective and more morally justifiable. Time and again he will come down on the side of the trader, leaving the preacher-converter scarified. One of the great pleasures of the digressions within his narrative is the ingenious ways he deals with what he perceives to be the missionary threat to the unenlightened.

But Maclean is addressing new Natal settlers only indirectly. His main readership is obviously that of *The Nautical Magazine* for which he writes – that is to say, the seafarers of the British merchant marine to which he belonged. They are the transport operators who at the time of his publication would have brought the Byrne Settlers to Natal, for example, and who maintained its main communications network with the Cape, London and the high seas of the British sphere of influence in general. They were the harbour-builders who would wish to add Durban as a port of call to the sea-route to India.

The Nautical Magazine did not often carry such extended pieces as Maclean's. More typically its pages included sketches or letters to the editor containing navigational and harbour details of interest to fellow sea-captains and pilots. Often these appeared under the rubric of 'Bottle Papers', some of which were actual messages of distress found in bottles. Hazards at sea are often tersely and technically described by contributors, as are the case histories of earlier and current shipwrecks. Typical titles by contributors are 'Remarks on the Principal Ports and Anchoring Places along the Coast of the Dominican Republic' (Apr., 1853), 'The North-West Passage' (Jan., 1854) or 'The Crimea' (March, 1855).

Maclean's first instalment, then, conforms to the typical *Nautical Magazine* item in, for example, its extensive quotation of King's account of the wreck of the *Mary* and in its description of Port Natal's dangers and opportunities. The first half of his title, *Loss of the Brig 'Mary' at Natal*, fits the bill of the magazine perfectly; in fact, it is merely an extended 'bottle paper' from the past, rendered by one of the few survivors of this typical disaster of the days of sail. It had the same fascination as disaster accounts have today. Later in the sequence Maclean expands far beyond this initial scope and intention, specifically when his narrative takes off from seafaring matters at the Bay.

In opening his narrative Maclean also takes the opportunity to introduce a historical perspective: the 'recent events' that precipitate the account are, he reminds us, predicated on the original events of 1825–28 which are his almost exclusive focus. The relationship between the scenes of his 'memory' and his present time of writing – a gap of a generation of very close to thirty years – is left unexamined by him, despite the fact that he establishes an implicit contrast throughout the work between conditions as they were then and are now.

Maclean had not kept up with affairs in Natal in any detailed way. For example, he seems not to know any of the highlights of Dingane's reign (although he knew the man), or that Port Natal had in fact been renamed Durban. As a result he does not make any specific connections or recommendations in what follows. His overriding concern is rather that his testimony not be forgotten in the history that is to follow in Natal. He insists that his successors there know and understand his story. Several later details give evidence that his vision of his past develops into becoming cautionary and even polemical, as he begins to assert a 'true' version of the Natal position *as he knew it*.

His opening project, however, is a simple one – merely to recount from memory 'those days' when Natal was 'little known to Europeans' and when, he reminds us, the 'invincible Shaka' held sway over the territory from Pondoland to Maputo. A substantial amount of what follows will detail the power and extent of the pristine 'Zulu Empire', poised as he saw it to meet the first impact of the incoming 'British Empire', of which he casts himself as a forerunner and representative. Hence the 'painted and romantic dream' of the recollections that 'pass in review' before him. Had not the Zulu connections become of interest once more, this dream would have 'passed away'.

Hence, also, his stress on 'the force of reality that early impressions are calculated to produce on the mind'. This insistence on the vividness, the hyperreality of childhood memory persists throughout what follows, giving rise to some of his finest passages. Yet Maclean's reminiscence is always tinged with a tone of nostalgia and regret – 'I mourn the change,' he says. Maclean knows that, just as his glorious and rather Wordsworthian childhood has vanished, so has the glory of that rival empire in which he so flourished.

In a very real sense the contest is set up from the beginning as between the two figureheads, George IV and King Shaka, rulers over the whites and the blacks respectively and, as he says, 'Little did they then dream that the successors of [our] king would rule over the destiny of the Zulu nation.'

Maclean is mistaken if he adjudges the Zulu Empire, if it ever was one, subdued by the British by 1853. Nevertheless, he quite correctly foresees as a forgone conclusion its reduction in the long term to vassal status. He neither celebrates nor decries the British penetration of the Zulu Empire of old; in fact, he remains temperate and resigned on the issue. He is far more concerned to analyze the process for what it was and is – a commercial and political inevitability. From this process he attempts to redeem a sense of old-fashioned honour and justice which he now feels may have become lost. Hence, later in the work, to substantiate his position he will give expression to some of his deeply-felt, passionately stirring outcries of conviction about human values. The actual discovery of these beliefs within himself – the mature man – is part of the narrative's great story.

That Maclean is choosing to back Britain above specifically Boer Trekker interests in Natal is evident when he accuses the latter of being 'rude and lawless', for example. To him the Trekkers, thanks to their weaponry, are also only too capable of conducting a 'deadly and exterminating war' against the Zulus – the Battle of Blood River (1838) comes to mind, though he does not mention this. But his antagonism towards Trekker control of Natal is far more deep-seated than his objection to their wild tactics. He knows that the Trekkers are only in Natal because they have rejected the British emancipation effort in the Cape – thus his fear of the 'extermination' of the Zulus. To Maclean the upholders of slavery are anathema, and British rule in Africa is preferable as a result. However, the point here is that, unlike many other writers on Natal, Maclean never pretends the Zulus have a chance should it come to a showdown between the heirs of King Shaka and King George. The submission of the Zulus is inevitable and they will not be able to withstand the white man, whosoever he be.

The dates Maclean gives for his insistent childhood dream – of 1824 and 1825 – are not quite accurate, nor could he then have been aged a perpetual thirteen. The wreck of the *Mary* occurred on 30 September 1825 (at which date he was ten years old), and he was not to leave Port Natal finally until shortly after King Shaka was killed on 22 September 1828 (by which time he was thirteen). He was, however, landbound on the south-east coast of Africa for almost exactly three years, as he says.

That he calls this period the time of his 'three years' residence among the savages' is of greater interest. Frequently he will give details like this to illustrate that he and his fellow castaways were thrown onto what was to them Zulu territory rather more as guests than as settlers. The use of the term 'settlement' in his title to describe Port Natal really refers more to the present state of the British interest than to his party's self-description. For us to call his generation 'settlers' in Natal, as many historians do, is a misnomer. It is the true settlers of around 1850 who need in his view to know about the earlier parties which he represents, who were, if anything, not settlers but precisely the maritime explorers and adventurers *The Nautical Magazine* was devised to celebrate and serve. Many further details will clarify his profile in this respect. The term 'residence' is also loaded; it implies occupation, not settlement.

Maclean's opening paragraphs also establish in a very real way the extent, and limits, of his capability as writer of this narrative. Accurately he remarks: 'Little connection . . . can be expected when narrating events.' However, this kind of disclaimer is common in such writing, and as the serial grows he becomes quite capable of organizing his material. But indeed the work is no systematic account, preplanned according to a scheme as, for example, one would expect to find in a book between single covers. His declared method is to follow the vagaries of recollection over 'a long vista of years'. He writes associatively, not systematically. His chosen discourse is thus more literary than scientific.

Possibly this is one reason why his text has not to date been found congenial to historians, because of the difficulty it presents in the extraction of simple facts – dates, places and events. But as a literary text – a childhood autobiography – it is not only unique in terms of our history, but in fact rather orthodox. Literary critics are well placed to respond to its depiction of personal anxiety, to its formal attempts to shape a 'tale' and to its general skill in dramatizing the great theme of the haphazard contingencies of providence. 'Mine, indeed, was a strange destiny,' Maclean will later remark, and the literary reader cannot but respond to a narrative prompt like this.

The third paragraph beginning 'I may here remark . . .' sets the pattern for what purports to be a spontaneous, unplanned set of interpolations and digressions, sunk into the forward thrust of the tale. In its supposedly haphazard randomness this discursive structure may prove infuriating to the contemporary reader. Later, large sections of instalments become digressions, or they carry over from one instalment to the next, so that his thread is sometimes difficult to follow. Sometimes, one may feel, he becomes wilfully obscure, even distracted. But rather than berating him for being unsystematic, we should perhaps accept that this mode is the *sine qua non* of what is ultimately a type of well-known romantic writing. His work is confessional.

His very insistence on giving himself the latitude to let his narrative line take him where his memory will freely go is illustrative of the character he creates for his younger self – buffetted about, put-upon, subject to fate. He is no encyclopaedic empire-builder with a scheme to comprehend the world; rather, this child of fortune, thrown into the eddies and currents of the storm (in his case literally), is one who must improvise his own survival.

In his last instalment he will finally call on his true literary predecessor:

> I had been greatly interested, as no doubt youths generally are, with the adventures of Robinson Crusoe, but the reality of my own were about to rival the fictions of Defoe.

Facts may be stranger than fiction, but to any real-life narrator the challenge of the heritage of fiction is overwhelming. The neat myth of castaway Crusoe who survives shipwreck only to win both the landscape and the indigenous population over to European methods of production – in short, the colonizer's allegory – is for Maclean far too orderly. Maclean sees that real life presents more complex challenges, throws up difficult variations outside the myth and is actually as ramshackle as his ensuing narrative. He eschews the shapeliness of fiction as well, although in his closing instalments he knows well enough how to orchestrate a climax with dramatic reversal.

At this juncture – where Maclean's account departs from the shape of fiction into his own pell-mell sequence – a literary decision must be made. Recording his childhood autobiography in this manner, Maclean wishes to illustrate many puzzling complexities of his actual experience which, for us, have altogether surprising conclusions. To give one example, the great drift of his narrative is not towards any satisfactory return home, enriched and rewarded; on the contrary, it is quite alarmingly a steady progress to the bosom of none other than Shaka himself. This unexpected structure – a trajectory into the very heart of darkness – runs counter to the adventure formula that will so flourish in later writers of Southern African experience (like H. Rider Haggard, for example).

This unexpected (and one might say almost unpatriotic) progress is well prepared for us in Maclean's first digression. He situates himself there as 'the little Mlungu' among 'my old native friends'. Friendship, warmth, caring for the Zulu people who received him become cumulatively and finally overwhelmingly strong. He leads up to saying it outright (and then reaffirms this statement in his later letter):

> I owe [the Zulus] a debt of gratitude that leads me to wish and to hope my countrymen, whosoever they be, will exercise that mercy and kindness toward them which I experienced at their hands in the day of their rule. Those are yet living to whom I am indirectly indebted for my life, and I trust their goodness will meet a just reward by kindness and forbearance at the white man's hands.

'Goodness', 'kindness', 'mercy' – these are Maclean's keywords, and his message is 'gratitude.' He intended these terms to ring with meaning throughout what follows. These are the values which give his work its conviction, and its very great poignancy.

Maclean's vision is also intended not only to be 'interesting' but 'tragical'. He writes, not triumphantly, but regretfully. His sense of the tragic is barely suppressed in what follows. The bitter-sweet memories of days gone by recur, they insist, one pushing the other forward until we have a document that is so contrary to our received expectations from the legend-makers that it is not too exaggerated to say Maclean's text demands not only a new way of reading, but a fresh attitude to the historical evidence he presents.

One of the surprises Maclean has to offer is that during his 'three years' residence' he becomes saturated in things Zulu. Here he mentions 'the eloquence of their language', which he learned perforce to speak (and later claims he spoke and probably still speaks better than any other white man). Later he will reveal that at one point in his life he had lost portions of his mother-tongue, English. Hence bits of his text have to be translated from Zulu. This is already evident in his description of 'the patriarch of the forest . . . stretched affectionately over the heads of the young . . .', for example. The sheltering tree is a common Zulu symbol for chieftaincy, often used in the praises of Shaka himself.

Here Maclean also calls up a natural, idyllic picture of the pastoral Zulu, with great stress on the peaceful harmony of the tribe. This version of Zulu life, implanted early on in the serial, must always be kept in mind as a contrast to the heroic, war-like version which Maclean was led to expect, and which later writers have often stressed to the exclusion of all else.

Maclean's reference to the accounts of 'recent intelligent travellers' is puzzling, and there are no indications in the text as to whom he may mean. One would have expected him to cite *Narrative of a Journey to the Zoolu Country* by Captain Allen F. Gardiner, R. N., first published in 1836 and Nathaniel Isaacs' *Travels and Adventures in Eastern Africa, Descriptive of the Zoolus, their Manners, Customs, etc., with a Sketch of Natal*, first published in the same year – but he appears not to know them. Certainly the omission of Isaacs is startling, for Maclean mentions him in his own account and the popularity of Isaacs' tomes had established them as essential reading on the early Natal experience. But Maclean seems quite unaware that his colleague had covered the same ground before him. Nor is he referring to Charles Barter's *The Dorp and the Veld, or Six Months in Natal*, published in London in 1852, the only other book-length work that fits the bill. Since Maclean visited the British Museum when he needed information on Natal, these oversights are inexplicable.

In fact, in the entire course of his serial Maclean cites only three other relevant accounts as being familiar to him – the two by the sea-captains King and Stout, and one by the missionary Kay. (The King text is of immediate use to him in this instalment.) It seems fruitless to speculate on why he does not take on Isaacs, whose work would obviously have annoyed him, when he so boldly and extensively takes on another source like Kay. Until further research reveals who Maclean's travellers might have been, this reference must remain a mystery.

Maclean's quotation from King in this instalment comes from the same source as that quoted by Isaacs in *his* first chapter. Although substantially identical, neither of them is averse to altering slightly the wording and punctuation in small details, which suggest minor inaccuracies in copying (always possibly compounded by typesetters). For both of them King's account of the wreck of the *Mary* is a set-piece, not to be outdone by them in penmanship and authority. Maclean's use of this source is slightly more extensive than Isaacs', which rules out any possibility of Maclean having copied it from him at secondhand without acknowledgement. In fact, Maclean had direct access to King's journal and other papers – as he later mentions, he was acquainted with King's surviving mother – and so presumably copied his version directly from source. As it is emphatically part of his intention in this instalment to vindicate Captain King from any detractors, the quotation is made in the spirit of admiring tribute.

Despite his unruffled and official style, many startling details emerge from King's account of loss and heartbreak. James Saunders King had indeed been on the first ship in living memory to enter the Bay at Port Natal – in April 1823, on his command, the *Salisbury*. Maclean was to confirm the details of King's survey and assert that King was justified in claiming to be the first cartographer of Port Natal above the claims of his rivals. This issue is a contentious one, as late in 1823 King had attempted to trade his map for the lieutenant's commission he desired, but which he unfortunately never obtained.

King acquired the *Mary* in Britain thereafter, with his mother – Maclean tells us – as co-investor. This is where and when Maclean must have been employed as his apprentice. According to *The South African Commercial Advertiser* of Cape Town the *Mary* was operating as a coastal trader by 21 January 1824 (when it arrived in Table Bay from Algoa Bay with a cargo of sundries) and its movements under various captains may be plotted thence up to its end. Its shipwreck was more than the 'unfortunate catastrophe' and 'disastrous adventure' King mentions, for it represented an immense financial setback for him and his backers, chiefly the merchant J.R. Thomson and Co. in Cape Town and even Farewell. King's reasons for salvaging as much as possible of the vessel and its cargo of trading truck are obvious enough, and the rest of his short life must be seen as a desperate attempt at recuperating his losses. Within days of Shaka, King was dead, too – at the age of thirty-three – so that the Zululand expedition was for him not only fatal, but a fiasco. Considering also that King's intention on the trip was to advertise the advantages of Port Natal to investors back at the Cape, the wreck was a setback indeed.

So for Maclean there were – confusingly for us – three kings in his life at this stage, the great King of Kings, King George IV (who ruled from 1820 to 1830) and Mr King, his captain. These were rapidly joined by a fourth and crucial one, His Majesty King Shaka, whose title he oftens gives in this capitalised way. There is also a confusion of Saint Lucias in what follows: the Saint Lucia to which King refers, as Maclean later tries to figure out, is at the mouth of the Mhlathuze River or more probably of the River Mvoti or at the Thukela (not the contemporary Saint Lucia estuary at the embouchure of the Mfolozis further up the coast). Neither of these should be muddled with the Saint Lucia island and Crown Colony in the Caribbean.

Twice King in his account thanks 'providence' for their rescue (Maclean fervently echoes this) and twice King raises the somewhat unexpected spectre of the alternative horror to being shipwrecked – being 'at the mercy of the natives' and having to give themselves up 'as their prey'. His apprehension that Farewell had been 'murdered' increases his anxiety. Compounding this fear is the very understandable one from which Maclean also suffers badly – that in being cast ashore they are indeed being hurled out of their element. No settlers these, King's seamen maintain every foreboding about being scuppered. From first to last they remain displaced from their 'floating home', fretful and insecure.

King's journal was obviously written after the shipwreck and for publication on his return to Cape Colony (see his account in *The South African Commercial Advertiser* of 11 July 1826, passages from which have been worked by the editors into the text of Fynn's diary). We may deduce that this fear of 'native' ambush is somewhat put on for effect. As Maclean's record makes clear, no member of either King's, Farewell's or any other party was ever maltreated by the subjects of King Shaka. King, after all, had had commerce with the indigenous people previously at Port Natal and had no reason to expect a hostile reception.

His motives, then, must be questioned. Making the 'natives' potentially threatening increases an impression of his own heroism in the eyes of the reader – possibly that is one reason. At the time of his publication there was a Zulu panic at the Cape. Another may be the give-away that assuming the 'natives' to be enemies, rather than allies, from the outset precludes any possibility of a relationship of accommodation and friendship (Maclean's great theme). At all events, King's psychology is far more aggressive than his protege's, and gets passed down to the child only as huge and longlasting terror of the land. Only with considerable effort will Maclean pull himself out of this attitude that was so convenient to King's project.

One of the now virtually obsolete words King has in his maritime vocabulary – 'necessaries' – has great resonance in the Maclean story. According to Isaacs, it was in the desperate quest for further 'necessaries' that Maclean would run to the shipyards of Delagoa Bay to enable the completion of the rebuilding of their ship. It is this aspect of the Maclean story which has been raised into the legend of 'John Ross', as we know, and those necessaries were essential items of maritime gear.

King mentions by name only one member of his crew: his all-important first mate, Mr Hutton (often in subsequent accounts spelled Hatton). From Maclean's account we may learn that the *Mary* was surprisingly undermanned – only sixteen beings, shortly fifteen, as one is taken by a 'tiger' on their first night ashore. Isaacs (1808–72), only seven years older than Maclean, is named by him as a 'passenger', although he was King's supercargo, employed to transact and account for trade at ports of call. Soon we will hear of a second mate, Norton. Only in the final instalment will we have the description of one of the seamen, Maclean's friend Ned Cameron. Other members of King's small party to this day remain anonymous.

When Maclean has quoted King's account of the wreck, he follows it with his own far more emotional one, in which many details corroborate or elaborate on King. To King's perceived threats of 'native' attack Maclean adds the threat of 'wild beasts.' In celebrating his fortune at overcoming the triple peril of drowning, ambush and being eaten alive, and to illustrate the faith he gains against 'despair', he quotes a stanza from one of William Cowper's 'Olney Hymns', better known by its opening lines:

> God moves in a mysterious way,
>   His wonders to perform;
> He plants his footsteps in the sea,
> And rides upon the storm. . . .

Maclean's mention that the salvage of the *Mary* included 'two six-pounder carronades' (short cannons) must be borne in mind in the light of his observations in Instalment Four about the 'wretched' state of Farewell's cannon. These weapons appear to have been standard equipment on merchant

'First interview with the natives at the watering place'.

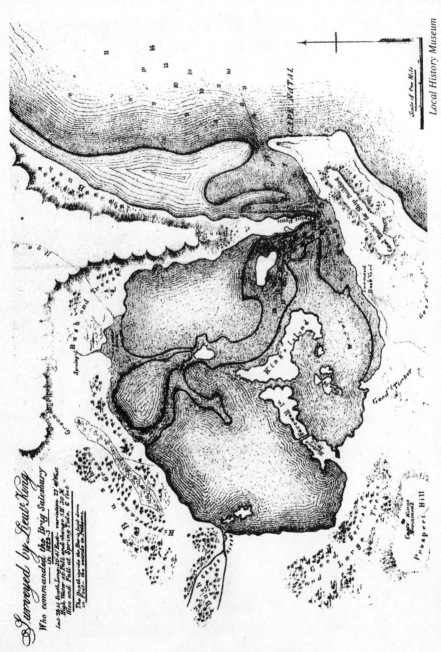

'Chart of Port Natal, surveyed by Lieut. King who commanded the Brig Salesbury [*sic*] in 1822–3'. Redrawn by W. Laughton in 1893.

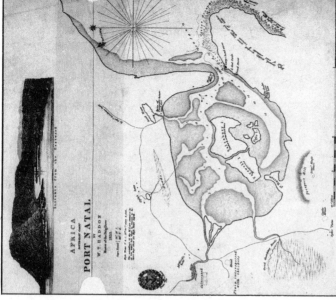

'Port Natal by W.T. Haddon,
Master of the Brig Dove, 1835'.

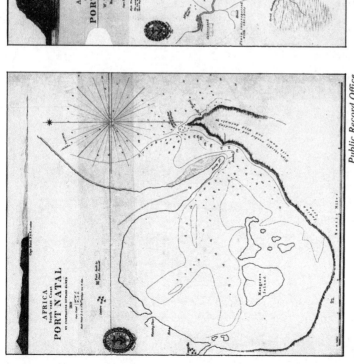

'Port Natal by Commander Edward Hawes,
1831'.

This Chart

of

Port Natal

from a Survey

of Mr James I. King of the

Brig Mary

is

presented to A.B. Becker Esq.

by his

most obedient Servant

Charles R. Maclean

Octr 15th 1854

In account of the loss of the Mary in the Nautical Magazine ? 185—

Title and dedication of Maclean's chart.
(The chart itself is reproduced as a fold-out at the end of this book.)

vessels of the brig type, as he will mention the same equipment used in his defence of his black crewmen in North Carolina in 1846. We need not conclude that King's vessel had been prepared with any particularly warlike features.

Maclean's concluding sentence to the instalment is delivered in true cliffhanger style. The twist it gives to their situation – that they were unexpectedly, even amusingly, made welcome by a ragged reception committee, and to receive 'some pleasing and interesting information' – is done with a cheerful flourish, very much in the 'to be continued' vein. This is clear proof that Maclean knowingly wrote his account for serialisation. Later evidence suggests that he even wrote parts of it piecemeal as the deadlines of *The Nautical Magazine* approached. Its improvised structure is thus understandable.

To summarise this opening instalment. Already Maclean's readers know, as he crosses the threshold from the seaman's world with other flotsam and jetsam onto the landmass of Africa, that the outcome of his childhood adventure will have certain results: his abiding love for the Zulu people, the proof of his faith in providence and, in general, a far more enriching experience that mere survival. While dramatising terrors, he is already asserting his disbelief in them. The experience of his life lies ahead of him, to be gone through.

Two

The serial resumes with the promised 'pleasing and interesting information' of Rachel, given in summary in indirect speech. Part of Farewell's original party of 'several Europeans and Hottentots', Rachel is English-speaking and so must have acquired her know-how in the recently anglicized Cape Town milieu. Rachel is also mentioned frequently by Isaacs, from whom one gathers that she may have been a slave who had earned her manumission. Isaacs also describes her as severely disfigured with the scars of smallpox. Generally written out of later versions of the Natal pioneering saga, she is in Maclean's text one of the best described of all the characters of his acquaintance.

Maclean leaves us with no doubt as to the crucial and powerful role Rachel played at Port Natal from 1824 onwards. She was the one of the reception committee (at first sight man or woman?) in her 'European garments' who hoisted the 'tattered rag' on a pole for the party's identification. (This is a significant variation on the handed down version of King planting a flagpole complete with ensign, claiming the beach as British territory.)

At all events, outside of the Cape Colony Rachel has an authority that that slave-holding society would not have permitted her. Not only does she behave like a madam, 'chastising' her servants with a 'cane', but as Farewell's representative at the encampment on the Bay she is left in charge of the efficient running of affairs while the menfolk of the party are away. She was a gracious and humorous hostess as well, and without hesitation Isaacs and Maclean fall in under her authority. Later references to her show that King's party comes to depend on her as well as their chief negotiator and provisioner. Maclean daily traipses to Rachel's stores for his sustaining milky breakfast. So the credit of being the first colonial trader to set up shop in Natal must go to Rachel the canteener, supreme in the domestic sphere.

It is Rachel who clarifies the position of the trading parties with respect to Zululand. Many important details emerge from her account. Firstly, it is clear from all of Maclean's record that both parties considered themselves temporary sojourners under the 'dominion' of the friendly King Shaka and might 'rest assured of his protection', words like 'dominion' and 'protection' being political in their implications. The 'hostile' chief of the Sikhunyana, against whom Farewell and company have joined forces with Shaka – but, as Maclean emphasizes, on a purely voluntary basis – is not mentioned by either Isaacs or Fynn. This detail is important to remember, as all the party leaders when later submitting their claims to territory in Natal at the Cape and making their cases to encourage annexation will deny that they had previously taken sides in any warlike adventures on the Zulus' behalf; indeed, in Maclean's polemic against Kay this information is vital.

The battle described by Rachel against the 'hostile chief' to the north who was 'not considered friendly to the white man' seems to have been a Zulu mopping-up operation against the Ndwandwes under Zwide. Sikhunyana was one of Zwide's sons. The Zulus under Shaka had first defeated them in 1819. According to Wright and Hamilton, Zulu paramountcy over the region dates only from then, so that we must bear in mind that Zulu hegemony was but freshly established in 1825. White participation in the wars that maintained the Shakan 'Empire' is an equivocal issue. Although Governor Somerset had forbidden Farewell's participation in any military campaigns as a condition of his permission to trade in Zululand, obviously the traders had no choice in the matter if they wished their trade routes to remain open or to expand. For Rachel this is the name of the game.

Secondly, Rachel immediately dispels the fears of King's party of ambush and attack. Cordiality, *bonhomie* rule at Port Natal in a way which is never stressed by later writers. Here the 'friendly' disposition of the local indigenous inhabitants is all-pervasive.

Two bold impressions emerge from Maclean's ensuing description of the harbourage of Port Natal, to which most of this instalment is devoted, if in a rather disorganised way. For a contemporary reader accustomed to the modern topography of Durban, Maclean's 'Port Natal' is hard to visualise in its uncharted wildness and extent. But Maclean's account of the fetid mangrove swamp which still exists in his imagination is a particular example of what in more general terms has come to be described as the appropriating discourse of colonialism, by which we understand a systematic taming and claiming of the scene is at work in naming it, measuring it, surveying it. The people of the unknown interior are likewise 'claimed' through description, placed and rendered 'other' by their differences. These two tendencies are familiarly and aggressively at work in the accounts of Isaacs and Fynn, both of whose agendas are headed by land claims and the reduction of 'others' to vassalage, and both of whom set about appropriating all the power of chieftainship from the beginning.

Although Maclean cannot escape this paradigm, in his account his perceptions are different. He was too young and dependent to stake out any part of it, for a start. His details of longitude and latitude are merely informative to seamen wishing a safe landing; he makes no claims for himself. Similarly, he accepts Rachel as a familiar (as he will accept all the other local people), hardly bothering to describe her. If anything, Port Natal to this milk-sated child is a verdant paradise. He can spend more time recollecting his primitive escapades with a troop of monkeys than getting on with the job!

His Bay of Port Natal is thoroughly cultivated and settled by the Mathubanes, what is more. They not only till its soil but harvest its fish in a long-established and efficient way, while paying their tribute in fealty to the Zulu overlords. This is drastically different from Fynn's and Isaacs' versions. While Fynn hardly mentions the amaThuli of Mathubane except to cast them as his fortunate retainers, Isaacs flatly contradicts Maclean:

> The tribe of which Mataban was chief had been subdued by Chaka, but having rallied the remains of it, with them he had sought a settlement between the forests, where they took refuge from the incursions of the Zoolas. The innumerable persecutions to which they had been subjected by their more powerful and sanguinary neighbours had tended to render them timid and apprehensive. On the approach of strangers they would flee with their valuables into the innermost recesses of the forest; where

they would seclude themselves until an opportunity occurred for emerging from their concealment. It was not therefore until after a lapse of some time, that the Europeans became acquainted with their neighbours; but when their retreat had been discovered, and the discomfited chief had seen the differences between the assurances of our party, and the predatory visits of his oppressor, he was not long in determining on a friendly alliance with us, and on living contiguous to our kraal. (pp. 25–6)

The differences between Maclean's and Isaacs' accounts are so glaring that one is forced to ask which of the two is plain lying. Maclean shows unproblematic collaboration with the amaThuli from the outset: they take the fish, while the Mlungus go for their favourite diet, the turtle, both sides getting the best of their collaboration. In Maclean they are no quaking refugees at all; rather, they are well-established settlers of the Bay, where, if anything, the sloppy hippos hold sway. Maclean's illustration of King's party's first encounter with the Mathubanes flatly contradicts Isaacs, as will the whole of his Instalment Seven.

Whereas in Isaacs and Fynn we find the colonizing discourse in full spate – the myth of the empty land into which the industrious power may expand, the putting on side of superiority to bring allies into fortunate submission, and so on – in Maclean this version is conspicuously absent. To Maclean the established kraals are the Mathubanes', on which through Rachel the castaways are dependent for flesh and grain. To Maclean *he* is the outsider intruding; even in the monkey incident he concedes that the luscious trees are theirs to harvest, while he stands up to his neck in a rising tide waiting for them to be done – a rather hopeless position for any would-be pioneer. What in Isaacs is serious business, to Maclean is an amusing and irresponsible romp.

In his further description of the Bay two areas of focus emerge as of immediate interest: trees for shipbuilding, hippos for ivory. The visual equivalent of Maclean's prose is indeed King's chart, which is equally interesting for its selection of detail: 'Good Timber for Ship-building' is inscribed over the Bluff; 'Hippopotamus Grazing Ground' is marked to the west over the swampy bushland at the mouth of what he labels the Congella; and from the northern landing place where Fort Farewell was located the note is 'Road to the Zulus' – these were the seafarers' interests in resources at Port Natal.

To a limited extent Maclean is curious about prior colonial claims on the Bay, as is evident in his taking the trouble reviewing Maxwell's little known account of 1706. But from this he deduces no more than that Natal was 'one of the most fertile regions on earth'. His concern is far more over whether or not the Dutch East India Company's entrepot at the Bay established 'a harbour for slave ships'. He concludes that this was unlikely, citing the oral evidence that 'no traditions existed among them of their forefathers ever having any traffic or intercourse with Europeans'. To this point we will have to return, as the issue of slavery is burningly close to Maclean's heart. Here we may register his relief that, to the best of his knowledge, the locals had not in that vicinity been subjected to this outrage, which is indeed one explanation of their hospitable peacefulness.

'The English River' Maclean mentions up at Delagoa Bay is the southernmost of many rivers emptying into that Bay, and only recently had it come to be known by that name. The man who had named it so optimistically was Farewell who, prior to his 1824 arrival in Port Natal, had attempted only a year previously to establish a British post there in competition with the Portuguese on the opposite side in the mercenary-controlled Lourenco Marques Co. As by then the abolition of slave-trading had occurred, and by international law Britain was empowered to search any trading vessels of the many nations that were signatory to the pact, Farewell established his beachhead as a supposed police post. But his real interests seem to have been the capture of the traditional ivory trade from the south. Feverish and ruined, he was driven away by the Portuguese company officials, and left his first fortification no more than its short-lived name.

Farewell's attempt at opening up Port Natal, then, must be seen as an alternative manoeuvre undertaken by him on his own initiative, with the flimsiest of colonial sanctions, to establish a base under British control in the general trade wars that flourished in the Indian Ocean in the wake of the defeat of Napoleon. Farewell was reliant on King's knowledge of the facilities and opportunities offered by Port Natal. Maclean makes much of their friendship, and it seems clear that with the dilemma of the wrecked *Mary* on their hands, they arranged a division of duties between them, Farewell responsible for trading in the hinterland and King for devising transport out of it.

That is why it is important for Maclean to establish the precedence of King's claim that his survey was 'the first ever made by any English navigator of this part of the coast of Eastern Africa'. Maclean revives King's claim over Owen's, not only because he feels King was unjustly overlooked by Townsend, but because the surviving Mrs King may stand to gain from her late son's stake in the development of Port Natal. One is reminded that the only other named survivor of the 1825–28 enterprise to make it out of Natal – Isaacs – was to pursue his much more persuasive claim with the Cape authorities, and in vain, for many years. Maclean is unaware that Captain William Owen had in 1833 published his claim in London (in his *Narrative of Voyages to Explore the Shores of Africa, Arabia and Madagascar*).

To drive home King's claim, rightly or wrongly, Maclean continued to rake up this issue. While Instalment Two appeared in February 1853, by October 1854, he had completed his own chart of Port Natal, drawn almost entirely from King's. This he presented, not to the Admiralty, but to A.B. Becker, Esq. (the editor?) to illustrate his contributions to *The Nautical Magazine* and to keep on file in their offices.

Since Maclean had not revisited Port Natal, we may take any alterations and additions he makes to King's original as coming from his own pristine experience, unmediated by any subsequent developments. Of all the maps of Port Natal as it existed for the 1824–28 parties, Maclean's is the most comprehensive from the seafarer's point of view. The two main flamingo-infested islands in the mudflats of the Bay are named there after the two initial survey ships, the *Salisbury* and the *Julia*. (The name Salisbury Island has stuck to this day.) In subsequent maps King, Farewell, Fynn, Isaacs, Ogle, Cane and even Hutton will variously have the islands and other strategic points under their names.

We must, however, question the accuracy of King's chart. Obviously he made a huge miscalculation in bringing in the *Mary*. Maclean also mentions that while waiting for Farewell's return, King and Hutton take the opportunity for further survey. Knowledge of Port Natal in 1825 was still amateurish and incomplete. The Bay must have seemed a swamp without bearing.

But not so for Maclean. His chart has additional features over King's original – his illustrations of three scenes of the Bay. The first depicts the three capes or points of the seaward approach to the promontory of the Bluff. The second shows the view of the anchorage from Salisbury Island. The third, entitled 'First Interview with the natives at the Watering Place', already mentioned, is a beguiling picture of ten crewmen of the *Mary* rowing past the Mathubane fishing enclosures to land at Congella. There they are casually welcomed by a seated black. A glen of trees and a beehive hut with other relaxed bystanders is shown against a park-like background. The scene is tranquil, pastoral . . . anything but the hostile nightmare he had been led by King to expect, and which Isaacs persists in portraying. It is the entirely appropriate visual analogue of his text.

That the debate about correct charts of Port Natal was pre-eminently important to the readers of *The Nautical Magazine* is evidenced by the editor's fractious footnote to this instalment. The maps of Commander Edward Hawes (1831) and by W.T. Haddon, Master of the *Dove* (1835), both kept and published by the Admiralty's Hydrographical Office, still extant, are indeed both sketchy and impressionistic. In reviving King's chart, Maclean was undoubtedly trying to improve on both of them.

There were, however, at least two further maps made of the area before 1853, and it is perhaps surprising that Maclean did not know of them. As both were kept in South Africa, this is further evidence that Maclean never returned to these waters. The first is John Centlivres Chase's of 1835, made personally by him by survey and copied by J.L. Leeb. (Maclean also seems unaware of Chase's *Natal Papers*, published in Grahamstown and Cape Town in 1843.) The second is the Tallis chart of 1851, which shows the entire coastline between Port Natal and Delagoa Bay, together with the region subdivided into divisions, its multitudinous rivers plotted, with Zulu territory pushed back to north of the Thukela as the last stronghold of 'Kaffraria.' The Tallis map summarizes the progress of British penetration in Natal with its renamings and relocations. Shaka's second capital of Dukuza will shortly be renamed Stanger, too, after Natal's first surveyor-general.

To Maclean the extent and boundaries of any Natal Colony are still unimaginable. He applies the term 'Natal' only very locally to mean the Bay and its immediate vicinity. To him the interior is not Natal at all, but generally Zululand . . . on which a small enclave had been found and shared.

The only other extant map of the Bay at that time is Fynn's rather childlike and eccentric drawing of the 'settlement', which places his residences and kraals to the south and west of the Bay, opposite Farewell's fort to the north. (Fynn seems to have made no impact on Maclean for he never mentions him.) This deployment of the first two white parties around the lagoon tends to substantiate the impression Maclean gives that the party leaders felt little need to shelter together in any threatened laager position (and incidentally vindicates Rachel's story). Indeed, when King arrives with the third party, as the next instalment shows, he instantly takes over another sector of the Bay's shore, moving from the point over to the Bluff, and never considers seeking refuge in Farewell's encampment. So much for the threat of hostile Africa.

This deployment of the three white chiefs about the Bay suggests not only that they did not feel the need to club together, but that there were certain rivalries between them. In due course these would come out into the open, and in the case of King vs. Farewell lead to outright hostilities. Later writers who suggest the unity of purpose and combined intention of the three great leaders in some pioneering effort greater than themselves are thus fantasizing about this very dispersed gathering of freebooters, subject to schisms and feuds, each out to grab what he could get.

The end of the instalment brings us an even firmer point than the above. On hearing a rumour that his friend Farewell may have been murdered at the Bay,

Maclean says, King 'resolved *while pursuing his course to the eastward* to call at Natal . . .' (my italics). If this is read correctly, and Maclean means what he says, then we arrive at the alarming realization that King, quite contrary to what we have always been led to believe, had not planned to reach Port Natal as the be-all and end-all of his voyage. Maclean suggests that this landfall of the *Mary* was merely a diversion on a routine coastal trading haul (probably with Delagoa Bay as its destination from Table Bay). In which case, we may conclude that King's enforced marooning at Port Natal was an accident, indeed, and that for Maclean — so celebrated today as a pioneer hero — certainly the last event he had planned on.

THREE

The shortest instalment of Maclean's serial, this is one of the most eventful. It advances the narrative line considerably. Two main actions occur: the defection from Port Natal of half of King's party, and the remainder's decision to assemble themselves as shipbuilders across the Bay. Throughout the instalment there is still no evidence that any of King's party intended to stay even temporarily at Port Natal. Their dispute is entirely over the best method of getting away from it.

After a fortnight stranded on shore with only a limited amount of the ship's stores of victuals saved, access to the ship's other resources — ironically, large quantities of 'grog' in the form of 'wine and spirits' — becomes the supposed cause of the contentious split within the King party. Maclean blames this dissension on the alcohol, and is disgusted by the base nature 'grog' is inclined to release in the seafaring 'class of men'. From this we may deduce an abstemiousness in his responses; truly, he is shocked by the drunkards' dissolution.

But from the way Maclean tells the incident we may also deduce a deeper dissatisfaction at work in the crew. Maclean is here nagging at a larger question which is of major concern to him in turn as a ship's captain. Having been flung out of their brig, under which law do they now fall? Does the orderly hierarchy of ship's regulations transfer to land and effectively function until they be restored back to their true domain, the sea? Constantly in Maclean the land has a threatening aspect – the evidently dissolute Farewell and the glamorous sensuality of the Zulus will try his morality even further – because it represents a collapse of maritime authority.

Mr Norton, the second mate, organizes a mutiny against King, in effect – shades of Fletcher Christian and the *Bounty*. Their disagreement is over prospects at Port Natal, and their focus the only craft they have that might conceivably make the long and perilous haul back to Algoa Bay (Port Elizabeth). Norton has six others of the men stacked against 'the captain and officers' – that is, King and Hutton and those who remain loyal to them. Maclean describes the revolt as 'disaffection and insubordination', but the point in this confrontation is that King's authority has broken down. He can only concede them the contested boat, although thereby losing half his skilled manpower and a significant part of his property. King is forced to accept their bargaining and release Norton and crew. The dry way in which Maclean concludes his account of their suicidal escape – 'they bade us adieu at Natal for ever' – suggests his feeling of good riddance, washing his hands of the affair. He implies they received the bleak and terrible end they deserved. (Isaacs, by contrast, says they got through, carrying messages for King.)

Yet Maclean's view is tempered by his real feelings when he gives vent to his tragic conclusions in the startling and illuminating paragraph beginning 'Men may become slaves of degrading and destructive passions. . . . ' Here we come closest to an outright statement of the older writer's code of ethics – that 'latent' in the hardest heart are 'tenderness' and 'generosity', which are activated by 'adversity'; that 'pure and self-denying love' transforms 'human nature and brings man nearer to his God', that all 'worldly distinctions' are levelled by innate 'nobleness and generosity of soul.' The realm of the sea, Maclean maintains, allows humankind the chance for these noble and spiritual decencies to become more evident. On land the gap between 'prosperity' and the 'poor' is greater, and it is the poor who may instruct us in 'noble instances of self-sacrifice'.

The moment of history caught here may be interpreted in several ways. The Scottish Low-Church spirit of the preacher and democrat, Thomas Paine, is clear here in honouring the worth of each individual believer, that is, the basic rights of man. The Royal Navy, although it had defeated Napoleon's revolutionary forces, had indeed been internally reformed by 1825: this is evident in King's own account (quoted in Instalment One) where he stresses that his first crucial decision about their common destiny during the shipwreck was handled by consulting 'with the officers and people, as their lives and the safety of the vessel entitled them'. King is scrupulous in recording the new, more democratic naval procedures and their results, an almighty concerted effort on everyone's part. (Which in turn brings him unstinting praise from Maclean as a leader of men.) Again, on shore, in this instalment, when the party has split into opposing factions, King reconciles himself to the situation by having his option 'mutually agreed upon'. The peculiar naval hierarchy – with Hutton, not King, as the key man – is now nevertheless subject to democratic procedures by which issues of common concern are settled by individual numbers and the vote. And the Norton party is independent-minded enough to go their own way.

The dramatic manner in which King's depleted party turns around on the issue, to see the Norton group off with such forgiving hearts, shows the remarkable extent to which Christian spiritual and secular democratic beliefs had meshed in the seaman's code. This was the British spirit of which Maclean was so actively convinced and proud – and it must be noted that by definition it is the very antithesis of that other condition of 'slavery' (a word which he uses with a very wide application to include both blacks and whites). The great debate here is whether or not this seafarer's code of Christian democracy may remain intact on shore.

King's decision to build the Townsend dockyard, then, must be seen as an attempt not only to reconstruct the salvage of the *Mary* into a safer ocean-going vessel than the longboat, but to restore the basis of his power. His own tragedy, together with others like Hutton's, is thus a playing out of a larger, but similar, drama to Norton's. The fact is that the Port Natal landfall was to mean the death of all but the last three of the *Mary*'s original complement – a heavy toll.

When at the end of the instalment the party is split further as King, Hutton and three seamen set off to pay their respects to King Shaka (thereby accepting his authority over them), the shipbuilders are reduced to a mere three (Isaacs, Cameron and Maclean). A deal is to be struck: 'beads and blankets' in exchange for dockyard labour. So desperate for assistance will King become that, as we will see, he will have the *Mary* rebuilt as Shaka's vessel. He concedes ownership over the craft in exchange for the right to sail in it once more.

In sinking the 'first post into the ground' and naming the site after his patron, Townsend (the same Townsend whom we know had denied King the credit for his chart in Instalment Two!), King is a man fighting – rather pathetically –for his reputation as a loyal Canadian back in the corridors of power as represented by the Lords of the Admiralty.

The wild dogs of Natal recur here, but more as an irritation than a threat. Hutton's pragmatic way of devising means of dealing with them is revealing of how the stranded mariners get down to coming to terms with these (and so many subsequent) hazards. Hutton is the child's most admired hero immediately to hand, and so his story is to be the best developed of all the individual stories in Maclean's account.

Here and in all his further actions Hutton behaves in an exemplary fashion, appropriate to his rank of first mate, leader of the men and in charge of all the practical functioning of their means of livelihood. Whether Hutton actually goes on the first expedition to Dukuza with King or not seems unclear, for he is certainly on the second expedition of the remaining members of the party. Yet Maclean says he and Isaacs were left in charge of the Townsend dockyard in King's absence. This seems a contradiction in Maclean's memory, not likely to be resolved.

The unfortunate attrition meted out by this stage to the party's dogs illustrates a further collapse in the human defences. Here Maclean's lack of detail is infuriating, for he gives us only a glimpse of one of the most extraordinary stories concerning himself. As regards the demise of their last dog, the Newfoundland (similar to the modern Labrador, black-coated), he remarks:

> This faithful animal was regretted by all of us, but by no one more than myself for, having fallen overboard at sea on the passage out from England, when on the Equator, the noble animal by jumping over after me saved my life. . . .

We may accept that the youthful Maclean was learning to internalize his emotions, but this stiff-upper lip style of recounting his rescue in equatorial seas, which confines such a major experience to a mere qualifying clause, is exceptionally self-effacing. The reader is far more haunted by the image of a non-swimming ship-boy saved from drowning by this helpful beast than Maclean obviously imagines.

He shares the distinction, by the way, of having been saved by a Newfoundland dog with none other than Napoleon, arch-enemy of his captain. This occurred when Napoleon tried to escape from Saint Helena, or so the legend goes. The *Mary* had put in at Saint Helena and collected Isaacs there, so perhaps the story was well known to them.

In the words 'on the passage out from England' Maclean incidentally gives us the only evidence we have of the *Mary*'s log prior to its arrival at Table Bay. Its home-port being in England (rather than Britain) suggests they embarked on this trip from London or another southern port (rather than from Glasgow). But that he once toppled off her decks and was saved by a Canadian, Indian-bred hound-dog . . . this is the very stuff from which his legend may be constructed afresh.

By the time Farewell returns from the interior in late October, King is obliged to venture forth. Tantalisingly, what transpired between the two leaders, apart from the mutual exchange of 'greetings', is left undescribed. Farewell loans his horse to King. This detail proves that King and Farewell were not joint-stockholders in a mutual company, but rather that each retained individual control over their own possessions.

The merry description Maclean gives of the departing delegation, memorably at sea on the landlubbers' means of transport, is one of the warmest passages in his account. Instead of names and ages, we have a generic description of three Jolly 'Jack Tars', ludicrously out of place as their rolling gaits are taken over by the oxen's plunging 'tacking and making stern bends' – a fine example of sailing-ship lingo transferred to a landsman's world, showing that like his confreres Maclean remained ever a man of the ocean waves. The convention of not naming these three tars except as Jacks later recoils on Maclean himself to his infinite disadvantage. When Isaacs describes him in turn by the generic 'John Ross' for red-headed Highland sailor (and also, incidentally, sometimes merely as 'Jack'), the convention was misread by later writers as a literal naming.

At the end of this instalment Maclean is truly in his stride and has a scheme to engage his readers through the next instalment. The 'brief description of Fort Farewell' that is to follow – to mark time until we have the results of King's negotiation at Dukuza – is a way of presenting his backlog of information in a dramatic way. Also, here we may notice he has changed into the present tense. The reality of his recollections has therefore moved to the front of his mind. He is no longer writing about his past, but is reliving it as if it were present and actual to him – and so more deeply moving for us.

Four

This instalment is notable for Maclean's first polemical digression, the very revealing and surprising onslaught against Kay. This takes over the middle section.

The framing description of 'Fort Farewell' is graphically clear and precise, but it is tinged with what now becomes Maclean's rather ironic tone, used to disabuse his readers of their expectations. The fort, he begins, is 'anything but what its name implies'. Its platform and embrasure are 'intended for heavy guns which never were there'. Playfulness intrudes: this is a very 'original fortification'. 'Nothing in my youth and inexperience could reconcile this wretched looking place with the name it bore', he concludes, and the technique of anticlimax reveals to us a wonder in reverse.

This process of deflation is coupled to a major theme: 'It might be naturally supposed that a feeling of security and confidence had not yet taken place in my mind as to the good will of our sable friends', he remarks with the benefit of hindsight. His intention is to show that for him as well 'time and intercourse' will reverse his anxiety. From here Maclean's project becomes the working out of his huge thematic scheme, of learning in the school of hard experience to love and let be – rather than to fear and distrust – 'our sable friends'. Everything that follows is related to this theme.

When his anger is finally provoked, it comes out against those who cannot conceive of – have never learnt – this fundamental element of human trust. For Maclean – simply put – human trust is to become the heart and soul of any life worth living.

That Maclean is familiar with and admires democratic values is evident in his description of how authority is exerted in the Farewell stockade (among whites), and how this is dependent on black acquiescence in servitude with justice – an equivocal point. Their makeshift system is ultimately patriarchal in its operation, as Maclean admits. A modern reader is sorely tempted to comment that the assumption of magisterial petty chieftainship in white pioneers, whereby each accumulates his own dependents from black society to bolster his rising command, is only too characteristic of the beliefs and practices of racial superiority, the very colonizing impulse in action on the ground. (Frequently this becomes projected onto the alien society, as if these were the only terms in which it may be seen, and by self-reflection the white man's behaviour is justified.) Certainly Maclean is a party to this system, and when he comes to describing Zulu society he will projectively see it as the most powerful example of patriarchal orders, headed by the mightiest 'tyrant' of them all, King Shaka himself. Possibly those are the only terms available to the whites; their comprehension does not include the possibility of wholly different social organisation. Often Zulu experts are only expert on themselves.

But in Maclean there is a contrary strain which militates against the Hobbesian world-view. In his paragraph describing the 'park-like' surrounds of Fort Farewell he finds 'a picture of nature which shed a soft and cheering influence over the mind'. In other words, the antidepressant effects of the unsullied wilds (with which he is now presented in abundance) call up for him very typical romantic responses. He suffers from all the melancholia and disillusion of romantic beliefs, too, even to the extent of remaining deeply solitary throughout his account. He is also saturated with the 'noble savage' strain of romanticism, which admires paganism for its 'natural' creed and its closeness to God's own environment. Faced now with thousands of stark naked and quite contented pagans, Maclean has seriously to consider if he should not step over into their domain in preference to the travestied version of his own that Fort Farewell represents.

This conflict within Maclean takes the form of his discussion of the two states of civilization and barbarism as they intersect at Fort Farewell, the case in point. To Maclean the distinctions are hardly clear-cut (and by the end of his narrative will have disappeared almost entirely). In taking on the Rev. Stephen Kay in what follows, he is urgently and somewhat resentfully determined to show that Kay's theory, that when in the contact situation the civilized man degenerates into barbarism, is flawed; in fact, untrue. The Port Natal survivors may have become uncouth and even unrecognisable to any who enjoy 'the comforts and style of a drawing-room', but this in no way implies that they lost what to Maclean is their key characteristic, their 'open and generous hearts of Englishmen'.

Kay (b. 1796) came to the Cape with the 1820 Settlers and was the Wesleyan preacher who by 1825 at Mount Coke had founded the second of the envisioned chain of missions designed to penetrate from the Eastern Cape frontier to effect pacification in the Transkei. Although unsuccessful there, Kay ministered to many communities inside the frontier before returning to London, where in 1833 he published the work Maclean cites. Its full title is *Travels and Researches in Caffraria describing the Character, Customs and Moral Condition of the Tribes inhabiting that Portion of Southern Africa, with Historical and Topographical Remarks Illustrative of the State of the British Settlement in its Borders, the Introduction of Christianity and the Progress of Civilization.*

Kay had returned to England as a corresponding member of the South African Institution, established to investigate the geography, natural history and general resources of the subcontinent. After summarising the works of Barrow, Lichtenstein and Thompson, Kay reports on the range and extent of missionary development in the Cape in order to reinforce his platform, which is the recruitment of more missionaries.

Kay's theory of how civilization should operate to spread itself is predicated on the conviction that his review of the state of heathenism in the southern African tribes

> reminds us of the degraded state of ancient Britain when Julius Caesar first invaded it; for in the present condition of the Caffrarian tribes is reflected, as in a mirror, the leading features of our progenitors; while

from our own history we may also learn the state to which such tribes may be elevated, by means favourable to their improvement. (p. vi)

Maclean is not the only commentator to pick up on Kay's theory that men would slip in and out of the reciprocal states of heathenism and civilization were it not for the missionary's effort at 'improvement'. Several Cape writers deeply resented his criticisms of the tendency of Christians in the bush to lapse in the rigours of their faith and to revert to their primitive prototypes – indeed, Kay's work provoked an outcry. Maclean's rebuttal essentially says, despite any theory, this did not occur at Port Natal.

Although Kay's account of Zululand in his Chapter 16 is indeed not derived from first-hand experience, Maclean took its allegations to heart seriously enough to check it thoroughly. Maclean's reference to the little-known Maxwell manuscript account in Instalment Two is triggered by Kay's own discovery of this source. From Maxwell Kay makes a far more elaborate point about the use of Port Natal in the seventeenth and eighteenth centuries as a slave-trading barracoon, exporting cargoes to Isle de France. If Kay is correct, then the 'Caffres' on Reunion island to this day are of Nguni-speaking stock. Maclean has already been replying to Kay without revealing this.

Kay even suggests that Farewell himself intended to maintain well-established slave-exporting procedures, and that King and all the rest in their desperation were deeply implicated in attempts to revive the trade. As Kay is writing after the emancipation of the slaves had been proclaimed in the Cape, we may assume that he could blacken Natal pioneers on this issue with impunity, and with a weight of popular condemnation on his side. So Maclean's rebuttal of Kay goes a long way further than we may imagine. At Fort Farewell, he states, there was servitude, maybe, but no slavery. His description of the site is as precise and extensive as it is because he wishes to reveal that no trace of the slave-factory, with all its grim architecture and equipment of whips and chains, was evident. (He knows the difference from having been to Lourenço Marques.) Of all sources, Maclean – so strongly anti-slavery himself – would not deceive us on this issue.

For the sake of the record, however, Kay is not the only missionary to suspect slave-handling activity on the Zululand coast. The French missionaries, T. Arbousset and F. Daumas in their work, which first appeared in English translation at the Cape in 1846 as *Narrative of an Exploratory Tour to the North-East of the Colony of the Cape of Good Hope*, give an extended account of an entire tribe of refugees from Shaka, complete with their cattle, being kidnapped and transported from there, never to have been heard of again (pp. 104–8). But Maclean seems not to know of their account. If he had, he would certainly have reacted to the luridly defamatory job they do on Shaka's life, using Kay as a source.

The contest between Kay and Maclean really has the effect of bringing slavery to South Africa as a burning issue. In Brookes and Webb the subject is not indexed; in Duminy and Guest it is mentioned only once as a problem of Zanzibar. At Port Natal in the 1820s it was *the* issue, and if this has not been reflected in subsequent history, then there is a vast omission. For both Maclean and Kay the slavery debate is at the heart of the matter of Port Natal from 1824 to 1828.

The contest between Kay and Maclean is also based on the relative merits of 'hearsay' as against the 'eye-witness' record. Maclean wishes to correct what 'will be handed down to posterity as a matter of history', as previously mentioned. Like many a fine poststructuralist, he believes that history is never written, only *re*written.

But Kay's account itself is based on other eye-witness records – King's account in *The South African Commercial Advertiser* and Farewell's Letter to the Governor of the Cape of September, 1824, are cited in Kay. (Isaacs' record and Fynn's various letters were yet to be published, and these in turn have to be read as reacting to Kay and much Kay-like criticism of many contentious aspects of their occupation of Port Natal, including its very legality.) The least useful reading of all this is the one that takes any of it at face value.

So the very name 'Port Natal' meant controversy over weighty legal and commercial issues which Kay skewed into an argument about religious principles and behaviour as they applied to the character and performance of his bloody conquistadors. Naturally Maclean was outraged. By going back to square one thirty years after the event – by simply and clearly painting conditions as they were – with the weight of empirical evidence on his side, he wishes to demystify this site of contest, and bring the whole story with a thump of common sense back into the framework of what his readers will easily concede did occur. While Kay villainizes the protagonists as brutish opportunists, fire-spurting assassins and sensualists, Maclean does not reply by valorizing them in the opposite deirection. His defence is far more subtle than that.

He has already established his own piety and high code of ethics. We know him to have been a thoroughly decent person, one who even in the case of Norton's villainy could find redeeming features and the lesson of forgiveness. Now, provocatively, he gives us a portrait of himself as a version of a civilized Briton becoming so 'heathenish' that he loses his posture (his 'air and gait') and even portions of his 'mother tongue'.

Kay is terrified of the white man when outnumbered and absorbed into native culture 'going black', so Maclean replies with the utterly shocking news that he spent most of his residence at Natal alone with the blacks, sunk in utter barbarity, and still has 'no shame in confessing' that, far from having his innate personality damaged, he thoroughly enjoyed and benefited from the experience! Kay's principles, Maclean implies, are really racial phobias, his contrary states of 'civilization' and 'savagery' no categories at all. Thoroughly on the offensive, Maclean recommends Kay direct his huge efforts to reclaiming his homeland, Britain, for Christ; he should keep his hands off the Zulus, leave them to their commercial friends.

Although this debate about suitable methods of colonization is left open here, Maclean and Kay really belong to different phases of the operation. Maclean was situated at the contact phase, when indeed, since the balance of power was entirely and overwhelmingly on the savage side, individual character, improvisation and an air of courtesy pulled the buccaneers through. After all, the tradition of three centuries of British endeavour to commercialise Africa rested on the limited establishment of coastal enclaves through which trade could flow — in terms of millions of examples of sound human flesh or, in this later variation, tons of ivory.

Since force was not yet operative (Farewell's carronades lie in the mud), the trading venture relied entirely on respectful mutuality established with the hinterland — that is why contact phase narrators are always quick to praise their partners as suitable allies (and Maclean's record, as we shall see, is unstinting in its praises of Shaka the king). Beads, bangles, blankets — these are the currency of the transaction — and Maclean even explains the value and function of the truck rescued from the *Mary* as acceptable currency.

During the contact phase, too — and this is unimaginable in later versions of it — the outnumbered traders assume the manners, customs and even the language of their partners — they lose their garb (in this case, most of their dress is lost in the wreck), and even enjoy their tatterdemalion caricatures of themselves. They go down on their hands and knees to enter huts and pride themselves on their rapid acquisition of the local language. To show what good chaps they are, they invariably take on native wives as well. When the Natal traders finally call for a missionary to Port Natal, we find Isaacs and Fynn fund-raising for one to take care of their staggering number of half-caste children before assailing any hinterland.

Kay in the Transkei, from which his limited experience is derived, belongs to the next phase in the process of colonization, which occurs once the adventurers of the trader-hunter phase have opened the way — explored the geography of the new land, mapped its resources and reported back on the amenability or otherwise of the encountered people. Kay's outpost was located in territory already partly annexed by the Cape by force of arms, reduced into magistracies which would control the Transkei for the next century, with the garrison near at hand.

Now dress, buildings, roads are rigidly and assertively European. Kay cannot abide the thought of the Zulus' nudity – imports of decorative beads that reveal the body's splendour and vanity give way to Lancashire cloth and worsted ware that cover its shame. Windowless huts and hovels are demolished in favour of four-square structures, most notably the church itself with its huge doors. Instead of learning the language and becoming absorbed in it, Kay under the influence of Moffat (with whom he travelled to Kuruman in 1821) is intent to translate it, serving it back to his parishioners in Christian terms – this is the entire function of the Society for the Propagation of the Gospel to which Maclean so scathingly refers.

Many further examples of ideological contrast may be extrapolated from these twin texts. Even Maclean's dietary descriptions are relevant here. Sourmilk and corn are to him utterly suitable foodstuffs – he even gives us the recipes for how to prepare them. To Kay the very fact that the indigenes were able to feed themselves perfectly adequately would be shocking. They are to be converted to their new staples, European bread and wine. To Maclean wine is wine (the cause of Norton's barbaric behaviour . . .), and the drunkard is Kay, high on his own vision of martyrdom, 'being devoured by a wild beast in the jungle, or cruelly butchered by the bloody hand of a savage in the deserts of Africa' – a view which Maclean himself once had, and has quickly overcome. We may enjoy his withering jibes.

Maclean is well aware of the British collection money that is needed to sponsor missionaries. But at Port Natal where European currency is never otherwise mentioned by him, the currency of glass beads is. The gradations of 'colour and size' he describes, with their equivalent values in livestock, suggest a long-standing agreement on exchange rates in a system of trade that was well developed. Maclean's values are far more worldly than Kay's.

At all events, while the furious debate of the day continues, we may extract from the digression a few scraps of information that Maclean drops almost by accident. As these are some of the very few tips he gives about the greatest part of his own story at Natal, we should consider them carefully.

The first is his reference in the middle of a larger sentence to his 'six months' absence on a long and somewhat perilous journey from Natal to Delagoa Bay'. This is the famous rescue run on which the legend of 'John Ross' is based and which we have seen travestied. The source is Isaacs:

... we were in want of many things which we might obtain from Delagoa Bay ... among other necessaries, we were greatly in want of medicines – when John Ross, Lieutenant King's apprentice, a lad of about fifteen years of age, acute, shrewd and active, was appointed to go the journey. No European had been known to make the attempt, and succeed in reaching that place from Natal. ... Shaka afforded us every assistance in sending off the lad, by at once giving him an escort to protect him and to furnish him with food on the way. ... John Ross is, doubtless, the first European who ever accomplished a journey (by land) from Natal to Delagoa Bay and back. When I look at his youth and reflect on the country through which he had to pass, and that he had to penetrate through wild, inhospitable and savage tracks, in which the natives had never been blessed with the sweets of civilization nor the light of reason, but were existing in a mere state of animal nature little exceeding the instinct of the brute; when I look at this, and also reflect that the whole surface of the country was infested with every species of wild and ferocious animal, and every venomous creature, all hostile to man, I cannot but conceive the journey of this lad as one that must be held as exceedingly bold, and wonderfully enterprising. (pp. 101–2)

Isaacs intercepts the young Maclean with King, and as we know gives a summary of Maclean's account on the same pages – the twenty days it took to reach 'English River'; the viciousness of the Shoshangane supporters about the Maputo; the kindness of the Portuguese who nevertheless felt Maclean was a spy for Shaka 'as no Christian would think of sending a boy like him that distance'; his encounter with the generous French slaver who furnished him with 'many useful articles gratis' at the company stores; the evacuation of his party from a hell-hole where the 'poor natives' were so 'subjected, in being chained together, and treated with such great severity and brutality' that he feared his Zulus would be seized and sold. ... this report in indirect speech sounds authentic enough. Isaacs also stresses the economic success of the trip – Maclean returned 'having only expended two dollars, and yet has as many things, of various descriptions, as ten of his people could carry'. It was Isaacs' job to keep account like this.

But the heroic little apprentice himself is far from fulsome in his own praise. The expedition, he says, took six months, as we know. Of the journey itself all he says is that it was 'long and somewhat perilous'. He seems to attach little importance to it if it receives such cursory mention.

Another scrap of throw-away is that 'occasionally' Maclean spent 'three and four months' residence with the king, during which he never saw nor had converse 'with a white man or woman, my constant and only companions being my rude native attendants'. This titbit connects up with his early announcement (in the second paragraph of Instalment One) that he was the eye-witness to 'many interesting and tragical scenes . . . during [his] residence among those savages'. Now we may say with certainty that he spent a very considerable portion of his three years in Natal residing, not at the Bay, but alone among the whites at King Shaka's court itself. Thus he was the *only* member of the Port Natal parties to live in the Zulu hinterland. Where other pioneers frequently visited Shaka and certainly spent much of their time roaming about his kingdom, Maclean lived at its heart. (We will find out the surprise reason for this later.) Maclean familiarly traipsed between the two groups, then, a negotiator to both sides. Alas, he will never in this serial expand in any detail on this.

His intention in mentioning these points is the immediate one of proving that the betwixt and between cross-frontier life he led did not induce any degeneracy or loss of faith in him, despite the fact that he joyfully celebrated sinking into assuming the manners, customs and morals of his environment.

The corrections he makes to Kay's speculations about the 1825 campaign against Sikhunyana, summarizing Farewell on his return, speak for themselves. As we would expect, Maclean's comments on 'the general rules of Caffrarian warfare' include careful mention of both Shaka's strategic skill and his exercise of mercy. His co-option of the defeated survivors into his forces as honorary Zulus not only explains his method of consolidating power, but also the means by which he acquires booty. Something deep in our Highlander clansman is stirred by Farewell's tale of cattle-rustling incidents like these. Kay need not have looked back to the advent of the Romans in the United Kingdom for examples of primitive British behaviour; events across the Border in Scotland would have given him a more recent historical parallel.

Another scrap of information is of extraordinary interest. The fact of Shaka's respect for 'courage' in his foes, Maclean says, 'will be illustrated by many other instances in these recollections in the memoir which I have attempted to give of this extraordinary savage chief'. If this is read correctly, it means Maclean had already written a discrete biography of King Shaka. If so, no such item (which logically would fit after the final instalment here) ever appeared between the covers of *The Nautical Magazine*. To our eternal loss, no life of Shaka by the one white individual who knew him better than any other has come to light elsewhere, either. *The Loss of the Brig 'Mary'* is written around the gap of this missing text. (But see later details on this issue.)

A final word on Maclean's observation that Farewell's 'Hottentots' played a visible and significant part in the action. This is a detail eliminated by many later historians, often for the coy reason that the description 'Hottentot' is considered racially offensive! – and despite the fact that even Isaacs recommends they be awarded honorary British citizenship, Rachel included, for their dedicated services. But 'Hottentot' here is not synonymous with Khoikhoi; Maclean means armed 'coloured' Christian converts who, like the Griquas elsewhere, played such an intermediary role between the whites and the blacks. This situation of collaborating in the frontier enterprise, at such personal loss to themselves, but with such loyalty to their conquerors, is exactly analogous to the situation of Shaka's own 'honorary Zulus' (Jacob, for example). Allegiances were not yet being formed along ethnic lines, in Zululand or at Port Natal. (Who were pure Zulus anyway, and who at Port Natal was of English stock? – very few, as it turns out.) Retaining the term 'Hottentot' here signifies the specific and irreplaceable role they played in frontier affairs.

Similarly, Kay's and Maclean's term 'Caffre' is retained in the text to refer in a general way to the people of the whole of the coast between the Transkei and Delagoa Bay. Spelled that way it seems less likely to convey any more recent pejorative sense. The very territory Kay and Maclean dispute on maps of their day was often designated Independent Caffreland.

FIVE

All the material here is a summary of Captain King's first four-week trip into the interior from late October to late November, 1825. Maclean's informants must be King himself, the three salts who accompanied him and possibly Hutton as well. Maclean corroborates their detail, where necessary, in the light of his own expedition of a fortnight later and many subsequent trips.

King's account establishes many points with which Maclean agrees. However, twice in its course he interrupts it to insert opinions of his own. Both these interpolations (the first a brief paragraph and the second an extensive digression) are crucial to our understanding of his emotional development through the analysis of his life experience. So his style in this instalment – of drawing interpretation from event – although consistent with his earlier practice, is here developed into its logical structure. This is the firmest way of convincing a reader, too.

What occurred to the King party between their send-off at the end of Instalment Three and their present return includes the following features: the well-forged nature of the route; the competence and loyalty of their escorts and guides; the dense population well-settled between Port Natal and Dukuza (so much for the myth of a deserted neutral zone between the two powers); the eager hospitality offered at stay-over points and the Zulu practice of welcoming strangers in a strange land; and the commonable nature of the domestic circle.

Their reception by the potentate with his 'hundred thousand warriors', supplicant as to their 'deity', is at first stiffly formal, then delighted, illustrating that there is a severe public Shaka the Ruler, who in private breaks down in casual pleasantries. (Surely this is highly projective, more suitable to a description of George IV.) The statement concerning their known world being divided between two kings is given in full here, as from Shaka's lips (though this may be a fabrication based on Farewell's view – obviously an entrenched part of the conversation).

The story of Jacob is crucial. (Bryant on p. 563 gives his correct name as Jacot Msimbini.) Jacob is peculiarly irksome yet nevertheless convenient to King, and his story is given here in more detail than in many other sources. King has a certain amount of resentment for the fact that Jacob would have conveyed to Shaka the 'black' view, prejudicial to white power and intentions. From Jacob Shaka learns of the resources of firepower of King George, as well as of the results of resistance: being 'vanquished', 'detention' and immurement on Robben Island. Although King is cast as Jacob's liberator, and scores much cachet for this, the tables have turned on him as he is now at Jacob's mercy. Unwittingly and ironically, it seems Jacob has only increased Shaka's awe of the British. Shaka is persuaded to sue for alliance with them rather than to risk confrontation (or so King would have us believe).

The logic is faultless: the means of effecting an alliance is an embassy; an embassy needs transport; hence Shaka's sponsorship of the reconstruction operation. When the Sothobe delegation eventually sets off for the Cape in the *Shaka* (the new *Mary*) on the critical voyage which Maclean promises to report for us (but, alas, on this point does not deliver in this serial), the outcome will be a disastrous setback to relations between Dukuza and Port Natal and, it must be pointed out, for Shaka's policy of cossetting and spoiling King George's representatives.

King's version of Jacob's story, which Isaacs retells, may also be interpreted in another way, for in essence its fascination for them is that it is *their own* story as well. In the Cape they are regarded as beyond the law, they too arrive in Zululand as castaway swimmers, and by being useful to Shaka have every hope of promotion to chiefdom, with its rewards of wives, body-servants and cattle. Of all the tales to tell about Zululand, this is the one with prospects that they enjoy retelling. But in Maclean's version Shaka is the one who makes all the decisions.

The (seemingly obligatory) demonstration of the superiority of Western arms over assegais is given, in King's version – through Maclean – in a rather downbeat and routine way. Other commentators tend to offer far more inflated versions of what, after all, is *the* cautionary spelling out on the traders' part of where the real strength lies.

The King summary ends with them having obtained Shaka's 'permission to return to Natal' – the concession to his sovereignty is assumed here, and great courtliness of behaviour suggested – with the express commission to make progress in shipbuilding. The mood of the trip seems frank and cordial – a successful compact concluded between the two great nations of beefeaters in the nineteenth century, the Zulus and the Georgians. The Shakan heartland is abundantly productive, well defended and highly organized. In the event the shipbuilding is protracted for two and a half years. Trashy and meretricious knickknacks are left behind to work their effect.

The effect, King would seem to be saying, is almost instantaneous. For only a 'few beads' more, even before they can return to the Bay, they have the nucleus of their own herd of cattle and 'two lads', the most loyal of servants . . . who devote themselves to little Maclean's service on the turn.

We must now consider how Maclean himself varies and extends King's story. In his first insertion (the paragraph beginning 'As a proof of Shaka's sentiments and concern for us . . .') we again come across one of Maclean's throw-aways: his subsequent status with Shaka himself. This casual mention advances the narrative with one huge bound: he is not only to meet King Shaka but become his confidant. He is to have a Zulu nickname, Jackabo, or little Jack. Shaka is to confide in him his feelings about the superiority of the whites, which Maclean the child must have been under considerable pressure to be an example of. There is a mirror image of King George's seafarers: to the Zulus, in the wonderfully hyperbolic way of their praises, they have the altogether dubious honour of being considered 'wild beasts'!

What is more, this insertion tells us with all the superior knowledge of hindsight that the Zulu kingdom is by no means monolithic; in fact, it is riven by distinctions of class. Shaka the royal may disagree with his council, who in turn may not be representative of the opinion of the 'common man' – here we have an all too rare glimpse into the Zulu polity where many opinions are entertained about how best to handle the British incursion. The success or failure of the

British venture is thus entirely dependent on Shaka's personal policy holding sway, and to him the British have to prove endlessly fascinating.

Maclean's second insertion (the long passage beginning 'The many sanguinary conflicts carried on between the Colonists and the Caffres on the frontiers, in which the latter were constantly and signally defeated . . .') connects up with his opening paragraphs in Instalment One and is written from his point of view of 1853. Here Maclean does not mince his words, his rhetoric sounding more familiar to modern ears than in many other passages.

His interpretation of the frontier wars as they have occurred meanwhile between the invading Trekkers and the Caffres in the contact zone is couched in terms of the abolitionists' cause. For border skirmishes we have 'many sanguinary conflicts'; for commando activity and retaliatory raids we have 'barbarities reciprocal and terrific'; in place of cordiality and friendship we now have 'atrocities'. Maclean even slips into calling the Caffres 'Aborigines' facing 'extermination'. We are tipped off to remember that the hands-off cause of the Aborigines Protection Society and the Anti-Slavery lobby in Britain were one and the same. Of the primarily Trekker wars of conquest in southern Natal Maclean has this to conclude:

> . . . many years of kind treatment will be required to blot out the atrocities perpetrated by people professing the doctrines of Christianity, that are not paralleled in the records of the most barbarous nations.

This hefty and dextrously delivered indictment dispenses with the practice of both the Trekkers and the warlike missionaries like Kay in the Transkei at one go.

Maclean's resultant advice to the British Colonial Office to exercise 'the strictest surveillance' in order 'to prevent the same abuses from being introduced into Natal' is, however, way off the mark. He seems to be unaware that, with Shepstone's location policy underway in the British areas of Natal by 1853, considerable dispossession of tracts of Zulu-held territory had occurred and that the might-over-right activity of rendering the 'original proprietors' into plantation labour on their very own ground had already made considerable and irreversible progress. His appeal to the superior power could only have fallen on deaf ears.

We are left in this instalment with a final detail about which subsequent writers have made far too much: the quaint invention that so vain was Shaka as he spotted a 'grey hair' in his beard in his first mirror that he would sell out his kingdom for a bottle of hair-dye – specifically Rowland's Macassar Oil, a cheap vanity preparation first brought onto the market from Indonesia by the

English East India Company. Today 'macassar oil' is better known as ylang-ylang, the basis of most perfume. King, ever the opportunist, sells this cosmetic preparation in the most inflated terms as a 'medicine' (read juju) that could 'prevent . . . effects of increasing years' – let us say, as the very elixir of longevity. Even a historian as sober as Leonard Thompson as late as 1969 cannot decode this detail: on p. 350 of *A History of South Africa to 1870* (Philip reprint, 1982), he deduces from this that Shaka 'seems to have become morbidly concerned about his health. The most urgent order he gave to King when he left on his embassy was to procure macassar oil, a hair tonic which he understood would rejuvenate him.' And Shaka was only in his late thirties and obviously in superb physical condition.

As aggressive white colonial writers were ever happy to stress the superstitious and gullible nature of 'heathens' and their credulity of witchcraft, it is only fair to redress the balance by pointing out that Maclean sees King posing as a great wizard here. His offer is, after all, only of that ultimate magic the missionaries will offer them in turn – the dubious guarantee of eternal life.

But Maclean sees this strategy for what it is – the trader's creation of 'artificial wants.' White man's magic, he seems to be concluding, is devilishly potent. Zululand must have been an extremely frustrating place to trade in, for the Zulus lacked no essentials which Europe could provide. Vanity preparations would have to serve.

The real issue is not hair-oil. It is emphatically, as Maclean sees clearly, a contest over the procedures and values of trade. The arrangement between the two Kings was businesslike.

Six

This central instalment is the longest. It briefly advances the main story by describing the urgency with which shipbuilding commences. While the 'little settlement' at Townsend fells timber and begins construction, many curious tribespeople are attracted to the scene, displaying a touristic glee going over the hulk of the *Mary*. Surely this is one of Maclean's most memorable passages. This encounter between the visiting locals and King's party phases into

Maclean's more general survey of all he came to know of the Zulus. His sub-title here might aptly have been 'A Description of the Zulu People', which will continue from here into the next instalment.

In general the tone of Maclean's account may be described in modern terms as more 'anthropological' than 'ethnological': that is, his evidence is gathered at first hand for the sake of its interest and information, and seems devoid of any racist theorizing. Mercifully, we are not in for any of the sensationalism, voyeurism or prurient indiscretions to which the more aggressively ethnological mode has made us accustomed in other accounts (Isaacs's and Kay's, for example). Maclean's account is devoid of that sense of difference, of othering for the sake of detraction, for as we shall later learn he is intent on keeping the Zulus very much within the family of man.

Where he compares his subjects to Europeans, this is often in a flattering way. His attitude is generally admiring and appreciative; his humour is genial, certainly not exercised at his subjects' expense. If anything, his sense of comedy is a very contemporary one, underlining genuinely absurd incongruities, as in the unforgettable passage dealing with the Zulu interpretations of the gaudy and fulsome figurehead of the *Mary*.

Early in the instalment he establishes the reverse view on the Zulus' part of the traders: that their ship is a 'wild beast that lived in the ocean' (Bryant, p. 582, gives 'sillwana' or 'isilwane' as iziLokozana, meaning beasts of the sea, or really deleterious animals). To the Zulus they are:

> a species of amphibious animals that lived within it. *At first* they imagined our clothes grew on our backs, that our flesh was soft and pulpy like that of an oyster or shell-fish, until they had convinced themselves by pinching it between their fingers and thumb that it was flesh and blood *like their own*, differing only in colour. (my italics)

We are set up to read what follows as a process of overcoming first impressions and familiarizing ourselves with − getting to know − his subjects. Of pinching, as a method of verification. This is not differencing at work, but overcoming difference.

Maclean's account of Zulu home economy and industry stresses the idyllic and pastoral rather more than the military aspect of his acquaintances. The Mathubanes volunteer to help, and are not coerced; nor is there a formal arrangement of payment in 'beads and trinkets' in exchange for work done. *Laissez-faire* is the policy on which all behaviour is based here, although the blacks themselves are by no means unacquainted with labour (pottery-making, smelting).

Incidentally, here is another indication of how out of touch Maclean is with later South Africa. He uses the words kraal and assegai, which by 1820 were entering the English vocabulary from the Portugese and Arabic respectively, but seems not to know the term knobkierie (for knob-stick) which was absorbed later from the Khoi and Dutch.

Maclean observes that:

> The general appearance of the natives of this part of the coast of Eastern Africa is so favourable, and particularly of the Zulus, who are a well made, robust, muscular and powerful race of men, perfectly devoid of the characteristic features that distinguish the African negro, that really with the exception of the colour of the skin they might justly rank with the most perfect European.

Writing in 1853, Maclean is pre-Darwin. Although he uses the term 'evolution', this is with no biological determinism in mind. Nor is he cursed with any later imperial ideology about nature red in tooth and claw and the survival of the fittest. His gaze is rather the seafarer's who has in mind a rudimentary and unfortunate stereotype of other African negroes as lethargic and submissive. Truly, this is the brutish heritage of the epoch of slavery. Athleticism and a healthy disposition, intelligence and a capacity for endurance – these compel admiration, and contest the ideals of the European. 'Manly', 'bold', 'dignified' – these adjectives recur.

Maclean's description of the Zulu way of life suggests that the roles of 'herdsman and warrior', among the men at least, are interchangeable, not yet distinctly separated into specialization. He stresses this point, with substantial evidence, throughout his description. This record is a profoundly different one from the picture given by later writers like George McCall Theal, for example, who in his book *The History of the Boers in South Africa* (1887) works up the Shakan Zulu polity as having been no more than a perpetual war-machine, a holocaust of blood-letting aggression. Theal's distortions become the basis of his 'mfecane' theory, which posits such extensive and lurid vortices of destructive, and even self-obliterating, action on the part of the Zulus in the 1820s that white usurpation of their power was not only inevitable, but morally necessary.

In Maclean none of this is so, and anyone still believing in the so-called mfecane will find precious little evidence of it here. The Zulu men's double personality – herdsman-warrior – is rooted in the seasons, suggesting a culture that could balance the two modes of existence; indeed, Maclean mentions this in his closing paragraph.

The description of the hyena hunt gives us a further future glimpse of what Maclean's life at Shaka's domain, attended by his two faithful lads, will be like. If the spoils of this shambolic affair were a mere three hyenas, that rather puts paid to the records of massive game-drives and wholesale slaughters Fynn and Isaacs indulge in. Maclean's point is that the Zulus themselves were inept at hunting and left it to others. The white traders, of course, were the monumental harvesters of Zululand's wildlife, and the elephant hunts mentioned later seem conducted in their honour in payment of debts.

The Zulu lore of the road is always an enchanting topic, which no traveller fails to comment on favourably. The courtesies of greeting and the ceremony of snuff-taking, whereby news is interchanged, give us an insight into a decorous and ceremonial society openly welcoming to 'strangers'. Not only cattle are the Zulu's riches, Maclean explains, but people. This seems a community in which it is a pleasure for the individual to exist.

Maclean never omits reference to the Zulus' military campaigns, and he will also when he approaches Dukuza be thunderstruck by a landscape of 'bleaching bones' and piles of human skulls. But here he says:

> Their fondness for their herds . . . would argue that they have been long a pastoral race, and that warlike enterprise has only emanated from the ambition of their chiefs, *not with the view of enlarging their territory by conquest*, but to enrich themselves with the cattle of their neighbours. (my italics)

Thus we have to revise much of the thinking that is automatically triggered by describing Shaka in conventional European imperialist terms. To label him the 'Napoleon of East Africa' (as Maclean does, quoting King, in Instalment Five) is inappropriate, for it projects onto him a European notion of the aggressive and antagonistic empire-builder. The name Napoleon, after all, to Maclean and his party, meant the land-hungry tyrant whose ambitions had affected the life and career of each and every one of them, and which it had taken the combined might of the British to defeat. Farewell and King were veterans of the Napoleonic wars at sea, and even Isaacs had been bundled out of London to the safety of Saint Helena before the villainous emperor was compelled to follow him into exile there. Shaka was no Napoleon, in Maclean's book. He was more a cattle-rustler supreme.

Maclean's Zululand thus far is a men's society. Nandi, Shaka's mother, supposedly the tyrannous matriarch who in other accounts is elevated to the stature of a vengeful Clytemnestra or Medea via Lady Macbeth, receives from Maclean but two mentions in passing. Other tribes of Caffres are distinguished from the Zulus by their attitudes to women, but in the true Zulu world women are confined to the domestic sphere, literally as hewers of wood and drawers of water. One extraordinary case of a woman's individuality is to come, however, and in the subsequent instalment the balance of Maclean's attention is redressed.

Maclean's account of the issue of religion/superstition among the Zulus is especially devoid of differencing. He observes that 'it is now pretty generally known that there are no people, however rude or barbarous, who have not some sort of religious notion. . . .' Would that this knowledge had become more prevalent after 1853, for it is on this issue that commentators really move into gear. For example, here is an irresistible quote from the sober R.C. Samuelson (in *Long Long Ago*, 1929) describing the role of abathakathi in Zulu society: 'They have no redeeming point about them, and are a counterpart to Bolshevists, Nihilists, Socialists and labourite communists' (p.293).

Isaacs' and Fynn's accounts of the Zulu faith start the process of denigration and are filled with an attitude of repugnance. Maclean writes far more as an insider, understanding the meaning and function of ancestor-worship, propitiatory animal sacrifice and healing rituals. When he comes to fatally loaded words like 'Evil One', 'Soothsayer' and 'Witch finder', he is scrupulous to give the Zulu terms, suggesting that there are no real English equivalents. Unlike Isaacs and Fynn, who are only too eager to deduce dubious pedigrees from these practices, Maclean resorts to a rather batty mystical view of 'successive evolutions of an extended series', and concedes that he does not know their origins.

Religious practice, in Maclean's account, is inextricably bound in with the oral culture of 'old men [who] take a pleasure in raking up the memory of the past'. Maclean mentions only one Zulu creation myth. Would that he had given us a fuller record of the performance of fireside epics that encoded both Zulu 'history' and 'tradition', and to which he was such a privileged witness. They are lost to us.

Indeed, as Maclean notes, they were becoming lost to the Zulus even then as the charismatic Shaka transformed their heritage into the new organization, incorporating all agglomerations of the past in his own praises.

The footnote inserted at the end of this instalment by the editor of *The Nautical Magazine* by chance throws up many vital issues and must be read as grimly ironic. Later we learn that Maclean was not in London in July 1853, when these events occurred, and the note was added to his text without his knowledge.

If in Zululand in the 1820s the whites were the great tourist draw, now by 1853 Zulu representatives in London have been turned into a living exhibition in the hands of the Natal entrepreneur, Mr Caldecott. Their praises are no longer made in honour of their own rulers, but of the great white Inkosikazi herself. She and her family attend their tribute and display of 'peculiar dances and evolutions' – not in their palace, but in the riding school . . . and Her Majesty's stables are all the Zulus are shown of the Empress' seat of power. Of course Maclean on their behalf was insulted at the tone of the advertisement and alarmed how power had so changed hands thirty years on.

We may digress here to consider one popular reaction to the exhibition of Caldecott's Zulu troupe at the Saint George's Gallery, Hyde Park. The reporter is Charles Dickens:

> What a visitor left to his own interpretings and imaginings might suppose these noblemen to be about, when they give vent to that pantomime expression which is quite settled to be the natural gift of the noble savage, I cannot possibly conceive; for it is so much too luminous for my personal civilisation that it conveys no idea to my mind beyond a general stamping, ramping, and raving, remarkable (as everything in savage life is) for its dire uniformity. But let us – with the interpreter's assistance, of which I for one stand so much in need – see what the noble savage does in Zulu Kaffirland.
>
> The noble savage sets a king to reign over him, to whom he submits his life and limbs without a murmur or question, and whose whole life is passed chin deep in a lake of blood; but who, after killing incessantly, is in turn killed by his relations and friends, the moment a grey hair appears on his head. All the noble savage's wars with his fellow-savages (and he takes no pleasure in anything else) are wars of extermination – which is the best thing I know of him, and the most comfortable to my mind when I look at him. He has no moral feelings of any kind, sort, or description; and his 'mission' may be summed up as simply diabolical. . . . The world will be all the better when his place knows him no more (pp. 107–8, 111).

When Maclean catches up on the impact of the Zulu exhibition of July, 1853 (in his Instalment Ten of February, 1855) we may fully understand that his response is intense. He must then have interrupted his pre-written text after the description of his party's first night at Dukuza to insert the most heartfelt words of his serial:

> What a change has now come over the land of the Zulu. The white man thus designated now rules his country, and it is no great prophetic stretch to say that the whole Zulu race will soon disappear before him, as the snow melts before the sun.

(His passionate direct address of warning to the Zulu people follows.)

To Maclean in 1855 the concept of the 'white man thus designated' is a novelty. In his own narrative he never uses the term 'white' to describe himself and has no sense of 'black' (he uses 'sable'). The very metaphor describing the Zulus as 'snow' poised to be melted before the imperial sun shows his complete lack of colour consciousness, for surely 'snow' is to any English-speaker the very epitome of whiteness.

To Dickens and the new generation Zulu savages are 'black', in all senses of the word. And to be exterminated for that reason.

SEVEN

Maclean's 'Description of the Zulu People', written before his return to London with his chart and his four final instalments, continues here with his attention given to the womenfolk, their physique, their role as child-bearers and tillers and their 'bouyancy of disposition'. Read by anyone who had seen the Dickens account it would have appeared most contrasting.

But the major part of this brief and exquisite instalment is the 'incident' he recounts in illustration of 'the extent and warmth of affection and gratitude of which they are so susceptible, and rarely equalled, in the history of civilized life'. The story of Dommana – her years of liaison with Mr Hutton – is far more revealing than that, and his most passionate passage yet.

Dommana's story is one of surprising chivalry between the traders and the indigenes and (one guesses) of deeply romantic love. In our literature, which has such taboos against the depiction of inter-ethnic personal transactions, certainly there is no other example like it dating from the nineteenth century. Here we have a tale that is unique in its sympathy and its power to engage our heartstrings. It is well told, too, with an orderly hold on dramatic power, a firm perspective and a wonderfully understated end.

Mr Hutton, the first mate, with his 'broad axe' – this doughty Yorkshire forester – we must now see as transformed into a romantic hero rescuing the heroine in distress. The incident of woman-bashing he witnesses, perpetrated by a Mathubane father who has already beaten his wife to death, is hideous enough. Hutton's intervention, at first, is charitable, and all condemn the man.

But as the poor eighteen-year-old daughter attaches herself to her saviour in perpetual devotion, crossing over from her people, more seems to be at stake than her gratitude. Indeed, her removal from her village with the consent of many of her friends to enjoy the company of an honourable man seems to suggest a marriage took place between them. In the light of Maclean's earlier description of gifts being exchanged in such a compact as 'indemnity to the parents for the loss of their daughter's services', the 'receiving of a small present in beads' seems to settle the deal satisfactorily between her father and Hutton.

We may smile at the role allotted to Dommana in the trader's society, in which Maclean has just remarked women are held superior to men. Dommana, an eager pupil, is instructed as a washerwoman. However, as it is time for all hands to the deck of the new *Mary*, we need not suppose that any of the men hung about Townsend dockyard in a state of inactivity. The community continued to operate in this industrious way for another two and a half years.

So Dommana's knightly 'protector' dies . . . and seeing that there is no life left to her, four days later she follows him, suiciding through grieving. The one is buried beside the other . . . in an unmarked grave at the foot of the modern Prospect Hill, where today only King's gravestone is commemorated. Besides being a stirring example of devotion, Dommana's story would have become legendary had the Shakan alliance come into being. Hutton and Dommana are the first lover-martyrs of that new Natal.

One senses Maclean's deep-seated grieving as well. 'Having also myself been a favourite with her in her recent happy days', he writes, even he is unable to rally the heartstricken woman to remain in the land of the living. Hutton, the individual, was her life.

Maclean veers off from this into a now-familiar anti-slavery tack, which we may read as his attempt at writing devoted Dommana's obituary. Alone and stranded, he is losing Hutton as well, who surely had been the young Maclean's benefactor. Maclean had also found another father figure, Shaka, who treated him as a child of his own and who was dead, too, as was his employer, King. All these losses burst out in Maclean as one overwhelming conviction: African bonds of 'affection' (he repeats the word) are an object lesson to European civilization. His cry from the core of his being is against all that is 'fiendish and revolting to humanity'; he means the way Europeans have treated Africans in history, not the other way round.

Isaacs is useful for dating here. He mentions Hutton's death (without a hint of any of the Dommana story) as having occurred after the death of King, just before the few remainders of the party finally departed for Algoa Bay in

October–December, 1828. Thus Hutton's burial is the deepest point in the chronology which Maclean covers.

Once the reader has let the impact of Maclean's anti-slavery outcry die down and come to terms with the powerful Dommana story, he or she should perhaps ponder why in 1853 Maclean still located all his anguish on the key phrase, 'African slavery'. Certainly in his youth he was familiar with the slaveholding of the Cape and all its ports. With his Zulu bodyguard he had escaped it at Delagoa Bay, then still one of the most active exporters of human cargo on the East coast, catering to the vessels of over a dozen different nations. Certainly also he was situated at the tail end of a trade which over three centuries had been responsible for the biggest forced removal in human history – the transportation under compulsion of no less than twenty-one million Africans from their homes.

There are two answers to this question. Firstly, Maclean himself did not feel that emancipation meant that the system of slavery had disappeared overnight. He was of the school that saw colonial expansionism as a refinement of the old system into new capitalist-inspired procedures that would merely enslave Africans by other methods. Secondly, with emancipation the old slave system did not necessarily come to an end outside the area of British control, or even within it. His own colleague, Nathaniel Isaacs, is the living proof. Having failed to institute or revive slavedealing at Port Natal or thereabouts, Isaacs succeeded in setting up a stockade for the Atlantic slave trade on Matacong Island off Sierra Leone, which functioned successfully right until his retirement in 1869, four years before his death. To us the impact of slavery on the history of early Natal may remain a closed book, but we may certainly understand the fiery urge behind Maclean's crusade.

The important detail to remember from Dommana's tale is that Dommana was no slave, nor was Hutton her master. She was not cast out on his demise, either. On the contrary, she was 'laid by his side in the same cold bed of death', which is surely the ultimate statement of their equality.

Christian burial, then, both for her and her lover. This is the new way, more humane than previous ways, including being left to be 'devoured by birds and wild animals'.

Their memory is immortal, his record of their life and tragic death an unexpected classic of its kind.

Eight

The remaining four instalments of Maclean's serial take us in one grand and accumulating sweep to the climax of the work, with its final and extraordinary twist. The material is arranged as follows: Eight: the journey of the leftovers of the King party towards Dukuza; Nine: their arrival at King Shaka's capital; Ten: their reception and interview by Shaka; and Eleven: the surprise reversal and upshot.

As Maclean has already summarized King's account of his journey, he need now give only the highlights of the trip made by the second half of the party. By comparison their delegation is less equipped, and they are in for a wearying trudge. The beach of the first day 'completely knocked me up', he says. Then comes one of the most memorable observations about himself being 'no great burden to my sable friend' who 'shouldered' him. We suddenly see a ten-year-old child with blistered feet, piggybacked by his willing bearer, the alternative being to be 'left by the way'. Maclean's Zulu guides and escorts porter him in turn. What a vivid image of the defenceless tot embarking on his great and dreaded adventure.

Further details are to be added to this self-portrait in due course (although it would seem incidentally) – his oversunburnt skin, his red hair. Maclean is physically of that distinctive Northern type unsuited to the subtropical summer, and suffers accordingly. Also, rather than a hardy adolescent, he is indeed a little mite if at this stage he weighs hardly more than the regular equipment of the 'rawboned fellows'.

Here Maclean emphasizes the hospitality of the conquered zone between the Port Natal sphere of influence and the mountains which are 'the boundary of Zulu territory proper'. We have 'good things and hospitality', as well received as 'the grateful shade of trees'. As a matter of pride, he duly insists on hobbling along, 'and struggled manfully to keep pace with my more robust ship-mates'.

Maclean's humorous paragraph about how willy-nilly he became the 'lion of the party', the star curiosity in the European's parade, is rather a give-away. Far from being self-indulgent – in fact, we may be delighted at the all too rare lapse in his reticence – this revelation is important to his theme of growing up among the Zulus as a learning process. At first he is resentful of the pinching and poking, but then he learns to submit to it. Having no alternative, he makes the best of it, turning his physical disadvantages to his own gain. The forthcoming incident where he is generously over-burdened with gifts more than he can carry as a 'mark of friendship and peace', wonderfully exaggerated, shows that he is learning to use his curiosity value, become his own man. We can feel the outcome; it is there in the warmth with which he writes.

Maclean's first regimental cattle-fold of the Fasimba age-set is a neat illustration of how the careers of herdsman and of warrior are combined in the Shakan social system. Wright and Hamilton in their chapter in *Natal and Zululand* are surely correct in identifying the amabutho system of male age-sets as 'designed as much to underpin the tenuous hold on political power of the Zulu rulers as to increase the efficacy of the force at their command: it was both an instrument of internal social control and a means of external defence' (p. 69). Similarly, Shaka's isigodlo establishment at Dukuza controls the resources of women to the benefit of the dynasty. Maclean gives extensive details of both organizations

Although Wright and Hamilton do not use Maclean as a source, there is no detail in his account of how the Zulu royals had so recently established themselves and maintained their control over the evolving polity that does not serve to corroborate their reconstruction. Their stress on trade routes within Zululand having been long established and influential in building royal privilege also coincides with Maclean's view. After all, while Shaka's porters are lugging our hero to the palace, they are also bearing a great prize – the ship's medicine chest – for the king's exclusive use.

What also emerges from the details he gives of the Zulu occupation of this territory is the scornful behaviour exercised by the conquerors over their subject people. There is much confirmation of the view that the Zulu hierarchy had to maintain itself by force: we have phrases like 'military despotism' and 'desolating wars' to describe the source of Shaka's sway. The piteous lot of the Maphisi 'remnants' is described in detail.

Here Maclean gives a key moral justification for the trader's presence: 'Our Zulu guides threatened these poor people very unceremoniously, and we had to interpose our authority to restrain them from committing acts of cruelty on these unoffending people.' Details like these serve to build up Maclean's case against the missionary view of the trader-adventurers. In miniature this comment substantiates Maclean's fuller claim, that he was able to intervene and persuade Shaka himself to be more merciful, which justifies their role in Zulu affairs.

By dropping phrases like 'I had occasion on one of my journeys to the interior' in the context of a description of hippopotamus hunting, or giving us generalized mention of future elephant hunting ('a most exciting and interesting spectacle'), Maclean is also letting us infer the end of his story before he gets there. We learn this route will become more than familiar to him in future. These are but hints, for at present he wishes to keep us in suspense about the success of this opening venture.

The descriptive details accumulate. We have techniques of the 'manufacture of native cloth from the ox hide', the use of the honey-bird in locating sweetness. The honey-bird description we may take as more than interesting natural history. This is like a parable, for the vagarious bird may lead the searcher to a reward or to sudden death. Maclean's message is: learn to trust. He faces the ultimate gamble, the judgement of his fate in Shaka's hands.

The weight of these descriptions builds up to his second polemic against Kay. Here he gives a far more systematic defence of the trader's position and in a far clearer way than previously.

This time the issue hinges on the rather dubious subject of magic/medicine – Farewell's accomplishment of a cure in the case which the Zulus had dismissed as hopeless. Whether the incident occurred as Maclean describes it, and as Farewell had previously informed him or not, we shall never know. But what is not in doubt is that the traders gave themselves out not only as merciful interventionists, but as workers of miracle cures. The key item in this party's baggage is the medicine chest of the *Mary*, with which Maclean will be entrusted. Medical wonders, then, are a humane and pragmatic way of presenting the message of 'civilization'. No surprise, then, that when all else is lost to them, Maclean has to make his dramatic dash to Maputo for medicines. (The terrible casualty rate amongst the traders must have disillusioned the Zulus somewhat on the score of European cures.)

The process of commercial colonization Kay refers to in Stout is of more than passing interest. Maclean seems not to be very familiar with the work of Stout, who is dismissed as 'an American writer'. Maclean accepts Kay's summary of Stout at face value. They are both referring to Captain Benjamin Stout of the American East-Indiaman *Hercules*, wrecked on the coast of Caffraria (at what is now known as Ciskei's Hamburg) as early as 1796. In 1820 Stout published his *Cape of Good Hope and Dependencies* in London, to cash in on popular versions of his account of the loss of the *Hercules* which had circulated in pamphlets stressing the awesome difficulties he and his crew experienced and his wonderful escape.

Stout's sub-title is instructive: *An Accurate and Truly Interesting Description of those Delightful Regions, Situated Five Hundred Miles North of the Cape, formerly in Possession of the Dutch, but lately Ceded to the Crown of England; and Which are to be Colonized, with every Possible Despatch, under the Authority of the British Government by Agriculturalists and Artificers of Every Denomination from the United Kingdom of Great Britain and Ireland.* As if this were not explicit enough, Stout appended *A Luminous and Affecting Detail of Captain Stout's Travels through the Deserts of Caffraria and the Christian Settlements to the Cape.*

Maclean is indeed writing directly in this line of yarning seafarers' eye-witness accounts of life-and-death experience. Stout's work was intended to serve as an inspiration to recruiters of British emigrants of 1820; similarly, Maclean's account offers advice on settlement in Natal some thirty years later. Stout warmly stresses Transkeian hospitality and amenability as propitious factors and goes on to the extent of proposing an entire scheme of penetration and settlement; Maclean, in stressing the same factors, but later on in the history, intends to bring matters back to the original scheme, blocking missionary interference. The only essential difference between them is their nationality – Stout's appeal is addressed to the Honourable John Adams, President of the Continental Congress of the United States of America, no less. Stout proposed an American slave-holding colony in Caffraria; Maclean would have been appalled.

Maclean's demolition job of Kay is explicit enough here. We may enjoy his ironic disclaimer, 'though I may not possess his descriptive powers, I have not been an idle observer of what was passing around me'. He is reacting with his own formidable pen against Kay's inimical theory, once again revising speculation in the light of experienced evidence.

He is also – oh noble thought – using the opportunity to celebrate the praises of Farewell the trader. His vindication is the epitaph of one on whom the grave might otherwise long have closed.

Isaacs' own account of this trip to Dukuza (in his Chapter 5) is so different from Maclean's that the contrast must give us pause. Making no mention of their having been summoned to appear before Shaka, Isaacs claims that the party started out to retrieve several tons of ivory Farewell had secreted away in a cache on the Thukela, and that the sixty porters were by then Isaacs' own. He then diverts to the imperial kraal for no particular reason other than to witness a mass of criminal executions! (Maclean says there were only three.)

Furthermore, Isaacs gives himself Farewell's one-eyed Rosinante which King had previously borrowed, which promptly dies under his weight. Then Isaacs co-opts one of Farewell's oxen which he would have us believe roamed freely over that intermediate land ceded by Shakan treaty to Farewell.

This contrasting version is but one instance of how drastically the Isaacs and Maclean accounts differ, often beyond all recognition. We may fruitlessly speculate on why this is so. Isaacs wrote a full seventeen years closer to the event and in the form of a diary kept at the time, while Maclean kept no records then (indeed, at that tender age was hardly likely to have done) and now writes at a far remove. Whose version is correct? Which must be discredited as a dissembler?

The Fynn records, at least in the published version, cannot reliably be called in to mediate, as we know his *Diary* is edited with Isaacs as ur-text. Alas, instead of correcting Kay, Maclean never set his sights on the one who seems to need adjustment most – Isaacs.

However, the relative veracity of both accounts seems to be a spurious issue at best. We must accept that quantities of fiction occur both in Isaacs and in Maclean. Their intentions differ, that is all. Isaacs is a self-aggrandizer wishing to illustrate what a push-over pioneering in Zululand was; Maclean is rather more self-effacing and pro-Zulu, wishing to express his doubts about the ease with which the Zulus were to be brought to heel. Thus, where Isaacs underplays the impact of the approach to Dukuza on him, to the extent of hardly mentioning it at all, for Maclean it is the most impressive and awe-inspiring sequence of his life. Where Isaacs is the shod and mounted swashbuckler, Maclean is his opposite – a barefooted pilgrim approaching in awed supplication.

Nine

Although our reading of *Loss of the Brig 'Mary'* is not touched by the following, it is as well to note here that for its original readers Maclean's serial was interrupted at this point and for the second time. Instalments One to Seven had appeared on time throughout 1853 in Volume 22 of *The Nautical Magazine* from the January issue through to the August (with only the May missing, but there was no May issue that year). Instalment Eight skipped out the September and October issues, to appear in the one for November.

Why Instalment Eight was held over by two months is readily established. In a piece dated Ship *Gilbert Munro*, West India Docks, 26 October 1853, which Maclean wrote for *The Shipping and Mercantile Gazette*, he gives a highly detailed account of a hurricane experienced on the ship's latest passage to London. This summary of his captain's log is intended as a contribution to the newspaper's debate about the lore of hurricanes and the usefulness of the new aneroid barometer in serving sailing ships to predict such onslaughts. The *Gilbert Munro* was hit early in September and limped into port at least a month behind schedule. In his piece Maclean praises not only the instruments of science but the epic 'energy and zeal' of his officers and crew, to which he characteristically attributes the 'preservation of the ship'. We may infer either that Maclean was writing his serial on board and had every reason to have missed his deadline, or that, if the instalment had previously been completed, he could not hand over the copy for the same reason.

This present instalment slips a bit further along, however, for no detectable reason, until the first issue of Volume 23 in January 1854. Then, between there and Instalments Ten and Eleven, a further really aggravated delay occurs, as *The Nautical Magazine's* readers have to wait over a year (until February and March 1855) for their final instalments. After the publication of Instalment Nine, the long silence from Maclean is punctuated only by his hopeful editor in the column of notes to correspondents: in October 1854, '. . . in our next text the continuation of the "Recollections from Natal" will appear' (p. 568); and then in November 1854: 'We hope to resume our "Recollections of Natal" in our next issue' (p. 624). When the serial does at last recommence, it is prefaced with a note: 'This has been suspended on account of the absence of the author, but we hope it will now be continued to its conclusion. – Ed.' Maclean gives no recorded reason for his failure to deliver.

The lapses are all the more curious because the last four instalments are very much all of a piece. The present instalment takes up directly where the previous one left off, and so on to the very end. They were obviously jointly planned and the continuity of argument and incident suggests an uninterrupted focus in the composition. Yet Maclean's commercial life saw to it that he was not in London to deliver his material on time, suggesting to us that, although conditions for writing his memoirs were less than ideal, he was under considerable pressure to get them down. (His further two serials for *The Nautical Magazine* were clearly pre-written in their entirety, so that contingencies of the wind and weather could not intervene. But in this one he is still a beginner at organizing an account which demanded more scope and extension than he was able to give it.)

In the instalment at hand, however, Maclean reaches new rhetorical heights as he continues to neutralize Kay. His sermon is a secular one, delivered with a fine control of invective. 'I cannot be silent,' he exclaims, developing his thrust to the extraordinary revelations of his climax.

We soon see that his saving of the reputation of Farewell (in the previous instalment) was but a prelude to clear the decks, as it were, for the far more difficult task of saving the reputation of Shaka. If we accept Maclean's reading of the first man, so his reasoning goes, how can we not accept his reading of the second?

In Kay's account the portrait given of Shaka is far more repulsive and cruel than Maclean leads us to believe. No wonder Maclean is so furious. Kay's Shaka is 'this inhuman being', this 'monster' full of 'murderous schemes', against whom in the end 'the revengeful feelings of his long-oppressed people burst forth with overwhelming fury, and suddenly put an end to their bloody

King' (p.404). None of this – Maclean states – could be further from the truth.

Kay's text is at the head of a long line of aspersive literature on the subject of Shaka which we need not go into here, but which it is worth mentioning luridly and fantastically persists with its character assassination as a legend of extraordinary tenacity and power, even today. It is white history at its worst.

Isaacs, interestingly enough, also takes on Kay, furiously rebutting his portrayal of Farewell and King as blood-drenched bandits, detail by detail. But when it comes to Kay on Shaka, Isaacs does a complete turn-around. He quotes the same passages as Maclean, not only letting them go uncontested, but approving them. Thus, on the issue of Shaka, Isaacs takes sides with Kay against the Maclean view, and the negative version of the Zulu king's life and personality becomes reinforced. Maclean's counter-version – his passionate corrective – when it finally emerged made no impact on any later writers. The Dickens view prevails today.

All Maclean can do to forestall the Kay fantasy version is hold up two key examples and reply that, if these are the evidence, the evidence is false. There was no 'massacre of innocents', for a start. Nor did Shaka kill husbands in his own troops in order to ravish their wives! . . . Maclean's rebuttals are firm and clear.

For us the stongest antidote of all is his climactic declaration:

> I have just remarked that I had extraordinary privileges. I may add more, that I had extraordinary power and influence with the savage chief. Mine, indeed, was a strange destiny. . . .

And then he explains the truth, that Shaka was prepared to listen even to the red-headed 'youth' who had been welcomed at his hearth, and who sat by his side. The effect is very revealing of how that Shakan alliance worked, and of his fondness for the little mlungu, Jackabo.

The 'biographical memoir of Shaka' is mentioned again as a separate text, but now Maclean comments that it 'may never meet the public eye.' However, we have here as if in preview of that memoir two observations that indeed upset the whole apple-cart of studies of the Shakan period: that Shaka had a compact of succession with his younger half-brother, Dingane, and that he wished none of his heirs to be placed to disrupt this. Other shreds and scraps that Maclean lets drop are sufficient to lead us to believe that the story of Shaka needs to be revindicated from scratch.

After the fireworks of his anti-clerical philippic, Maclean wisely lets his anger subside to resume the threads of his narrative. Wisely, he lets his story carry our emotions further. The boy dressing up with his carefully preserved 'clean frock and pair of ducks' over his ragged gear, their cresting the mountains of Bulawayo (killing-place), facing magnificent Dukuza (the hide-away) in the wildest 'grandeur.' The reference he makes to his 'brave companions of the sea', raptly viewing the spectacle with him, is from Carlyle: 'Providence has given to the French the empire of the land, to the English that of the sea. . . .'

So, patriotically, the 'king's wild beasts' enter into the heart of Zulu power.

It is early December, 1825 – coincidentally in time for that year's Festival of the First-fruits.

(At this climactic moment the serial went into abeyance for the next thirteen months.)

Ten

Although it appeared over a year later, in February 1855, this instalment continues directly from the previous one. The footnote which gives Maclean's response to the editor's attachment to Instalment Six of the advertisement about the Zulu exhibition in London appears now.

Maclean's next note about the Wilmington incident also has everything to do with the point of his serial. Essentially this note is an abbreviated summary of the more extensive report which did indeed appear in *The Anti-Slavery Reporter*. The issue of Friday 1 May 1846 contains this piece, headlined 'The Liberty of British Subjects Invaded in the United States'. Drawn from Maclean's even more detailed 'narrative' submitted to the Lieutenant-Governor, dated 'Brig *Susan King*, Saint Lucia, 24 February, 1846', the report gives key passages of his protest and complaint to the Colonial Authorities about conditions for British seamen in the *antebellum* South. *The Anti-Slavery Reporter* took the opportunity to publicize excerpts, saluting Captain Maclean as a man of 'firmness'.

Maclean, it seems, intended to precipitate a showdown at Wilmington about the treatment of his black crew. Here is his speech to the U.S. harbour authorities:

Gentlemen, the laws of my country happily make no distinctions in the colour of the skin; my men are free subjects of her Britannic Majesty; and what a libel (I fearlessly said) it is when you call this a free country! what a profanation of the sacred word LIBERTY! . . . these men are free British subjects, and I am their employer, and consider myself also their protector; and I am resolved to dispute their being taken from under the protection of that flag (pointing to the British ensign at our peak) without a cause. You are in reality making war on the liberty of British subjects when you would incarcerate us in your dungeons, who are guilty of nothing save coming to your port for the lawful purpose of trade. This point I shall dispute, and if I am wrong, I will suffer for my temerity; if right, I fear not but my sovereign and country (insignificant as I am) will visit with ample retribution any injustice done me.

According to the newspaper report, after Maclean refused to surrender his black crew members under local slave-state law to the harbour authorities, they were somewhat more than regretful. They organized in retaliation to prohibit *their* blacks shifting cargo for Maclean, 'under pain of twenty-nine lashes for every time they were detected on board.' Maclean concludes that 'I was by this measure subjected to great inconvenience and delay in the loading of my vessel.'

One may admire his steadfastness and solidarity with his mixed crew, and the point of principle that under British maritime law discrimination on grounds of skin-colour was illegal. His definition of the terms 'free' and 'LIBERTY', 'protection' and the 'law' interrelate to illustrate that he considered his men had equal human rights to exercise their business, with himself cast as their protector. In advertising that thanks to his Lieutenant-Governor his case had been taken to the British Government itself, he wished to force public attention to the habitual abuses of slave societies where they still survived intact. Clearly he also believed that British authority, if it exercised 'high-minded zeal and a sense of duty', could be an invincible force in having discriminatory laws repealed in territories with which Britain had commercial treaties.

These beliefs project forward in this instalment to the situation in Natal nine years after the Wilmington incident. In *Loss of the Brig 'Mary'* Maclean's opening appeals to authority and to the new settlers of Natal implicitly remind them, not only of the law of the British Empire, but of their duties with respect to 'people of colour'. The flag Maclean flies in his first venture into print in 1846 is flown here once again. As we shall see, his last appearance in print (in 1875) makes essentially the same point, so that for his thirty years as a writer he stuck to his theme of liberty meaning non-discriminatory practices.

His address directly to the Zulu people in the present instalment, preceded as it is by his prophecy of Zulu collapse, bursts through the narrative in the same heightened rhetorical vein he used at his address to his crew at Wilmington. It is worth considering in some detail for what it reveals of Maclean's beliefs and why, after hearing of the Zulus in Britain, he has such anxiety about the condition of Natal:

> People of Zulu, I leave this record of you in the day of your greatness as a nation. None of you may ever see the greatness of mine, but its influence is already surrounding you. I write this in testimony of my gratitude for the many favours I received at your hands. It is too much for me to expect that a revolution in your habits, so great and so opposite to all you have been accustomed, can be effected in your generation without doing violence to your happiness. The white man's notions and yours differ widely on this point, and I am concerned for you in the struggle. But I look forward with hope that your successors will enjoy the advantages and benefits which you cannot appreciate.

As 'this record' refers to *Loss of the Brig 'Mary'*, we learn that in addressing the Zulu people of 1853 he now intends it to be taken up by them as a document with which they may recall the day of their 'greatness'. This implies a measurement of how their empire has been reduced in the face of the 'greatness' of his. The impending 'revolution' as the transition to British rule occurs will cause 'violence' to their happiness, and the 'struggle' to accommodate and adapt will confer currently unforeseeable 'advantages and benefits'.

In the midst of expressing his concern Maclean interposes the key sentence which so powerfully justifies his project – that he writes in 'testimony' of his gratitude for past favours. This is his enduring tribute, which is repeated even at the end of his career. Read by his audience of British authorities and new settlers, this sentence makes the point that any lack of advantageous and beneficial circumstances meted out to the Zulu people would not only be dishonourable, but ungrateful in terms of *their* code of conduct.

He continues, clinching his whole case on the cause of the anti-slavery lobby:

> I am a decided advocate for your liberty, in common with that of the whole African race, and rejoice that my country has been the first to acknowledge that right, and has set the example of your freedom to the rest of the world. Other advantages will follow: the Genius of universal emancipation has set her foot in every land, before which slavery must be

for ever trodden down. The work is begun, and the pseudo-Christianity that reduces you to the condition of the brute creation is fast losing ground. Greater and more talented minds will rise to vindicate your rights as members of the human family . . . .

So Maclean's fervent ideal is to promote the spread of human rights in the known world in what we recognise as a truly democratic (and he says essential Christian) spirit. This is official British policy, he continues (even if in the less ideal colonies such policy was diluted and even inverted!). It is worth taking a stance to defend; and it is inevitable.

Furthermore – and ironically – Maclean's crusade involves the complete dismantling of the Zulu social system in the respects in which it in turn does not comply with the democratic ideal. He is not in favour of a hands-off policy, nor was he ever, even at his most cowed in his original encounters. The idea that he himself had the power to nudge Shaka into more just and merciful practices derives not only from his Christian tenets, but we now see from his political liberalism. He sees his role in the great transforming drama which contact precipitates as mediatory, in the service of the best ideals of his frequently defaulting nation.

Thus his critique of Shakan Zululand, although often garbled and contradictory, really focuses on aspects which militate against the introduction of 'universal emancipation'. The treatment of the Maphisi, the entrapment and servitude of the royal women, the cruelty of summary execution – these are but three of many examples. Above all, the deified autocrat, Shaka himself, is heavily criticized for his dictatorial wielding of might. . . . And so on.

But this is not to say that Maclean is doing the same job of blackening Shakan Zululand as Kay, Isaacs, Fynn and a mighty host of subsequent commentators. Their strategies proceed by insult, treat the culture as an undifferentiated (often classless and raceless) mass, sow confusion and misunderstanding; ultimately block interpretation itself. By contrast, in every word he writes, Maclean proceeds from the assumption that every facet of the Zulu system is entirely understandable to Europeans. What is more, they *are* 'members of the human family'; any pseudo-Christian attempt to 'reduce' them to brutality is not only a consummate crime, but a strategy of exclusion (besides being illegal). Maclean feels free to wield his rhetoric on behalf of a politically influential lobby, proceeding from his belief that the Zulus are as logically amenable, as socially responsive – and as elegible to pursue happiness as any other human beings. (Compare this passage to the Isaacs passage quoted in the commentary to Instalment Four.)

The young Maclean's 'state of fear and anxiety' at first meeting King Shaka, back at Dukuza in December 1825, as recalled in 1855, is thus caused by his terror that Shaka may turn out after all to be – as Kay says – some mad 'inhuman being'. Maclean's build-up to the physical appearance of Shaka is deconstructive; it sabotages his own worst fears. 'Shaka was worshipped as a deity, and was believed by the Zulus to have supernatural powers,' Maclean says. But his following remark could not more succinctly reduce Shaka the God to the human level: 'No one of his subjects doubted his having these powers, but he did himself.' The deflation could not be more adroit. As Maclean was destined to become Shaka's 'first physician in the seraglio', he ought to know.

That King's second party arrived at the height of Shaka's arrangement of the First-fruits ceremony of that year seems to us more than fortuitous. Maclean is orchestrating heavily. Obviously we are in for the full extravaganza – 6 000 warriors in attendance, plus more regiments arriving, the sight of Shaka in full regalia dancing in the season of harvesting, peace and abundant prosperity – this is all the stuff of the mandatory climax of a spectacular display.

But throughout his pulsing description Maclean does not lose sight of its significance. This is no bewildering pagan fertility orgy, no bloodletting sacrifice to Mother Earth, etc., although his description of the court imbongi is rather unfortunate. Here the gathering is clearly about the consolidation of the chief's power and about how he exercises it – principally through the control of the food supply. When Maclean says the text of the celebration is the new Zulu 'corn-laws', he means far more than some superstitious agricultural taboo. Maclean is a Scotsman, we must remember, fully aware of how the application of English Corn Laws up to 1846 had precipitated his Highland home of eighteenth-century agricultural clansmen into reorganization by industrial capital, with all the shifts in control of the mode of production that that painful process entailed. Through a few such laws his own homeland had been cleared of people to make way for sheep. Maclean knew exactly the power of the ceremony which centralised control of the people's means of subsistence.

The entry to the threshold of Shaka's 'throne' ('a large roll of matting') is masterfully done, the chorus of yes-men intended to show the subjection and the concurrence of the varied crowd. The traders' first public interview with Shaka is rendered verbatim to stress its importance. This is the only time Maclean uses dialogue extensively, complete with gestures and the deployment of the characters in respect to one another. The dramatic effect is to engrave every detail on the reader's memory. This is testimony at its most vibrant. He has great difficulty with translation, trying to avoid Shaka's speech coming out as pidgin. Even if he did not understand their dialogue in their first encounter of

1825 he would retrospectively, thanks to his later familiarity with Zulu, have been able to reconstruct it.

A further note on Maclean's Zulu needs to be made. Since Shaka the king had been on the first Zulu throne for only a short while, and consolidated Mthethwa power over the Ndwandwes only the month before, we may speculate on how widely familiar the Zulu dialect was, not only to the traders, but to the host of 100 000 new Zulus. The imbongi, the ritual singing, the very preciseness of the language used – these all suggest a linguistic transaction was taking place at Dukuza on that day that had everything to do with Shaka's establishment of the norms of his paramountcy. As the great display of dancing overcomes any linguistic glitches, so Ned's initiative as a performer wins the greatest enthusiasm of all. Fynn is always claimed later on as the great Zulu linguist and hence 'expert', but Fynn never gives the sense of having understood the meaning of ritual occasions quite the way Maclean does.

That Shaka now takes time off from his onerous duties, following the Zulu 'etiquette', to single out Maclean and fondle the little pik's exceptional locks is the most telling detail of all – an all too human bond is being formed. Then Maclean is required to show his 'agility', which he does by running and jumping with all his 'might and main, seeing that it pleases him'. Surely this is one of the most delightful moments in our frontier literature, so extraordinary in its techniques that we can only be won over. (The further incident when Maclean's nose is put out of joint by Cameron's rival display only reinforces the sense of Maclean's authenticity.)

Maclean's final paragraph here is a reprise in simpler terms and concrete imagery of the principles which he established early in the instalment. It serves to clinch the clarification of his beliefs:

> The first law of nature and the first right of man, that no man should starve while his neighbour has abundance, is recognized by the Zulus in the fullest extent. I verily believe that were there but a handful of corn in a village it would be equally divided.

ELEVEN

The final instalment of Maclean's Natal recollections appeared in March 1855, and nothing in the text suggests that it is planned as the work's conclusion. In fact, like all the other instalments, it concludes with the phrase, 'To be continued'.

Further evidence that he had promised more instalments is found in his editor's understandably plaintive remark at the end of the same issue (Vol. 24, No. 3, p. 168): 'Will Captain Maclean look after his adopted, and send us timely matter.'

However, no further word of *Loss of the Brig 'Mary'* is traceable in *The Nautical Magazine*. Natal as a topic is not again mentioned in its pages until July 1863, when an item called 'A Few Words about Natal' appeared. This comments that the new colony, 'An enlarged edition of Devonshire under a more sunny sky, ought to furnish everything that an emigrant could wish for' (p. 479). This promotional piece erases the Zulu presence from Natal by not presenting it at all. Rather, we now have an edenic paradise, cleared of its wildlife as well, in which the new settler is invited to plant and prosper alongside the friendly minority of Boers.

For Maclean only a decade before the 'Zoola Indians' – as the index to *The Nautical Magazine* persisted in labelling them – remained intact and complete at the pinnacle of the glory of their empire. He and his party stepped into this 'new world', witnessing its utterly alien parade, its sumptuous display of camaraderie, feasting and might. In British accounts that is how little time it took – from 1824 to 1863 – to shift from first intimidated contact to writing the Zulu people out of the record. But the Zulus would return to the public notice in the 1870s with a vengeance.

In this final instalment every aspect of Maclean's description questions whether the Zulus are to be that easily dismissed as a significant power in south-east Africa. He may maintain that George IV's military resources vastly outweighed King Shaka's, but by the height of the festivity he estimates no less than 50 000 trained and skilled warriors are in attendance. Their dances are 'novel, grand and wild' – but they are also terrifying to the traders.

A few seemingly arbitrary executions, conducted at Shaka's will and in the most gruesome manner, traumatically terrify them further. Maclean's bad dream of the previous instalment carries through in his nightmare language. Typically and for ever the maritime man, in his imagery he suggests their spectating at the display is for him a second drowning: the white shields of the palace bodyguard arrive 'like the white crest of a wave'. At the climactic twist in the final paragraphs of this instalment – when he learns that he is to be stranded at Dukuza – he writes:

On this intelligence being communicated to me, my heart sank within me, and I nearly fainted with the idea. At the horror of being left alone in the midst of this wild and terrible scene, cut off from all communion, all intercourse and even the sight of civilization, my heart sank with despair. Compared to it, my recent shipwreck, and the very waves that had threatened every moment to swallow me up, were comparatively insignificant. Great was my despair when, on the following day, my shipmates took leave of me, as I thought in all probability for ever.

He has forcibly crossed the 'gulf' between the civilized and the savage, been swept by the second storm in ten weeks onto the fatal shore, washed up (like Robinson Crusoe) yet again to survive.

In this finale Maclean does to a certain extent have it both ways. His narrative surges to its horrifying climax, yet at the same time we know that the abandonment is his good fortune. We already know that he comes to terms with it and prospers over the next three years, that in his new home he will become a figure of influence. From being a dependent tiddler he will grow into adolescence, capable of advising the king and even being part of gruelling trading expeditions (to Port Natal and to Delagoa Bay). He will, we know, learn more Zulu than any other of his compatriots, and come to consider himself an insider in their affairs.

His forced familiarity with the Zulu kingdom will cause him to abandon even the crucial debate about 'civilization' and 'savagery', which previously he had thought separated them. He says,

> Were I called upon to state in which condition the most happiness existed, I should, from the knowledge I have of man in both conditions, bear testimony to the Zulus being the most cheerful and happy people of which I have had any experience. These opinions may not be orthodox, but are at any rate based upon experience.

Maclean carefully prepares us for this great reversal of attitude. He says that 'sympathies for the unhappy and deplorable state of the savage' are − simply − 'mistaken'. Shaka is 'liberal', Shaka is even 'indulgent'. Shaka obviously spoiled Maclean silly, pampering him as no white man had. The result is his unorthodoxy.

Maclean's tactic is both subtle and sophisticated. He depicts all the outward terrors of first acquaintance, while forewarning us that they are an incorrect reading of the situation. That first touch of his bizarre head of hair, where Shaka tames this young 'wild beast' like a dog, winning his confidence, begins a process of reconciliation within him which profoundly changed his views.

Maclean must learn to outlive his heritage of hostile and prejudicial stereotypes. Like Ned Cameron, he must take his opportunity before King Shaka, win approval and enjoy his reward. Also like Ned, he must learn to assume the songs and dances of 'Quashie' (the archetypal free black) and role-play successfully in what (following Maclean) must have been one of the most theatrical courts on earth.

Perhaps Maclean could not continue his story, for, if he had described his youthful conversion and maturation as a savage, who would really have believed him? If he had managed to convey the gist and meaning of his new life, would it not be dismissed as a young man's fancy? Anyway, in English there are not the words to describe this gybe in his progress. Other writers he knew, like Kay, make an unholy mess of portraying life across the frontier. Are the British interested in anything more than the touristic view of life out there? (If he did write the Shaka memoir, could he get it published?) Perhaps Zulu modes of being were inexpressible . . . and he left them in his memory as his private possession. That glory had passed for him with the death of King Shaka and his evacuation from Port Natal, just as his youth had passed.

The least we may deduce with certainty is that the experience of his Zulu childhood and youth, between 1825 and 1828, produced a lifelong devotion to emancipationism in the adult Maclean. On that point he stands committed.

Once he had left Zululand and returned to his element – the sea – he found the island of Saint Lucia at which he could combine his career and his alliance with the 'African race'. The warmth with which he writes of Ned, 'a seaman who had served his time in a West Indiaman', shows his affection for the 'Jamaica trade' – indeed, dragging (or droghing) sugar became the mainstay of the rest of Maclean's life.

If by 1855 Maclean let *Loss of the Brig 'Mary'* come to an abrupt end, marooning his readers, that is not to say that during the rest of his lifetime he would not have another go at completing his recollections, when the time was right for his revelation and his final plea that his testimony be heard in Natal.

TWELVE

The editor takes the opportunity here of appending Maclean's letter to the serial, *Loss of the Brig 'Mary'*, to serve as a 'final instalment.' This twelfth item remarkably brings the earlier suspended narrative to closure, while providing many definitive and final statements of Maclean's views of his Natal experience. The letter first appeared in the London *Times* of Tuesday 3 August 1875, under the heading 'Among the Caffres', although the entry for it in the *Times* index is 'Maclean's Excuse for Langalibalele'. On 12 August of that year the Secretary of the Aborigines Protection Society backed Maclean in the same letter column.

So the controversy around the Langalibalele case is what brought Maclean out of cover from Saint Lucia. The sudden coming to prominence of the name 'Langalibalele' in the British newspapers attracted his attention and caused him to deliver his last word on the subject of Anglo-Zulu relations.

The aged Langalibalele who became embroiled in the headlines was the hereditary chief of the amaHlubi, a tributary group to Shaka. They had twice been forced to remove from their ancestral grounds up in the catchment area of the Buffalo River – once from what became Klip River Territory allocated by the Trekkers in 1847 to themselves, and then under Shepstone to the Bushman's Pass area in the foothills of the Drakensberg, where they were placed as a buffer against Bushman incursions of white stockholders. When Shepstone as Secretary of Native Affairs subpoenaed Langalibalele to Pietermaritzburg to explain the accumulation of guns his people had acquired on the diamond fields, and he had thrice refused to attend, 'rebellion' was suspected on the part of the amaHlubi. Natal's notorious panic ensued.

Far from opposing the colonial forces, the amaHlubi attempted an exodus from Natal over the Berg. Langalibalele was caught and subsequently tried, and by the 1875 of Maclean's response had been sentenced to life imprisonment on Robben Island, his people dispersed. Lieutenant-Governor Pine (who was later dismissed for his handling of the affair) and Shepstone, it now seems clear, stacked the case against Langalibalele in such a way that an injustice was perpetrated against him through their ignorance of 'native character, policy and tradition' – this is Maclean's view, although it was hardly the view of the 18 000 Colonists he feels should have known better. Colenso, the heretic bishop, turned the mistrial into a *cause célèbre* in London, even publishing a book about it in 1874. Maclean sides with him as one who had 'studied' the Zulu people 'more closely and earnestly' than their administrative overlords. Carnarvon, the Colonial Secretary, indeed subsequently returned Langalibalele from imprisonment and arranged for some compensation to his people. This is indeed an example of a higher justice having prevailed. The amaHlubi never recovered, however.

Since the Langalibalele of history was born in 1818, it is not possible on the grounds of age alone that he was the same person who headed the Delagoa Bay delegation in the 1820s. He is not the same individual whom Maclean imagines to have been his friend and benefactor. However, the name 'Langalibalele', meaning scorching sun and referring to any birthdate coinciding with a period of severe drought, may have been common in Shakan Zululand and not restricted to members of the amaHlubi group. Maclean is mistaken here in fact, if not in spirit.

The 'Langalibalele affair' had brought Natal back to public attention in Britain and Maclean seized the opportunity to champion his cause of 'kindness and forbearance' towards the Zulu people. Certainly he feels the ugly business sheds no glory on the officials and settlers of the colony, who acted out of ignorance and unjustly, bringing their administration into disrepute.

But, although Maclean claims always to 'have taken a lively interest in what has been doing in that part of the world', he is deeply out of touch with the scale and even the impact of events. While he imagines a reciprocal and even-handed balance of power may still be restored between the British and the Zulu interests in Natal, that a mutual partnership will prevail, the Langalibalele incident was one of a concatenating and complex sequence of events which would lead to the ultimatum that would precipitate the devastating Anglo-Zulu War. The showdown – that would cause Disraeli's memorable tribute to the resisting Zulu people: 'They beat our generals, they convert our bishops, and they write "finis" to a French dynasty' (quoted in Brookes and Webb, p. 108) – was about to occur. Maclean has no sense that the Zulu would ever be provoked into taking up arms in defence of their territory, let alone lose it to British invasion. Yet this is only five years thence.

Although his letter must certainly have been read in Natal, this researcher has turned up no reaction to it in the local press. Although a typed copy of the letter is held in the Natal Archives in Pietermaritzburg and in the Killie Campbell Africana Library in Durban among the Fynn Papers (with the note 'by Charles Rawden Maclean, the real name of "John Ross"'), it seems not to have been used by many later historians, either. One exception is Donald Morris in *The Washing of the Spears* (p. 96), who comments:

> . . . on the off chance that this [Langalibalele] might be his friend John Ross wrote a letter in his defence to a Natal newspaper. He described his trip and the good service Langalibalele had rendered. His own true name, he added, was Charles Rawden Maclean; he had taken the name of Ross when he ran away to sea at the age of twelve.

Apart from the fact that Maclean does no such thing in his letter, which is to London – he was never aware that he had been dubbed 'John Ross' in the first place! – Morris's reading is fanciful. Once tangled in a mythological construct, it seems, historians like Morris are hard put to escape it, or to follow the evidence step by step through to its inevitable conclusion.

As if there were any doubt left about it, Maclean's letter at least establishes once and for all that *Loss of the Brig 'Mary'* is indeed by himself. His last paragraph of the letter, quoted from the opening of his very first instalment, giving his source, establishes this conclusively, and for us completes the grand cycle. Since the letter also establishes that he was part of a 'party of 30 warriors charged with the escort of the writer to the Portuguese settlement at Delagoa Bay', he is 'John Ross' as well.

In order to restore Maclean's own view of his life and role in Zululand we should work through his letter step by step. Much of it is summary of his previous narrative, but even his summary is of interest. He writes in 1875 almost exactly a half-century after the original events, rather poignantly as 'now the only one living, of the small band of Europeans who first had intercourse with the Caffre tribes of Natal'. As an old man, his recall of 'the fields of many adventures and privations in the days of my youth' is for us unbearably tender.

Then Farewell had gone to Natal 'on a trading expedition for the purchase of ivory' – this is plainly said. Another such expedition of trade is the Delagoa Bay trip, organized by King Shaka and sponsored by him in alliance with the traders. (The view that 'John Ross' travelled alone to outwit the Zulus is thus untenable. Nor is this trip the highlight of his life in Zululand – it is mentioned only to stress how 'nobly and faithfully' the original Langalibalele and his men performed 'this duty'.)

'During four years of my residence in Natal, three years were, with little interruption, passed at King Shaka's residence,' he continues. (Thus, after the First-fruits Festival of Instalments Ten and Eleven, after December 1825, he was based for the most part at Dukuza. This substantiates his claim that he became more intimate with the Zulu polity than any other member of the 'band'.)

Then comes the most revealing section of all:

> [Shaka] kept me with him first as a *sort of rare pet animal*, on whom he bestowed *a large amount of genuine kindness* and, I must add, a *large share of indulgence.* . . . (my italics)

Although we should not speculate too far on the nature of the Shaka-Maclean relationship, he certainly wishes us to know that it was based on affection and kindness. At first Maclean seems to have been regarded as a court curiosity (a 'pet') – a bizarre amphibious little beasty in the Zulu eyes, to be educated into human status.

But then the relationship grows and changes, according to Maclean. Insofar as Shaka is interested in Maclean at all, it is as a 'confidential companion.' The core of the many secrets they traded can only have had to do with the true nature of the white man; thus, for Maclean an advisory role on what was likely to be the Port Natal response to any particular initiative on Shaka's part.

A further interpretation may be deduced. In keeping Maclean at Dukuza (first the one, then the later site) for his curiosity value and letting him exhibit himself to the passing parade of Zulu subjects, Shaka was not only extending extraordinary privileges to Maclean. Surely he also meant to familiarize the Zulus with the whites. If only three months before the Zulu view was that they were mythical beasts that ate their own children, as Maclean describes it, having Maclean on display at Dukuza as a meat- and milk-guzzling child like any other child could demystify hosts of inland Zulus.

Furthermore, that Maclean became a friendly, amenable and efficient trader himself as he grew up, proved to the Zulus that the bond with the whites was advantageous to both sides. The very few authentic details we have of the Delagoa Bay trip illustrate this: Maclean traded with Britain's Portuguese associates, and even the French, while defended by his Zulu accomplices, and all parties reaped the benefits. (This is the Georgian-Shaka accord at its most profitable.) In reminding us that he was not 'slaughtered' – quite the contrary – Maclean is stressing the usefulness of his role at the interface, and how it was only from that position, no matter under what peculiar and to his memory rather dream-like circumstances, that influence could be exerted. This admittedly is a very condensed view of the Shaka-Maclean link; presumably for months and years on end, like the band at Port Natal, the parties continued to pursue their usual business of living normally.

Maclean's account of the trip of Ambassador Sothobe to Algoa Bay is also of interest in this respect. We know from Isaacs that Maclean accompanied Sothobe to Port Elizabeth and back, so that he is not speaking from hearsay. As Sothobe's arrival in the Cape is better documented than almost any other Natal event of 1825–28 (see Isaacs' Chapter 14 and the official documentation on which it is based), Maclean's version is of crucial interest. Undoubtedly he feels Shaka's deputy was snubbed; that the mission to the white authorities was a disastrous setback, both for the white traders and the Zulus. (Nor was this the only delegation Shaka sent to King George's officials.)

The timing is important. In the New Year of 1828 the *Mary* was relaunched as the *Shaka* or the *Elizabeth and Susan* and Sothobe returned with the news that, not only had he been deported from the Cape but that the white man's strength was 'insignificant'. By then Maclean must have relocated to Port Natal – indeed, this is the time the joint deaths of Hutton and Dommana to which he was an eye-witness occur there – for he speculates about the impact of Sothobe's message on Shaka ('he could not . . . have carried back to his master any very high notions. . . . '). He was no longer at Dukuza to hear Shaka's reaction to the failure of the accord.

Since, as Maclean says over and over again, Shaka pinned his external policy to this accord, we must see that its collapse contributed to his downfall. In fact, within months he would be killed off and replaced by Dingane, whose policy towards white adventurers (as we know only too well from the slaying of Piet Retief and party) was less staked on mutual collaboration with them. As in the Transkei earlier, Zulu policy changed from collaboration to resistance as the pressure of white claims increased. The very fact that the survivors of the Natal parties, including Maclean himself, quitted their stations on the demise of Shaka, and that Farewell when he attempted a return was killed, indicates how Zulu policy with regard to whites shifted. Nor was Cape policy ever what they imagined, for the brave *Mary* was confiscated from the pioneer remnants when it finally evacuated to Port Elizabeth and was used thereafter to collect guano.

We may then conclude that the white presence at Port Natal was deeply implicated in maintaining Shaka's personal power (in the shape of their representative, Maclean at Dukuza). They were also implicated in his death when they failed to interest the Cape Colony (and, indeed, King George himself) in the viability of their arrangement. Shaka fell for lack of *British* support.

As Maclean does not see this kind of power-play is also the downfall of Langalibalele – this is Maclean's blindspot – he could hardly have projected that view backwards to the circumstances of his own youth. Like many a fine liberal, he has no sense of *realpolitik*. To his dying day he remains somewhat innocent with regard to the awesome workings of international policy and trade. With regard to the destruction of the amaHlubi all he sees is 'a great mischief, which time only can repair.'

For policy, in fact, Maclean substitutes morality. This was the basis of his whole savagery/civilization argument, and of his antagonism against what he perceived as religious bigotry. He defers to wiser policy instead of contesting the fact that its misapplication on the ground is destroying the vision he loves most. . . . And we are left with his repeated plea to his countrymen, 'whosoever they be', to 'exercise mercy and kindness'.

Perhaps it is a sufficient indictment of colonial policy in Natal to conclude that – on the grounds of morality alone – Charles Rawden Maclean indubitably found more 'mercy and kindness' in the hands of the Zulus than in those of his own people in the days of his youth.

Bibliography

WORKS BY CHARLES RAWDEN MACLEAN

'The Liberty of British Subjects Invaded in the United States,' *The British and Foreign Anti-Slavery Reporter*, London (1 May, 1846) – includes 1 500 word excerpt from his report to the Governor of Barbados.
Loss of the Brig 'Mary' at Natal, with Early Recollections of that Settlement, The *Nautical Magazine*, London (Jan., 1853–March, 1855).
'Law of Storms,' *The Shipping and Mercantile Gazette*, London (8 Nov., 1853) – 2 000 word letter.
Notes on a Voyage from England to Balaclava in the 'Gilbert Munro', Late Store-ship at Hyder Pacha, The *Nautical Magazine*, London (Oct., 1856–Feb., 1857) – four instalments.
A Voyage to the West Indies, with Notes on Saint Lucia, The *Nautical Magazine*, London (July–Dec., 1857) – four instalments.
'Among the Caffres' (Letter), *The Times*, London (3 Aug., 1875).
'To the Editor of the *Observer*,' *The Saint Lucia Observer*, Castries (18 Sept., 1875).

WORKS BY STEPHEN GRAY

'The Real John Ross,' *Living*, Johannesburg (Oct., 1987).
John Ross: The True Story (Johannesburg: Penguin, 1987).
'South African Fiction and a Case History Revised: An Account of Research into Retellings of the John Ross Story of Early Natal,' *Research in African Literatures*, Austin, Texas, Vol. 19, No. 4 (Winter, 1988).
'John Ross and Slavery,' *English in Africa*, Grahamstown, Vol. 17, No. 1 (May, 1990).
'Saint Lucia: Dearly Beloved,' *The London Magazine*, London, Vol. 30, Nos. 9 and 10 (Dec., 1990–Jan., 1991).

WORKS QUOTED

BRYANT, A.T., *Olden Times in Zululand and Natal* (1929) (Cape Town: Struik, 1965).
BROOKES, E.H. and C. de B. WEBB, *A History of Natal* (2nd ed.) (Pietermaritzburg: University of Natal Press, 1987).

The Diary of Henry Francis Fynn, Stuart, James and D. McK. Malcolm (eds.) (Pietermaritzburg: Shuter and Shooter, 1969).

DICKENS, CHARLES, 'The Noble Savage' in *Household Words* (1853), *Reprinted Pieces* (London: Dent, 1921).

Dictionary of South African Biography: Vol. 1, pp. 286–7: Francis George Farewell; Vol. 1, pp. 400–2: Nathaniel Isaacs; Vol. 2, pp. 363–4: James Saunders King; Vol. 2, pp. 383–4: Langalibalele; Vol. 2, pp. 655–7: Shaka; Vol. 4, pp. 270–1: Stephen Kay; and Vol. 5, p. 659: 'John Ross.'

DUMINY, ANDREW and BILL GUEST (eds.), *Natal and Zululand from Earliest Times to 1910* (Pietermaritzburg: University of Natal Press, 1989), particularly John Wright and Carolyn Hamilton, 'Traditions and Transformations' (pp. 49–82).

ISAACS, NATHANIEL, *Travels and Adventures in Eastern Africa (Natal)* (1836), Louis Herman and Percival R. Kirby (eds.) (reprint) (Cape Town: Struik, 1970).

JACKSON HAIGHT, MABEL V., *European Powers and South-East Africa* (London: Routledge and Kegan Paul, 1967).

MORRIS, DONALD R., *The Washing of the Spears* (London: Jonathan Cape, 1966).

Index

Page numbers in bold type refer to Maclean's own works (39–137); other references are to the Introduction (1–33) and to the editor's Commentary (139–202). Zulu words and names are given in modern orthography and filing is by stem not by prefix. For example *amaHlubi* is filed after *Helicon*.